POLITICALLY INCORRECT

POLITICALLY INCORRECT

THE AUTOBIOGRAPHY

PETER DE VILLIERS WITH GAVIN RICH

Published by Zebra Press
an imprint of Random House Struik (Pty) Ltd
Company Reg. No. 1966/003153/07
Wembley Square, First Floor, Solan Road, Gardens, Cape Town, 8001
PO Box 1144, Cape Town, 8000, South Africa

www.zebrapress.co.za

First published 2012
Reprinted in June 2012

3 5 7 9 10 8 6 4 2

Publication © Zebra Press 2012
Text © Peter de Villiers and Gavin Rich 2012

Cover image © Gallo Images / AFP

PUBLISHER: Marlene Fryer
EDITOR: Ronel Richter-Herbert
PROOFREADER: Bronwen Leak
COVER DESIGN: Sean Robertson
TEXT DESIGN: Jacques Kaiser
TYPESETTER: Catherine Coetzer

Set in 11 pt on 14.5 pt Adobe Garamond

Printed and bound by Paarl Media,
Jan van Riebeeck Drive, Paarl, South Africa

ISBN: 978 1 77022 421 6 (print)
ISBN: 978 1 77022 422 3 (ePub)
ISBN: 978 1 77022 423 0 (PDF)

Contents

Foreword

While sitting in my little house in France in late 2007, when I was playing for ASM Clermont Avergne, I got a call from South Africa asking whether I would meet with newly appointed Bok coach Peter de Villiers in Cape Town in January 2008. I had never met the man before and wondered what it was about. Even back then, many had an opinion about Peter, but few really knew him. I believe this is still the case today. Well, we eventually met and I'm sure you know the rest!

I worked with Peter for four years, and wherever I go, people ask me about him. My response is always the same: 'Let me explain to you who Peter de Villiers is by telling you this: In all my years as a player, I have had many coaches – some good, some bad and some okay – but at the beginning of my four years with Peter, I met a man who always seemed happy (quite out of the ordinary for a coach!), and in those four years I watched him grow as a person but remain the same man, still smiling!

He was the only coach ever to send me home from a Bok camp during training – so that I could go and see my boy, who was ill. I didn't ask to leave – at training he just sensed that my mind was elsewhere and asked around to find out what was wrong. He was told that my kid was ill. He called Charles, our manager, aside and asked him to book me a flight home – without even discussing it with me! Now this is bizarre behaviour for a coach, but it was one of the many lessons I learnt from Peter. His explanation was, 'Rugby can be a very important part of your life, but don't make it your whole life. Maintain a balance, as your family will be there long after your career is over.'

I know we didn't win the Rugby World Cup in 2011, but I know in my heart that with Peter as coach and with the plan we had, it had been possible. However, the margins are small and we missed out. But I don't remember Peter for that – I remember him for what he meant to us as a group. Do yourself a favour and ask any player he coached since 2007 which coach they would invite to their house for dinner in 20 years' time, and I'm pretty sure most of them will say, 'Peter.'

JOHN SMIT
APRIL 2012

Foreword

This book is a fundamental part of South Africa's recent (post-1994) history. It will be a disservice to the characters, and primarily the primary character, to read it outside of the above context. The reflections and descriptions in the book must be understood against the general theme of the victorious nature of the human spirit.

When Peter de Villiers became South Africa's national rugby coach in 2008, he had lived in a post-apartheid society for 14 years. At the age of 50, he had lived as a victim under the oppression of apartheid for 36 years. He represents a special generation of South Africans who have lived their lives mostly pre-1994 and only slightly post-1994. This generation carries both the burdens of the past and those of the future of our country. Peter's appointment was a great moment in rejuvenating our belief that critical gains were being made in the building of our nation.

When Peter became the South African national rugby coach, he entered both the national arena of rugby and became a role player in the highly competitive international rugby scene during this professional era of the sport. This was a major challenge for which he was more than adequately prepared.

At the time of his appointment, Peter had a deep knowledge of the game both as a player and as a coach, as well as incredible life experience, having learnt to play rugby under shamefully under-resourced conditions. Yet he had an unwavering commitment to South Africa's nation-building project. These attributes were critical to him fulfilling the role to which he had been appointed.

Throughout his rugby career, Peter de Villiers was an avid rugby player – playing the game at Noorder Paarl High School, for his club Young Gardens in Paarl (where he both played and coached) and for the Boland provincial team – and rugby coach in the schools where he taught. Rugby was always in his blood, just as it flowed through the veins of his community and family.

The commitment to South Africa's nation building came from Peter's experience of living in a community that had experienced the destruction of its cohesive core through the Group Areas Act. These experiences make those of his generation a special kind of South African, one who has lived under the harsh reality of state oppression and suppression but who is also able to embrace the future of our country with a deep sense of gratitude.

Peter has lived the reconstruction of those disrupted communities, as many of us did in Paarl and in many other places in our land. Our generation has experienced the social pathologies that seem to be inevitable in this kind of reconstruction of broken communities. These are the things that make Peter thrive – seeing our nation flourish and grow and present itself in the most glorious blossoming. It gives him a tremendous sense of satisfaction to experience our children reaching their full potential.

As a professional teacher, Peter was known for his irrepressible commitment to making things work. He was prepared to walk many extra miles and to make personal sacrifices to give of his best to those whom he served as an educator (learners, fellow educators, parents and the community at large).

Added to this, we had a South African Springbok rugby coach steeped in his religious faith and the traditions followed by the community that had shaped him and the family who had nurtured him. It is therefore of fundamental importance to see this book as critical literature in post-1994 and post-apartheid South Africa. It is a functional part of the remaking of South African society, a story of the triumph of the human spirit.

Springbok rugby coach? Yes, but that is but a part of a much bigger picture. This book presents a truly South African story and is a critical step in understanding the normalisation of our society.

COURTNEY SAMPSON
ELECTORAL COMMISSION OFFICER, WESTERN CAPE
APRIL 2012

Author's note

When we met at a coffee shop at Cape Town airport in June 2011 to start the discussions about the possibility of doing this book together, I greeted Peter with the following words: 'I always suspected you might be mad, but now I know it.'

I'd taken my cue from Peter's agent, Hilton Houghton, who, when he phoned me to ask if I might be interested, told me Peter had said I would pack up laughing. I didn't laugh, but I did ask Hilton if he was sure he had the right guy. I was known to be the Springbok coach's biggest critic.

But that was part of the reason Peter wanted me to write the book: his line – that I had kept such a close watch on him during his tenure that I probably knew his career better than he did – made sense. I remember thinking that it said something positive about him that his mind worked like that.

As a journalist, though, you value your independence, and while readers, coaches and players often like to pigeonhole rugby reporters as either positive or negative, in reality I have always observed only one mantra – 'write it like you see it'.

If working on this book meant that I would lose the right to write it like I saw it – which was particularly important in a World Cup year – then I didn't want to enter into the relationship. However, my reservations about writing the book were eroded when, at our first meeting, I told Peter that I didn't want to endorse him, and he responded by giving me an emphatic assurance that he was not trying to 'buy' me and would not interfere with my independence.

He was true to his word, too, and even allowed me to blow off a bit of my own frustration at him when we met to do a book interview shortly after he had announced his team for the World Cup quarter-final in Wellington. I was convinced he was making a massive mistake by starting with John Smit ahead of Bismarck du Plessis, and sometimes I wear my heart on my sleeve.

When he asked me why I was looking so angry, I told him exactly what I had written in my internet column a few hours earlier – in my view, he was throwing away the World Cup. Instead of arguing the point with me, Peter said that he understood why I felt the way I did, but he had made a commitment a long time ago that he had to honour. I told him I was getting stuck into him on Supersport.com and in my *Weekend Argus* column, which he said he accepted, as he knew I had a job to do.

His reaction illustrated just how much Peter had changed from his first year as Bok coach, when he reacted defensively and a touch tetchily to any criticism. The truth is that long before the prospect of a book arrived on the horizon, Peter and I had started to get on well on a personal level. Our relationship was helped by the changes he had made to his management team, particularly with the appointment of Rassie Erasmus, who provided the attention to technical detail I thought was required.

There are many different ways to coach and many different styles of coaching, and by Peter's last year in charge I had started to appreciate his special way of managing the players. We can only speculate, but I believe there was merit when Peter was quoted as saying, 'Together Rassie and I could conquer the world.' De Villiers and Erasmus complemented each other's strengths and covered each other's weaknesses.

I had by then also grown to admire his stubborn refusal to be moulded into somebody that he didn't want to be. I have seen so many Springbok coaches undergo a personality change when confronted with the pressures of the job, but in Peter's case you could argue that Peter de Villiers stayed Peter de Villiers to the point where it almost became a character flaw.

After the Twickenham win against England in 2010, Peter, when asked if he feared for his job, made the point that he didn't care, as he didn't appoint himself. That struck a chord with me, and from that point on, mistakes that were made on Peter's watch were blamed on those who employed him. As you will come to realise when you read this book, his job was made so much more difficult by the lack of support he was given by his employers.

In the process of writing this book, by spending time with Peter, I came to appreciate the role he played in breaking the mould and by making the Springboks seem more accessible to a wider audience and to all the communities. This was drummed in over and over again in the reactions of the car guards in Port Elizabeth, the street vendors in Paarl, the Indian waiters in Umhlanga Rocks, who all wanted some of his time, to get his autograph, to be photographed with him, to the extent where it was sometimes almost impossible to get any work done. It was a reaction quite unlike any I had witnessed in the company of previous Springbok coaches.

The emotional scenes at the Springbok farewell in Johannesburg and again on their return from the 2011 Rugby World Cup may well in time be recognised as Peter's legacy more than the quarter-final exit from the competition or the winning feats of 2009. When it comes to the nation-building aspect of the Springbok coaching job, his departure undeniably leaves a massive void.

I thank Peter for giving me the opportunity to help him tell a story that is so much more than just a rugby story, and write a book that is more than just a rugby book. I hope I delivered on his expectations. Thanks, too, to my editor, Ronel Richter-Herbert, for helping to make the end product readable. And thanks to my wife Anna and children Kate and Peter for their patience during the many long hours when my mind quite clearly was somewhere else.

GAVIN RICH
APRIL 2012

Acknowledgements

I dedicate this book to my parents Peter and Hilda de Villiers to acknowledge the long nights they spent on their knees praying until we got home safe and sound, for their unconditional love to this day, for the book of life I read by observing them every day, and that the wider community can also experience some of the fruit of the spirit that we were exposed to. You are true leaders, as people tend to follow your example. You never sent us to church, though to this day, you are a living testimony to the true course to prosperity in life. You taught me to appreciate what I have and to be true to who I am, and to love and believe in myself, because you made me understand that I am made in the image of God. In you I had all the friends I ever needed, for in the unwavering, principled manner you disciplined me, you gave me more than money can ever buy, and today I can say that if God ever granted me the privilege to choose my own parents, you would be whom I would choose. Your faith in God overshadows any desire man can have. May God grant you more happy days together in addition to the 60 you already have. God bless.

I also want to thank my family, my friends and the whole of South Africa for all the support I received when I was entrusted with the opportunity to serve my country at the highest level. You made it an interesting learning experience and, although it was at times a painful process, you allowed me to make mistakes. Most off all, you made me believe in what I was doing, just as you perhaps came to believe in my efforts. I wanted to make the Springboks the people's team – not least because you make such a huge contribution to the team with your support. I always tried to be the people's coach – to inspire the people of this country to become the best they could be, and to do so while being true to themselves.

A special word of thanks to SA Rugby for taking the bold step in appointing me as the Springbok coach. By doing so, they inspired many South Africans and spread a message of hope across all cultures. My appointment happened against all odds, and in the process SA Rugby made history. Sport has an extraordinary power to unite, and we are blessed to have it in our lives.

To God Almighty, thank you, Lord, for choosing me to do such an important job. It could have been anyone! But You carried me through and were always true to Your word. Knowing what our abilities are comes from You, and You love us regardless of how we perform, which eliminates the need we have to perform for others and frees us from allowing other opinions to control our decisions.

Then, to all the sponsors – personal and team sponsors – who created an environment in which it was so much easier to focus on the job at hand. You will never really know how much you add to the success of the team. We believe that we always did our best to represent your product to the highest standards, and we are grateful for your support.

Thanks to everybody else who worked tirelessly behind the scenes to help make the Boks successful, whether through analytical contributions or by motivating the team. Our country is a better place because of all those who were prepared to help our nation building without other people knowing about it.

To Gavin Rich, you were my strongest support in the writing of this book. Be assured that I know how you gave your all to the process, sometimes even to your own detriment. And thanks to everyone else involved in the publishing process – you are people with extraordinary abilities.

Lastly, I hope we, as South Africans, don't let slip the opportunities we are given, as we had after 1995, to unify our lovely country. Let's use our opportunities, as we may not have many others.

PETER DE VILLIERS
APRIL 2012

1

Even the bad days are good

You don't experience much quiet when you are the Springbok coach. So when silence descends on you, you know it won't last long. Soon enough, the voice in your head is back: 'Should I perhaps have done that differently? Did I make the right decision?'

In 2009, as the team celebrated clinching the Tri Nations with a win over the All Blacks in Hamilton, I chose to sit in silence. Instead of running onto the field to celebrate with the players, as my assistant coaches had urged me to do, I stayed behind to be by myself. I wanted to think. I wanted to reflect on what we had achieved and where we still had to go.

These were the players who had won the World Cup two years earlier, and they had now also won a series against the British & Irish Lions and a Tri Nations title, thereby confirming that they were indeed the best team in the world. This was their moment. Like I had done when the South African under-21 team I was coaching won the IRB Junior World Cup in Argentina in 2005, I chose to stand back. Intrinsic to my coaching philosophy is the view that it is not about the coach – it's about the players. The coaches are there only for the players; there would not be any coaches without them.

I know when people need me, and they don't need me when they win. When you go onto the field to join in the victory celebrations, you take the focus away from what has happened in the match. It's the players who play the game, and winning is the just reward for the hard work they've put in.

That night in Hamilton, alone for those few minutes before I joined everyone in the changing room, I felt elated. But I also felt a little empty. I had coached the players to get this far, but how would I motivate them for the next challenge? How would I keep them at the top?

Two years later, also in New Zealand, I would again sit in an empty coaches' box and speak to the voices that echoed in the silence, and I would recall those minutes I had spent on my own in Hamilton. It was just one memory among many in my four years in charge of the Springboks. This day in October 2011 had been tumultuous for me – and for South African rugby – so I sat in silence as the Regional Stadium gradually emptied under an unusually still and clear Wellington evening sky.

This time I was experiencing a scenario quite different from the one in Hamilton. Now there was no point pondering where the Springboks and I would go from here. My journey with the Boks had ended in the cruellest way imaginable, in a World Cup quarter-final we had dominated but which Australia had somehow managed to win. This was the full stop to my career as Springbok coach. There was no point in speculating on what might have been, or on where we had gone wrong. This was the one occasion where you didn't get the opportunity to learn from your mistakes, or were given another day to make up for them. In fact, the next day we were going to board the Boeing 747 that would fly us back to South Africa, to the angry reception that I was sure awaited us. In my first year in the job, I had been booed after a Tri Nations game at Kings Park. I expected a similar reaction now.

To be honest, I was terrified. I didn't feel as if my shoulders were broad enough to carry the load. I felt as if I had failed my country. Springbok teams aren't supposed to be knocked out in the quarter-final of the World Cup. But before we could board the flight home or face the media in Johannesburg upon our return, there were other important matters that needed seeing to. I had to address the players, and I also had to attend what would probably be my final post-match press conference.

Press conferences were never easy for me. No matter how many times people tried to warn me or coach me to do otherwise, I always found it nearly impossible to avoid answering a straight question with what I thought was an honest answer. And I suspected that Bryce Lawrence, the referee who had played a bigger role than anyone else in knocking us out of the World Cup, was going to be a hot topic.

I knew I should try to skirt the issue and maintain my dignity by not blaming the referee, but before the tournament it had been said that referees would determine the outcome of games, and I hadn't quite realised at the time how accurate that prediction would turn out to be.

Quite a few things went through my mind as I sat there staring into the middle distance, at the empty green field and the sky beyond it. And because I have to be honest, I have to admit that this was one of the thoughts that went through my mind: If unscrupulous bookies had not on occasion failed to get what they wanted from cricket players, thereby bringing betting into the open, perhaps we would still not know that match fixing existed in that sport.

Perhaps it is naive to think that match fixing doesn't exist in rugby. At the World Cup, we heard of instances where people were betting as much as £400 000 on a game. So it did cross my mind that my team might have been targeted. Some of the things that had been happening in the tournament just didn't make any sense.

The previous week, Welsh referee Nigel Owens had done world rugby a huge disservice by letting Samoa get away with murder against the Springboks in a decisive pool match. Afterwards, the International Rugby Board (IRB) had apologised to me in private and also congratulated the players and management on the diplomatic way we had handled the situation. But they never said anything publicly. Instead they just continued – as is their wont – to concern themselves with 'illegal' branding on headgear and mouth guards and issuing fines to players who contravened their rules.

Instead of censuring Owens, the IRB rewarded him with a quarterfinal. Why would you reward a referee for the way he had performed in that Bok/Samoan match?

These issues had my mind in turmoil as I left my seat and headed out of the box to start the long walk down the steps and into the bowels of the concrete stadium and its maze of corridors. Bryce Lawrence was normally a cocky ref, always ready to rebuke the players and put them in their place. But in this game he had kept on apologising to John Smit and Victor Matfield for infringements he was inexplicably missing.

But as I thought about the outcome of the game, I remembered that I believe that you get only that which is meant to come your way. Sometimes, there is no point trying to find a reason why some things happen. If you do, it often just causes you more pain. People will find a way to justify their actions, even though you know they aren't really justifiable.

These thoughts were milling through my mind, and I had no idea how I was going to deal with them during the press conference. I knew that people were betting big money on our games and I knew what I was tempted to say, but I was well aware that if I said anything about it, it would create a massive international incident. And our World Cup campaign would then end in an undignified exit.

Before going to the press conference, I went to the changing room, where the players were inconsolable. The tears were flowing freely. Everyone was gutted, completely gutted. I could not have asked for more from the players than they gave. I was immensely proud of all of them. And yet this was where our journey as a team was going to end. No, we were more than a team; we were a family. Our defeat was one heck of a thing to accept, particularly when we had so clearly been the better team on the day, and when it was so obvious that the referee had been the biggest factor in our loss ... There was anger, and lots of it. But where could one direct that anger?

As had happened after all the losses during my tenure, there would be criticism afterwards for mistakes the team had made and for perceived wrong decisions on and off the field. Criticising us for going for posts when we were awarded a penalty instead of kicking for touch was perhaps justified, but hindsight is a perfect science. During the game, when we looked at the momentum we had in our favour, it seemed just a matter of time before we would break through and take control of the game. And if the referee had made the right decisions, this would surely have happened.

So although I couldn't criticise our decision-making on the field, perhaps we should have adjusted our game when we saw how the referee was interpreting the rules.

In the changing room, none of the players who had played in the game looked me in the eye. I walked from one to the other and thanked them all individually for their efforts. Not one of them looked at me directly. If you studied the missed kicks, the marginal forward passes, the cynical Danie Rossouw interference at a line-out that had led to the Wallabies' winning penalty, there were enough reasons to absolve individual responsibility, to say, 'Hey, *I* am not to blame.'

But rugby is not about individuals. We were all in this together. We had gone into the tournament as a united group, and we would leave as a united group. I was determined for that to happen, but I still didn't know what to do next. Needing to buy some time, I asked Jean de Villiers to lead the players in prayer.

When Jean finished, I still didn't know what to say, but I thought, 'Damn it, I have to say *something*.' So I cleared my throat. Of the few guys who were looking at me, most were management members and non-playing reserves.

'When I look around this room at all of you, I feel I have failed you guys, and for one reason only,' I said. 'I always promised you that I would be there for you and that I would stand up for you, but now, when you need me the most, I can't do anything. I can't change the scoreboard, and in the end that is all that counts. Everyone will remember that the final score was against us when it mattered most. I feel I have failed you, because now that you need me, I can't do anything for you. That makes me a failure today in this huddle.'

I gathered myself before continuing.

'But if you look at the journey we have been on together, you should all be so proud. And I am proud of what I learnt from you and could give to you. We went through a lot in the past four years, but nothing could break us or drive us apart, not even now that our journey has come to an end. We, as the management, tried to create an environment in which you could grow, which I believe you have all done.

'If you grew as a person on this journey, you can feel proud to have been a part of it. So let's go out there tonight and be proud of the fact that we all gave our best. The plans we laid back in May worked today. But we could never have foreseen that the referee would be so influential that he would stop us in our tracks. That is why we never got to fulfil our destiny.'

The words came from deep within my heart, but my head was still all over the place. Later, I said to the media that the changing room had been only one degree better than attending a funeral. So many questions needed answers, but it was like trying to get to the bottom of why an accident had happened. Knowing why a car has hit you won't undo the damage done.

The success of our game plan could be measured against how much the Australians had been forced to kick in that match. They had been unable to play their normal game – we simply hadn't allowed them to.

With the experience you gain as Bok coach, you start to anticipate the questions you will get at a press conference. But this time, there was still no clarity in my mind. Usually when you lose, it's because you played badly. You can blame the line-outs, for example. But we had dominated their line-out … we had dominated *everything*. So the question kept nagging: How was I going to get through the press conference without blaming Bryce Lawrence for our loss?

First up was a television interview. It didn't go well. You can't hide your face when you are being interviewed on television.

As I neared the room where the media were waiting, I thought to myself: 'Come on, this might be very bad for Peter de Villiers, the team, the country and the hopes you helped create that are now dashed. But what is *your* purpose? Your purpose is surely to be a true leader. Going out with complaints will achieve no purpose.'

So I knew that this would be the one occasion where I would have to be like other coaches: I would have to be politically correct in whatever I said. Of course I knew they would ask me about Bryce Lawrence, and if he was not to blame for our loss, who was?

The Australians certainly weren't to blame. They had played the game clean and straight and had defended well. They were rightfully elated that they were through to the semi-final. It wouldn't be fair to begrudge them their happiness. I resolved that no matter what happened at the press conference, I would congratulate the Aussies and wish them well on the way forward.

In the end, because every rugby fan had witnessed Bryce Lawrence's inventive refereeing that day, there was no need for us to make a point about it. In fact, we weren't even quizzed particularly aggressively about the refereeing. My skipper, John Smit, and I congratulated the Wallabies, and of course it had been John and Victor Matfield's last game for the Springboks, so a lot of focus was deflected towards that. According to media interpretation of what I went on to say, I had also had my last game in the Springbok camp. And that became the main topic at the press conference – not Bryce Lawrence.

I was asked what plans I had for the future, and I can't recall saying that I was going to resign. I just said that I knew it was time to go, and that I had always known that my contract would come to an end in December 2011. As no internationals had been planned for after the World Cup, my job was effectively over. It was time for me to move on. And in more ways than one, as I couldn't wait to leave the whole bad experience, and what I was feeling, behind.

This was one of the reasons why I didn't approach Bryce Lawrence after the game. There would have been no point to it. Having it out with him would simply have prolonged the agony. And I don't live in the past. I have never done that.

I was asked to sum up my career as Springbok coach. 'It's been one hell of a ride,' I said. 'One hell of a ride.' And so we left our final press conference with our dignity intact, although a storm was still raging inside me.

And it certainly had been quite a ride. I consider it both a massive privilege and an honour to have served my country, but for most of the way it was a pretty tempestuous ride, as there had been so many highs and lows. I experienced many wonderful times, but also much anxiety and frustration, and sometimes even heartache. Hell, I can't emphasise enough how much intensity and emotion the job entailed.

But my philosophy, which is underpinned by my deep faith, has always been that everything happens for a reason. Whenever I greet people, my stock phrase is always, 'Even the bad days are good.' And although many people probably got extremely angry with me at various stages over my four-year tenure, often justifiably, I really do believe that. Rugby is a big part of my life, but in the end it is just a sport. It is not my whole life.

Even the bad times are good – yes, probably even the moments right after a gut-wrenching defeat like the one we had suffered in Wellington on that eventful Sunday afternoon.

One of my parables got me into hot water in the build-up to the 2009 British & Irish Lions series, when I said that between the pit and the palace, the Biblical character Daniel had to go through a '*moerse* load of *kak*' (a huge amount of shit). That was true for me too. Looking back now, it's quite obvious that many of the problems I encountered were determined on the day I was appointed.

That day, in early 2008, was supposed to be the most exciting and happy moment of my life, but it would end up far from being so. Much of what happened then was a microcosm of events that would unfold over the next four years.

When Johan Prinsloo, the then chief executive of the South African Rugby Union (SARU), phoned me to tell me I had the job, I was, of course, thrilled.

'We want you at our offices to make the announcement,' he said. 'You are the coach.'

I had had an anxious month over the Christmas holiday period waiting for that call, so when I heard those words, all the breath was expunged from my body and I was suddenly light-headed. *I had the job* – the dream I had cherished from the time South African rugby had unified in 1992 was being fulfilled. Johan told me to keep the news under my hat until it was announced, but that I must come down to the SARU offices for the media briefing.

Driving to Newlands from Paarl on a bright Cape summer morning, I could scarcely contain my excitement. Hell, the guy from Paarl was the new Springbok coach! But SARU had a shock in store for me. When I got to their offices, Johan met me at the entrance and told me that there had been a change of plan. The provincial presidents weren't happy with the decision the technical committee had made. They wanted to vote again, and this time it would be the presidents – effectively the SARU board – doing the voting and not the technical committee.

I was ushered into an office and told to sit and wait. It was there that the same silence I was to experience later on enveloped me. Although I was anxious, I also found calm in the tense quiet of that empty room. I remembered my mantra: 'Whatever will be, will be.' If God wanted me for the job, they wouldn't have a choice but to appoint me; if He didn't, they would convey that message. From the beginning, my attitude had been that the job was not mine to keep – I would just be the care-taker for four years, serving my country to the best of my ability.

There was nothing I could do to swing the vote in my favour. If the presidents voted against me, then that would be it. It crossed my mind that I hadn't even told the people back home that I had been appointed. Therefore, if the vote went against me, who would ever know that I had, for one brief, wonderful moment, been the Springbok coach?

So my Springbok coaching career started off rather badly.

I had no idea why the technical committee had been overruled, as it had interviewed the candidates, conducted the tests and voted for me 7-1. The only person who had voted against me was the chief executive of the Sharks, Brian van Zyl. Overruling the committee effectively meant a vote of no-confidence in its members.

I eventually won the day … not by much, though. The board voted 11-10 in my favour, so it was immediately apparent that there was much opposition to my appointment – and the president voted against me. But no matter, as soon I was put in front of the media. My new bosses hadn't even discussed my remuneration or any other aspects of my contract with me. I answered the reporters' questions … and then I heard the president of the union say that I was an affirmative-action appointment.

Here is what Oregan Hoskins said on 9 January 2008, the day of my appointment:

'I want to be honest with South Africa and say that the appointment did not take into account only rugby reasons. We took … the issue of transformation in rugby very, very seriously when we made the appointment.'

What the hell was that supposed to mean? How was I supposed to react to what he'd just said? Oregan later told me that Morné du Plessis and Johann Rupert had advised him on what to say. They had probably meant well, but where was the backbone you would expect in a strong leader? I can't imagine that rugby leaders of the past, such as Dr Danie Craven, would have been swayed so easily or would have tolerated being told what to say.

I was very angry. And I was just as angry with Oregan's next statement: 'South Africa has a black coach now – that is fantastic for the game in all parts of the world.'

With those words, Oregan permanently pigeonholed me as an affirmative-action appointment. He was helping form the perceptions that would make it so difficult for me to be accepted by the rugby public, the media and other stakeholders. After that, each and every criticism that came my way was underscored by what Hoskins had said: that I was not given the position for rugby reasons only. I thus didn't deserve to be the Springbok coach.

I immediately realised what a setback this was, and that I would face a massive challenge in trying to convince the rugby world, including the players, that I was representing everyone and not just black people, that I was not there to serve a specific agenda, and that I was, black or not, the best man for the job. Knowing this directed my response to a reporter's question: 'The [perception] that I am the first *black* coach must end now,' I said. 'Players … must understand that they will stand an equal chance [of selection]. If they are good enough, talented enough and work hard enough, they will play for the Boks … The word "transformation" is a bit of a swear word with me. I'm more concerned about a change of attitude than a change of colour.'

I suppose I was naive. In fact, I was naive about a lot of things, like the motives of the people who'd initially supported me. But we'll get to that later. Before my appointment, numerous media articles reported that SARU was under government pressure to make up for the 2007 World Cup transformation 'disaster', as government called it, when just two black players, wings JP Pietersen and Bryan Habana, had played in the final.

So it was short-sighted of me not to realise that race would play a big part in the discourse. From the outset, though, I was determined to be *everyone's* coach, not just a coach for a particular community or race group. It was one of the reasons why I wore a Bulls blazer to SA Rugby (Pty) Ltd headquarters on the fifth floor of the Sports Science Institute at Newlands for the media announcement. Some people thought the gesture arrogant, as Heyneke Meyer had been the other big contender for the job, and he was coaching the Bulls. So they thought I was trying to get at Heyneke. But that wasn't the case at all. I wore the Bulls blazer because, at that stage, my stint as assistant coach to the Bulls in the 2002 Super 12 had been one of my most senior rugby positions.

And, as I explained to the media, I wore the blazer because I wanted to make everyone feel included. As I lived in the Cape, people could easily think that my allegiance lay with Western Province. By wearing the Bulls blazer, I was conveying the message that I was not aligned to anyone and that everyone was equal in my eyes. I might have said it a bit tongue-in-cheek, but it was important to me that everyone felt included.

So when Oregan said what he did, it dampened my excitement and made my job as a unifier a lot more difficult. I had lived and strived for the position of Bok coach all my adult life, but to then hear that I had got the job for reasons other than just rugby … I felt as if someone had punched me in the guts.

Needless to say, Regan's statement did nothing to increase my respect for him. Nor did it quell my suspicion that the SA Rugby administrators did not want me as the Bok coach, and that they would try to force me out at the first opportunity.

It's very difficult working for people you don't trust. This lack of trust, as well as the feeling that I never really had their support, was to direct a lot of my decision-making and behaviour over the next four years. It was also one of the major reasons for making the senior players my sole support group later on.

I had really wanted the day of the announcement to be the last day I was referred to as a 'black' coach. Although I did see myself as breaking the mould and offering hope to the black kids in the townships, to be seen always as the 'black' coach would also put unfair pressure on me. And I was already putting enough pressure on myself. Focusing on the colour of my skin made me feel tainted, as if everyone was judging me as a black man who was a coach, instead of just as a coach who happened to be a black man. I didn't want to look for an easy way out if I made a mistake; I wanted to be judged on my coaching abilities alone.

The upshot of Oregan's words was that everyone perceived me to be a political appointment. I had to decide how I was going to live with that. I was no different from, say, the traffic cop who becomes the chief of traffic because of the colour of his skin when everyone knows he's not the best traffic cop in the department.

Surely things could only get better from then on? Well, it did get better, for as I said, I had a wonderful ride. I also like to think that I made the Springboks more accessible to all South Africans. But hell, there were far more obstacles than there needed to be, and so many of those had been placed there by my employers on that very first day.

But the experience of getting through those initial hours taught me that no one can take away one's destiny. It was an important realisation, as it helped me to know that whatever had brought me to the position would carry me through. With the pain of being told that I wasn't really good enough for the job came the knowledge that the person I was and the qualities I possessed – for which SARU had appointed me in the first place, surely? – would equip me for the task ahead. If I'd had a speech prepared for that day, I would have not been able to deliver it. Oregan's comments would have left me speechless.

But my community in Paarl, where I have lived for most of my life, celebrated my appointment with great joy, which immediately lifted my spirits. I had difficulty getting to my house, as all the roads near my home in Paarl were blocked off until about 3 a.m. the next morning. It was one hell of a party.

Of course I recognised the significance of my appointment to the black communities – in their collective mind, I was breaking down race barriers. Although South Africa had had a black president since 1994, many still considered Springbok rugby the last bastion of Afrikanerdom, an exclusive club championing white supremacy. In a previous era, a black person becoming a Springbok coach was akin to a Jew taking over the running of the Gestapo.

As it turned out, some of those who helped me in my bid to get the Springbok coaching job didn't understand a few things about me. Firstly, the Springbok emblem was very important to me. In fact, had the Springbok emblem been abolished in my time as coach, there would have been a big court case, as I was never contracted to be anything other than the *Springbok* coach. That's the job I applied for. That's the title that was printed on the application form and, eventually, when it was finally signed, on my contract too.

Secondly, I didn't want to alienate anyone. I was adamant that I didn't want to represent only black people; I wanted to be respected by everyone in the country; I wanted to be there for *all* my countrymen. I mention this in the context of the time, when some factions feared my appointment to be the first step in getting rid of the Springbok emblem. I was considered to be the agent of dark forces that were out to ruin South African rugby and, in the words of former Springbok captain Corné Krige, take the game into 'seven lean years'.

Breaking down these misconceptions was my immediate and most important goal, but the words of Oregan Hoskins had ensured that I would start my Springbok coaching career facing even bigger challenges.

2

Learning through hardship

It's probably safe to say I had a different upbringing and background from other Springbok coaches and most Springbok players. The social and political crime of apartheid ensured that this would be the case, but I was fortunate to have been born into a strong family unit and was given a solid grounding by my parents.

There was also religion, and my strong faith in God has directed most of the decisions I have made in my life.

I am the second-oldest child in a family of five children. My father was a disciplinarian who did not believe in sparing the rod. My older brother, Joseph, was my childhood hero, and I followed him through much of my youth. He was extremely talented and was good at everything he tried.

At primary school, Joseph would compete with the teachers at table tennis and cricket. He was a great athlete and a natural rugby player who could make spot-on decisions and big tackles, and he scored tries seemingly at will. He was strong-willed, but because he did not talk much, he was often misunderstood.

The bottom fell out of my world when Joseph was sent to a high school in another town. After that I had to learn to survive on my own, and I was no longer in my comfort zone. Joseph did, however, leave me with a strong work ethic, as I had not been given his talent and therefore had to work so much harder to achieve good results.

My older sister, Elisabeth, was a bit like my father: it was very important to her to stay on the straight and narrow. All of us knew how to fight for what we wanted, but Elisabeth always had that extra bit of will power and never took short cuts. It must have been tough for her living with brothers who were only interested in sport and didn't really care about what happened around the house.

My little brother, Hilton, was overprotected by my mother, as the baby in the family often is. He showed outstanding musical talent, but it was his sense of justice that made him special. As a young man, he fought tirelessly against apartheid, which cost him dearly in the workplace. He was denied promotion on a couple of occasions, and was also sacked a few times, mainly because he insisted on always speaking his mind. I suppose to some extent all of us siblings have this characteristic in common.

My younger sister, Melony, was a combination of both my mother and my father's personalities. Everyone spoilt her and, like Joseph, she had outstanding sporting talent. She obtained provincial colours in three sports codes at school. We didn't have a lot to show the world in terms of material possessions, and there was nothing that made us different from other people, but we loved and cared for each other, and the values and norms instilled in us by our parents were a binding factor.

Looking back, I was fortunate to have grown up in an environment where the three essential pillars for a good upbringing were in place: the family and home environment; the school, which lays the intellectual foundation; and the church, which is directed towards spiritual growth.

Because of the circumstances of the time in the country we lived in, coloured people's sporting achievements did not make the national news or get championed beyond the communities in which we lived. But that did not mean that rugby was a big thing only in the white community. In fact, far from it. Because of the harshness of our everyday existence, rugby became an important part of life in the black communities of the Western Cape. It was a way to establish oneself in the community, to gain recognition, and the matches were played with great passion and intensity.

If you were talented, you could set yourself up as the next hot topic in town. Our world was small, and while our achievements did not make the news beyond the borders of our towns, we took them very seriously.

Rugby, as a community-driven sport, had a way of making you feel good about yourself, and it was a feeling you couldn't get from anything else. If you performed outstandingly, you and your teammates could inspire the people, and they would go to work and church with their heads held high.

These were the days before the Group Areas Act, and social clubs were born from the rugby clubs in our communities. Black, white, coloured, Christian, Jew and Muslim lived happily together, solving the problems of the neighbourhood as a unit.

In a predominantly working-class community, it was the rugby players' task to put on a good show on a Saturday afternoon so that everyone else's problems could be alleviated, if just for a while. A Saturday afternoon at the rugby was an outing for the whole family to enjoy and to look forward to all week.

This big weekly event was the reason why everybody went to town early on a Saturday morning to do their shopping, and that was where the big build-up to the afternoon's game began. Even if you were playing that day, you had to go to town to help the rest of the family carry the heavy bags back home. You'd bump into your team's supporters there and they'd make you feel special, because the game meant so much to them. They would greet you and say, 'Hi, how are you? Are you ready for today's game? Don't worry, we will win today; that other lot will never be able to beat us. See you later; I still have a lot to do before the game.'

At the same time, you would also run into players from the opposing team and their supporters. Of course you knew these people well after years of rivalry, and they would make their presence felt by trying to unsettle you with negative talk. A conversation with one of them would go something like this: 'Hi, what are *you* doing here? Shouldn't you be spending the last few hours of your life with your family? 'Cause you know that you're dead today, don't you? So I'll see you this afternoon for the last time. But I can't talk now; I have things to do.'

As I reminded the world rugby media during the British & Irish Lions tour of South Africa in 2009, rugby has always been a contact sport – but even more so when *we* played. There were no height restrictions on tackles, and vigorous rucking, with feet all over the poor opposing player's body, was part and parcel of the game.

The surfaces we played on were not always conducive to great rugby and sometimes resembled a railway track. Today they are, in fact, considered suitable only for stock-car racing. Those conditions lent credence to the slogan 'no normal sport in an abnormal society'. The playing surfaces were so bad, they were notorious for causing injuries without the players even going on the field – some of them would take one look at the surface they were about to run onto and suddenly be too injured to play.

When we were playing away, we made use of lorries, buses and anything with four wheels that could move forward without going up in a puff of smoke to get to our destination. We usually overcame any obstacles – nothing could dampen our enthusiasm for rugby. Wire fences separated you from the fiery, passionate crowd who arrived in their thousands to watch their local heroes, and they normally left no stone unturned in their attempts to break you down mentally.

And everyone would do just about anything to pressurise and influence the referee. Hah, you think I had trouble with referees later on, as in Wellington in 2011 with Bryce Lawrence? Well, I can tell you that where I come from, games were often determined before the kick-off, depending on who the referee was and where the game was being played. So don't talk to me about the role home-ground advantage plays in determining the result – I know all about it from my youth. That was just the way it was.

These were tough times, but rugby provided valuable life lessons and built character. We learnt many things, but perhaps the most important was not to pay heed to people who looked down on you because they had more material wealth than you. On the sports field everyone was equal and your talent was all that mattered. We realised that wealth was only a temporary, earthly advantage and should not dictate your life.

In spite of the dire conditions, the communities spawned some extraordinarily talented sportspeople, and it was a crying shame that the laws of the land prevented them from competing for a place on the international stage. I am not saying that all of them would have been successful, but now we will never know, which is tragic.

What a big country South Africa seemed to me then, a land of milk and honey, and yet so many of us were only allowed to *look* at what God had created, as to touch and share was forbidden to us. As sportspeople, our common experiences bound us together and we grew very close. If someone was badly injured in a game, the bus or lorry would stop off at the hospital on the way home and no one minded waiting for the injured chap to get help. It was a caring community.

Times were hard and life was tough, but in those days it was bearable, as the law that would scatter us to the four corners of the town had not yet been passed by the all-white government.

Before the Group Areas Act, we lived in Paarl itself, in a place called 'Die Ou Tuin' (the Old Garden). In 1948, a rugby club by the name of Young Gardens was established – everyone who lived in Die Ou Tuin played for this club, and the whole community helped to develop the club into something we could all identify with and be proud of.

Then, in 1950, the Group Areas Act scattered us all over the town, ironically for the purposes of building sports fields for white people, and most of the new generation – perhaps they should be known as the 'missing generation' – was moved to a place called Amstelhof. It was an awful place for any human being to grow up in or in which to raise children. There were no parks or playgrounds; just stones everywhere. Most of the street games took place on rock-hard surfaces. You had to develop extraordinary skills not to fall or get tackled. The bigger boys didn't care if they hurt you, and many a night you were afraid to get into the bath because of all your wounds.

The gravel roads were our playgrounds, and we had to contend not only with our direct opponent, but also with oncoming cars, pedestrians, the police and our neighbours, who were angry at the government for dumping them there. One road was later tarred, which meant that everyone came to play there. But it was also the main thoroughfare, so there were always cars moving along, often at considerable speed.

Some people who lived in Amstelhof were not sport lovers. Like us, they didn't want to live there, but they allowed their grievances and unhappiness to rule their lives. We therefore had to be accurate in our execution of whatever sport we were playing, for if a ball went into one of those people's gardens, it never came back.

The Group Areas Act didn't only break up the community – we also had to rebuild our beloved rugby club, which we are still struggling to do to this day. We had to walk great distances to attend meetings and practices, and sometimes we had to change the venue in order to accommodate everyone. Some people grew disillusioned because of what we had to go through just to play the game and keep the club together, but our passion for rugby was much greater than any obstacles we faced.

Most of our young players, thanks to the vision of their parents, went on to tertiary institutions, with the result that we had a strong, disciplined rugby club with educated members who could debate a point responsibly. So, through the rugby club, we saw the birth of a new crop of leaders within the community.

Obviously, we vehemently opposed apartheid. Our parents weren't happy with that at first, because, apart from fearing the state, they had also been a bit brainwashed. Although we managed to successfully confront most of the challenges that came our way, unfortunately the law was a massive obstacle to overcome. Every time we thought we had achieved one of our objectives, something else would catch us unawares. It was a frustrating time, made even more frustrating by the successful policy of divide-and-rule that the government employed.

While we all wanted to be part of the international arena so that the top players in our community would have a chance to play international sport, many of us couldn't see the way clear to do that when the country we lived in was governed by the laws of apartheid. That was why the old South African Rugby Union (SARU – not to be confused with the body currently running rugby in this country) aligned itself with the anti-apartheid movements in 1973. It was necessary to make changes in all spheres of life, so it was pointless competing with white people on the sports field if they did not see you as equals off it.

Thus, when Dr Danie Craven, the president of the white South African Rugby Board, co-opted some of our leaders, such as Dougie Dyers, into being 'semi-included' in white rugby, it caused division among our people, and the South African Rugby Federation (SARF) was formed as a rival to SARU.

Suddenly we were no longer united against one enemy, the government, but found ourselves becoming enemies of each other, with the supporters of SARU and the Federation having fierce differences of opinion. Yet while we regarded SARF as sell-outs in the sports arena, we had to rely on each other whenever we clashed with the state apparatus in the form of the army or police, and fight side by side. It was a very unsatisfactory situation.

So most of us adopted the slogan of the South African Council of Sports, which said, 'no normal sport in an abnormal society', as we realised we'd have to make sacrifices if we wanted to effect political change. We were banned from participating in any sport sanctioned by the regime.

These were bad times indeed for our community, particularly for those of us who stood by our principles. Some of us were very talented, and sometimes we couldn't help but wonder whether it was worth sacrificing the few opportunities we had to showcase our talents for a principle. But then we were given a reality check when we were treated like inferior human beings in the shops or on the streets.

Many of the players at Young Gardens Rugby Club were clued-up about the political situation and, as a result, the club became another victim of the political conditions in our country. The young guys' sentiments differed from those of the older generation, many of whom were on committees and held positions that enabled them to attend the big matches, often in hospitality boxes. Naturally they were reluctant to give up those privileges, apparently unaware that they were there for the collar and not the dog. Those of us who saw through this window-dressing were seen as rebels.

So, after a lengthy debate on whether or not we should stand by our principles, the club was split into Young Gardens SARU, of which I remained a part, and Young Gardens Federation. It was a difficult decision, as we had a lot of respect for our elders, but we could no longer make decisions based on sentiment. We reasoned that one day people would ask us what we had done to help bring down the system … what sacrifices had *we* made? We wanted to be able to respond honestly and with a clear conscience.

But it split Paarl, and even some households, into two camps. We only realised much later just how much animosity had sprung up between us and how much trust and respect we had lost for one another. This is one of the reasons why it's so difficult for our communities to perceive someone like Danie Craven as an icon.

My school halfback partner and I played well together, and we felt that we were destined for great things on the rugby field, but now we found ourselves in different camps and our relationship broke down completely.

Because of the infighting in the community, my father stopped watching rugby altogether. I never had the privilege of having him come and watch any of my rugby games, although I went on to play at provincial level. But I always knew that he was one of my biggest supporters.

I have to confess that I once secretly went against his wishes when he forbade me to play rugby after I brought home a bad school report. I carried on playing regardless. My brother helped me in the subterfuge, as I would leave the house on the pretence that I was supporting him. I was simply too passionate about the sport not to be a part of it.

* * *

On a different note, I was very fortunate that my parents were able to afford an education for me. For a while, the teaching profession's passive attitude to the riots of 1976 made me doubt my dream of becoming a teacher, but I later came to understand the restraints they were under, and that made up my mind for me. The decision, however, required a lot of deliberation, and it was only after the deadline for applications had expired that I decided to apply to Perseverance Teachers Training College in Kimberley. Two weeks after the tertiary institutions opened for tuition in the new academic year, I received a letter saying that my application had been successful. So I set off by train to Kimberley to fulfil my dream.

Initially, the rugby side of college did not go well, as at the trials I didn't even make it into the B-side. There were two scrumhalves who had better rugby CVs than me, and they kept me out of contention. But I got my chance late in the second half of the trial. I must have impressed someone because I was selected for the final trial and then to play for the college prestige team alongside some excellent players.

I went on to play for Griqualand West under the capable leadership of the president of SARU, Abdul Abass, who was well respected for his leadership abilities and his firm decision-making.

And I had the privilege of playing my provincial rugby under the guidance of the best rugby coach ever, Piet van Wyk. Piet understood both the needs of the player and what the word 'team' meant. He was always fair, but he did not make decisions based on sentiment. And he had an amazing ability to motivate and inspire a player to play for him, as well as the ability to say something straight to your face and so make you understand your role and responsibilities towards yourself, your teammates, your province and the wider community. I learnt a lot from Piet that I applied later when I, too, became a coach.

When I was first selected, I displaced a local guy who had played for his province for more than 10 years. Needless to say, it didn't make me the most popular person in Kimberley. I had to prove to the people why I had been selected, which demanded hard work and lots of dedication. But I enjoyed the pressure, and gradually won everyone over.

I was also honoured to represent a zone side selected from a combination of Griquas, Natal, Transvaal and Northern Cape players. Unfortunately, I don't remember the experience with great fondness. There were no funds available, so we couldn't get together for any preparation. We all travelled to Port Elizabeth separately, and we only joined up once we arrived there, with the players meeting their teammates for the first time the night before the game.

We spent most of that night on indoor board sessions, where we discussed calls and moves for the next day's game. It was the only time that I can recall staying in a hotel as a player. I think SARU must have obtained sponsorship from the Alabama Hotel, but unfortunately we couldn't get any sleep that night because it was located on one of the busiest entertainment blocks in the city.

I later returned to Port Elizabeth to play in the Springbok trials. The rugby was very competitive and of a high standard. The best black players in the country were attending the trails, and people came from far and wide to see their heroes playing. Although I did not make the team, the experience I gained, the intensity of the games and the pressure to perform stuck with me afterwards and helped me grow as a person.

Those were great days, but then came the moment I was forced out of rugby for reasons unrelated to the sport. Some students at the college were being treated unfairly, and I stood up for them. As a result, I had a huge fight with the matron of the hostel, and it turned quite ugly. Not being from Kimberley, I was on the back foot from the outset. Her two sons stepped in to defend their mother and put me in my place.

When I doubt my facts, I consult, but when I have no doubt that I am right about something, then nothing will convince me to change my mind. I am prepared to die for my principles. And this was one of those occasions. It got quite scary, though. On the Friday night of the week when all this transpired, I faced death for the first time as a gun was pointed at me from just one metre away. I was helpless, but I refused to apologise. Fortunately one of my mates, Jimmy, had a plastic cane. Goodness knows where he'd got it from or why he had it – I really don't want to know. But one smack of the cane on the man's shoulder was enough to make him forget he had a gun.

I couldn't go to the rugby grounds for quite a while after this incident. Finally the provincial coach came to find out why I wasn't playing, and he rescued me. After that, my rugby career at Griquas proceeded uneventfully, and although I did not make the national team, I was selected for the South African College XV. I received great offers to stay in Kimberley to further my careers as both a teacher and a rugby player, but I felt it was time to pay back my parents for the sacrifices they had made in supporting my education.

So I went back to Paarl to take up my first teaching job. Before I could start teaching, though, I was made another offer – one that resulted in a lot of soul-searching and led me to confront my principles and beliefs head-on. I had a rugby guru, who had coached and influenced me at junior level – I used to refer to him as the 'black Danie Craven'. Dumpies Ontong had a special way about him, an instinctive knowledge of rugby, and he commanded massive respect. Some of the tactics Dumpies taught me at under-14 and under-15 level, I later saw France doing at international level.

While I attended the Springbok trials in Port Elizabeth, Dumpies got in touch with me to find out whether I would be interested in playing for Western Province Federation. Dumpies had switched from

SARU to become a WP Federation selector. My decision to move back home had not been influenced by rugby, so it came as a big surprise to me when I arrived at Paarl station and Dumpies was waiting for me. I hadn't even told my parents I was coming home, as I had wanted to surprise them. How Dumpies knew I was on that train will forever be a mystery to me. I had to attend a wedding in Upington, and my intention had been to come home for only four days before setting off again.

But Dumpies took me for a drive, and he tried to do a hard sell on me. He told me about the benefits of playing for WP Federation. They were moving out Attie Lategan as their scrumhalf and thus had a place for me. I told Dumpies I would think about it, which I did.

Eventually I called him. I told him that I wasn't a politician and had no intention of becoming one, but that one thing I knew for certain, and that was that the system in South Africa was rotten. By playing for Federation, I would be colluding with the establishment, which I just couldn't do. I told him I wanted to make a contribution on the SARU side. There couldn't be normal sport in an abnormal society.

But that didn't mean that I agreed with everything that was happening at SARU either. As someone who spoke his mind, I wasn't very popular and never had many true friends in rugby.

One issue I remember clearly was the controversy around my first game for Boland, against Western Province. The game was to be played on the same day as the annual Easter club tournament at the City and Suburban grounds. I was captain of my club, Young Gardens, but instead of people phoning up to congratulate me on being awarded the captaincy, I had to put up with verbal abuse. They thought I should withdraw from the Boland team and play for my club instead.

Luckily the club game was scheduled to be played a lot earlier than the Boland game, so I got around the problem by playing for my club first and playing the provincial game later – two games on the same day.

I stopped playing rugby in 1987, by which time I had already had my first taste of coaching while working as a teacher. I enjoyed coaching the pupils in all the different sports codes, and I soon enough realised that sport afforded me the opportunity to make a difference in society. Seeing the passion the kids had for sport, I put extra effort into helping build tennis courts, a mini-athletics track and a cricket pitch. I went to factories and got the materials needed, such as ash for the tennis court. I located a suitable, unused rugby field next to a factory and worked damn hard to ensure that it became playable, something for which I was highly commended by the principal of the school where I was teaching. Our teams did not always win, but I loved the look of fulfilment in the eyes of the kids when we did.

I had some difficult experiences with children, teachers, parents, principals, inspectors and the police during my two decades as a teacher, but it all helped prepare me for my next challenge, which was coaching rugby. Let me say, though, that the rationalisation of teachers, which entailed the retrenchment of so many good teachers in order to save the government money, was a mind-numbingly stupid decision that has set both the teaching profession and the country back by years. The education of our youth should be a priority and should be allocated a much bigger budget than is currently the case.

With rationalisation we not only lost very good teachers, but also the intellectual property we require to keep the profession on the moral high ground. Everyone who knew how to work hard to get to the top left, and those who had no experience of hard work were promoted without having proven their abilities. So our matric results will remain a problem until sufficient effort and expense are poured into teaching.

All of this made me so depressed that I lost my passion for the profession.

My disillusionment with teaching and the problems our education system was encountering made my decision a few years later to make rugby my career much easier.

3

A brief taste of the Springboks

My entry into coaching at senior club level happened through Young Gardens. I achieved some success in my new role, and when the country was united in 1992 and it became possible for all race groups to be represented in a national team that would soon be sporting the colours of a democratic country, I decided I wanted to coach the Springboks.

I wasn't stupid, though. I realised that as a black coach I would be perceived as lagging behind white coaches and I would battle to be treated the same as them. So I resolved to lift myself to the same level as my white peers. I decided to obtain the kind of qualifications that no one would be able to dispute.

After giving it some thought, I concluded that Wales had been the nation that had most captured my imagination during my younger years. They played the kind of rugby I enjoyed the most. Guys like JPR Williams, JJ Williams, Phil Bennett and Gareth Edwards were my heroes. So I resolved to attend some coaching courses in Wales.

I approached the bank for a loan, and then set about raising money for the purpose of going overseas. But you can't get money for doing nothing, so I organised a black-tie function at Paarl Rock Cellars, where former Springbok captain Morné du Plessis agreed to be the guest speaker. And so I raised enough funds to further my overseas coaching dreams.

Once in Wales, I met up with John Prince, the national rugby team's coaching coordinator. Wow, what a guy! He helped me a great deal, and with all my newly acquired knowledge, I even managed to impress people on the coaching course with some of my ideas on how the game of rugby could be advanced. Whenever I see him, John always mentions the ideas I suggested while on the first few courses.

I completed my Level 2 coaching course in Wales, but you have to be invited back to do Level 3. Fortunately they didn't waste any time inviting me, so the next year, following the same process of raising money in order to sponsor myself, I managed to go to Wales for another few months. I had to take unpaid leave from my teaching, so it did cost me some of my own money.

In 2010, when I was in Cardiff with the Springboks for the June Test, they gave me the paper I had written during my Level 3 course on how the game will progress in the future. So much of what was written in that paper had turned out exactly as predicted. They gave me 94 per cent for that paper.

I was then invited back to do Level 4, which was a higher-graduate coaching course, and again they seemed to be impressed with me. They hadn't known me from a bar of soap before I started attending the courses, so I thought it was a strong endorsement of my coaching abilities that I was able to do so well in a foreign country, and it made me feel like I was ready to progress further. As part of the Level 3 and Level 4 courses, you spend time with the national teams to see how coaching is done at that level. Thanks to that experience, I now had the confidence to coach at a higher level.

But I was in for a shock when I got back to Paarl and invited the 13 clubs in town to send representatives to two Saturday coaching seminars, where I wanted to share what I had experienced in Wales. I wanted to give something back for the sponsorship I had received and which had enabled me to go overseas. On the first Saturday, a few people turned up, but on the second, no one pitched.

I was so disappointed. I took all the material I had prepared and burnt it. I heard that the people were saying, 'What makes him think he's such a big deal that he can come back and tell us how to do things?' But that hadn't been my intention at all. I just wanted to share what I had learnt.

I think my propensity for doing everything my way and still confronting injustice made people think I was a politician. Let's say I was standing in a shop and people were waiting patiently in line to be served, and then a guy came in wearing a smart suit and the shop assistant gave him preferential treatment over everyone else – that sort of scenario seemed so unjust, and it really irritated me. And I always reacted to it when it happened in my presence.

But it meant that I was constantly frustrated, and my attitude didn't go down well with the people around me. So I decided to change my approach and not wear my heart on my sleeve any more. I deliberately made a show of being light-hearted. I hid away the fact that I was seething because of some injustice by giving everyone the impression that I was a fun guy who wasn't bothered by anything.

You can't inspire anybody if you're angry the whole time. And a frustrated life is no life to lead. The number of people who, after sitting down with me, have said, 'Now I see the real Peter de Villiers, and he is different from the Peter de Villiers I thought I knew,' would take days to count.

But back to rugby: due to my successes at club level, I was appointed to coach the Western Province Disas team, and from there I moved up to coach the Western Province B-team. In 1997 I was in charge of an extremely successful WP B-team that did well in the old SA Cup. Earlier that year I had been privileged to be invited to shadow Carel du Plessis and Gert Smal, then Springbok head coach and assistant coach respectively, in the build-up to the British & Irish Lions tour of South Africa. It was a great experience and an introduction to the Springbok culture, and it allowed me to witness the pressure under which coaches at that level have to operate.

So, having had this experience, it didn't come as a complete surprise when, later in the year, before the end-of-year Springbok tour to France and England, I was invited to a meeting with Nick Mallett and the South African Rugby Football Union (SARFU) chief executive, Rian Oberholzer. Nick had just taken over from Carel, who had been sacked following a difficult first year in the job.

Nick told me he wanted me to go on the Springboks' end-of-year tour as an assistant coach. Naturally I was extremely excited about this turn of events, but first I needed to know a few things. Was I going as an *official* assistant coach, on the same level as the other assistant coaches, or was this just one of those development appointments geared towards helping me learn more about rugby coaching?

I wanted to know how it had come about that I had been chosen to work with Nick, as I did not know him and he didn't know me at all. Nick and Rian told me that they were impressed with my achievements on the rugby field, which was all that mattered.

But I made it clear to them that I would go as an assistant coach and nothing less. I did not want to be a token appointment. If that was their intention, then I would rather stay at home. Nick was adamant that I would go as an assistant coach, and I believed him. When I received my blazer, it felt as if I had been transported to another world. I looked at the badge first and there, underneath it, were the words written in gold – assistant coach.

I was very happy that all the sacrifices I had made were paying off, but what I did not know was that although we were all assistant coaches and thus equal, one was more equal than the other. My excitement about the position did not make me lose focus on reality. I knew I was going to work with high-profile players who had made it to the top and had been there for a while, which was going to be a big challenge. But I looked forward to inspiring them to reach even bigger heights.

Alan Solomons, the other assistant coach, was close to Nick, and I suppose you could say that I was naive for not knowing what would happen. Once we were on tour, Nick and Solly were inseparable. They spent a lot of time socialising together, but, even so, I sensed that Solly felt a bit threatened by me. Jake White would experience a similar situation in 1999, when he was hounded out of his job as the Boks' technical advisor/video operator.

Dick Muir was in the 1997 end-of-year team. It was his swansong as a player, and he had earned his Springbok colours in the nick of time, because the following season he would be injured while captaining the Western Stormers during their turbulent – and ultimately failed – first season in the Super 12, and would be forced to retire. Dick and I had a chat on the tour, and together we came up with a plan on how to use Os du Randt more effectively in the game. Our idea was communicated to Nick, who took our advice. And it worked.

I also discussed a few backline moves that I thought might suit Percy Montgomery's style of play with the other coaches. At that stage, Percy was a bit wild. He was still a young player and it had been his first full season of top rugby. He had played most of the year at outside centre, but then, when Justin Swart was injured before the second international of the tour, against France in Lyon, Percy switched to full-back and played almost all of his rugby in that position from then on.

Dick agreed with what I was saying about Percy, but for some reason my suggestion drew a chilly response from the coaches. That was the last time they allowed me to work with the players. I quickly picked up that I had been sidelined. I wasn't stupid. And naturally I was angry and frustrated. So, as I wasn't being used, I decided to concentrate on doing some coaching courses during the tour, which I did after hours so that they didn't interfere with my professional responsibilities with the team.

But hell, it wasn't an easy situation to take, and I felt insulted. I think part of the problem was that Nick and Solly used to socialise together, but then when they invited me to come along, I refused. I just wasn't into that sort of thing. Nick is a very forceful personality and he doesn't easily accept people saying no to him.

On three occasions he asked me to join him and Solly for a few beers, but I didn't drink. I thought that they might be using the drinking sessions to discuss me behind my back, and that they wanted to keep me in my place by offering me drinks. So I told them that if I had something to say to them, I would rather do it sober. In my view, you can't be honest with someone by having a few drinks and then afterwards blaming whatever you said on the alcohol. I've always preferred to fight my battles sober, but Nick took exception to my stance.

On the day we were flying out of France to start the British leg of the tour, I approached Arthob Petersen, the team manager, at Charles de Gaulle airport.

'Arthob,' I said, 'I'm going home. I've had enough. I can't allow these people to misuse me any further.'

I knew there were a lot of people back home who felt I was their representative on the tour and they would have expected me to stand up for what we believed in. I would have felt that I had let them down had I just accepted the situation and carried on regardless. I told Arthob that I could pay for myself to come to France if I wanted a holiday, but that the understanding had been that I would be undertaking the tour as an assistant coach.

My words started one hell of a fight. And we had it out right there at the airport in front of everyone. Nick is not good in situations where he feels he has to defend himself, and to say he got hot under the collar with me would be putting it mildly.

Rob van der Valk, a long-time aide of Nick's who was on tour as a logistics manager (Arthob's role was more ceremonial), intervened in the argument, but Nick did not calm down. He said, 'Why are you so upset? Why are you causing trouble now? You have done some really good things and you helped us a lot with Os.'

Rob said I mustn't be selfish and always just want everything for myself. But I was adamant. I told them that if they were going to put me in charge of something, they must have the confidence to trust me with the responsibility. I told them that if I was going to do a job, I was going to do it properly or I wasn't going to do it at all.

I was happy that I had I stood up for myself. I didn't want any favours from them – I just wanted to be respected as a professional who knew what he was doing. Otherwise, what was the point of being on the tour in the first place? But they didn't want to see it my way. They must have had their reasons. Perhaps it came down to our different backgrounds, or maybe they just didn't believe in me.

Although I eventually agreed to stay on for the rest of the tour, I felt I had been misinformed about their intentions and that they were still trying to pull the wool over my eyes, and we had quite a few fights during the remainder of the trip.

My relationship with Nick had actually not been great from the beginning, mainly due to a newspaper interview I had given before my appointment as assistant coach. Nick had got the Springbok job at a time when I had thought Carel du Plessis was doing okay. I didn't agree with all the negative criticism about Carel's coaching, and the Boks had won the last Test he coached, against Australia, by a big margin. (The Boks beat the Wallabies 61-22 in Pretoria.)

So I believed that Carel was starting to achieve the kind of game he was aiming for, and after the Boks' victory over Australia, the *Paarl Post* asked me for my opinion on whether Nick Mallett should replace him. I said that Carel had not been that successful on the scoreboard, but then neither had Nick.

Mallett was coaching the Boland Cavaliers at the time, and he had been criticised by the media. The Cavaliers may have improved a lot under him, but while they were more competitive in their games against bigger opponents, they still didn't win many matches. So it wasn't as if Nick's team had won a handful of trophies or achieved measurable success in that sense.

Early on in the tour Nick confronted me about what I had said in the newspapers. He told me that talking to the media wasn't acceptable and that I was being disloyal. But I had said those things long before I was appointed assistant coach. My comments had only come to his attention afterwards.

Despite all the drama in his management team, Nick did well with the Springboks. He had his own style of doing things. Although it wasn't a style I would follow myself, the players liked his approach and he got results. He was forthright and sometimes even harsh, but his tactics seemed to work. He was an excellent coach, as a matter of fact. The Boks won every game comfortably on that tour, including a record 52-10 win over France at Parc des Princes and an equally savage thrashing of England at Twickenham. Mallett's team was seen to have turned the corner, and they would go on to equal the international record of 17 consecutive victories.

When I got back to South Africa, Rian Oberholzer called me in, as did Sas Bailey, who was in charge of development at SARFU. Arthob had obviously told them what had happened at the airport. They asked me what had made me so unhappy – they wanted me to spill the beans on why some of Nick's management members had clashed on the tour.

But I didn't tell them anything, as I didn't think it was the right thing to do.

'You didn't employ me so that you could send me on tour to spy on people,' I said. 'I was there to assist Nick. That is what I was employed to do, no more and no less.'

Needless to say, Sas and Rian were both quite angry with me. They might have had information they wanted to use against Nick and Solly, but, if so, I wasn't going to be their snitch. I really meant what I said to both Rian and Sas – I was there only to assist, and in keeping quiet I was being loyal to the squad.

So what if I felt Nick had not treated me all that well? If I hadn't been man enough to stand up to him, I had no right to expect anyone else to fight the battle for me. That was the way I saw it. Later, when Rian somehow got to know the whole story, he asked me why I hadn't told him, but I just said that I couldn't talk behind anyone's back.

All in all, it had been a disappointing experience for me. I had wanted so desperately to make a difference and to be a representative of my people. I wanted to pave the way for those who would follow me.

What I learnt from that experience was how *not* to treat those you are working with. It is a lesson that will stay with me for as long as I work with people.

4

From pillar to post

When I returned from the Springbok tour in 1997, I was still a school-teacher, but I was having grave concerns about continuing my career because of the rationalisation of the teaching profession. In my view, the importance of the education system was not being respected enough and was, in effect, being downgraded.

So when Western Province offered me a job, I readily accepted. After all, rugby was my passion. Up until then I had coached Western Province teams, but not on a full-time basis. I was offered the position of development officer at WP, which was obviously a few notches down from where I had been as a Springbok assistant coach. Nevertheless, it was a proper, full-time rugby job and I couldn't have been happier, as it was a great opportunity for me to further my rugby ambitions and to work in a sport that had kept me spellbound since I was a little boy. It was also a chance for me to make a difference by improving the lot of black rugby players and to further the drive towards equality.

So what could possibly go wrong? As it turned out, and as I learnt very quickly, quite a lot, actually. The problems started when I found out how much more Alan Solomons, who was employed as the senior WP coach a couple of months after I had taken up my job, was earning in comparison to me. I knew he had to deal with a lot more pressure than I did, but that was not the issue. I also didn't think that he was being overpaid, for that was not the case. However, the vast discrepancy between our respective pay cheques showed that what I was earning was ridiculous.

So I approached the WP chief executive, Theuns Roodman.

'How the devil did you work that out?' I asked him.

Theuns's response was that Solly had been a lawyer in his previous career and thus had to be paid significantly more than me. 'You were only a teacher before,' he said.

But Theuns then offered to increase what I was earning. Again, it was just ridiculous, as the money they were offering was pathetic.

The next bone of contention was when Solly brought in Adrian Kennedy from New Zealand as his assistant coach. I've never really liked the idea of hiring foreigners to work with top South African teams, as I believe we should be doing more to nurture and develop our own coaches. I also can't see how a foreign coach can have more passion for a South African team than a local guy.

When Adrian arrived at Province to help Solly at the Stormers, Theuns introduced him to us as follows: 'This is Gert Smal [the Western Province coach], this is Hennie Bekker, and these are the rest of the boys,' and he waved his hand to include everyone else in the room.

So I went to Adrian and said, 'Hi, I'm Peter de Villiers. I am not "one of the boys"; I'm Peter de Villiers.'

I quickly filled Adrian in on my background and the teams I had coached. Of course, the Province administrators weren't happy that I was talking to Adrian, but then they had never treated any of the teams I coached with anything approaching respect. Because they never prioritised the WP B-team or the Disas, it made it hard for me to get buy-in from the players when I wanted them to put some passion into their work. I constantly had to figure out ways to try to make the guys feel more important. I remember being called onto the carpet by WP president Ronnie Masson, who accused me of being difficult after I had complained that the selectors weren't making enough of an effort to watch my team play.

At the time (1999), work was being done on Newlands Stadium, so the Currie Cup games were played in Stellenbosch. But *only* the Currie Cup side and the under-21 team played there, while the B-side routinely got banished to another club venue or field.

That might have been acceptable had the selectors made the effort to come and watch our games, but they never did. I complained, saying that my guys in the B-side were often called to fill in for the A-team players when they were injured, but neither the selectors nor the coaches ever came to watch them play. How, then, could I motivate my players to make a special effort?

Because of this situation, many players preferred to play for their clubs rather than for the Province B-side. They'd rather play for Maties on a Saturday than for the provincial representative team. This attitude was a sad indictment of the state of affairs and not at all good for WP rugby.

So I decided to become really aggressive about transformation and make the team black. It seemed like the only thing to do, otherwise you had to question what WP were getting out of the B-team, given that the players didn't really want to play for the side.

And we became very successful with that predominantly black team. Gradually the other players in the side also started to take some pride in the team, and they enjoyed the brand of rugby they were starting to play. Robbie Fleck and Louis Koen were two players who went on to bigger things who really appeared to relish their apprenticeship in the WP B-side. And Chester Williams also came to play for my team and had a good time playing for us. He wanted to be in the team.

But my Mondays consisted only of arguments when I tried to get better treatment for my team from the WP administrators. I told them that they were always ready to listen to everyone else, like first-team hooker and long-time stalwart Andrew Patterson when he complained about problems on the seniors' bus trips, or take note of the smallest niggles suffered by the first team and act immediately to rectify the problem, but they didn't care two hoots about us.

During this time, a club called me and asked if I would like to be nominated as a selector. I said yes, and was placed on the shortlist with Peter Jooste and a couple of other guys. But I soon realised that I would replace Cassiem Jabaar if I was appointed, and he was a real legend of non-white rugby in our country. I didn't want to stand against my own people. Cassiem had a lot of experience and I felt he needed to be part of the system. I'm not saying that had I stood I would have beaten him, but I didn't want to run that risk.

So I informed Theuns that I wanted to carry on coaching, but he told me that I couldn't be both a coach and a selector. I assured him that I would rather be a coach than a selector, and he asked me whether I knew what I was giving up. I couldn't see his point – his logic made no sense to me. When you are a coach, you still get to select, as it is an important part of the job, but it doesn't work the other way around.

When I turned down the chance to run for one of the selection positions, I was told that there was no guarantee that I would coach the B-side again. But I was emphatic and told Theuns that I wanted to be a coach, no matter what.

The message, though, was clear. They didn't seem to want me to continue coaching the B-side and instead wanted to sideline me, which they proved by trying to talk me into being a selector. I think they thought I was too strong-minded and stroppy as a coach. People high up in rugby did not like it when I stood up for what I believed in.

Then Phil Pretorius came to Cape Town and we had a very interesting meeting, during which he asked me to join him at the Bulls for the 2001 Super 12 season. WP were so eager for me to meet with Phil, they even set up the meeting! It seemed that they had already signed me away to the Bulls, which only reaffirmed that they weren't interested in my services. I was even more convinced that this was the case by the fact that they had never commended me for my successes with the South African under-19 side, which, by that stage, I had been coaching for three years. We'd hardly lost a game in that time.

So all in all they had an odd attitude towards me, which really bothered me. I felt as if they wanted me to get down on my hands and knees and thank them for the opportunities they had given me. I was grateful, of course, but I also figured that my hard work and coaching abilities had helped get me to where I was.

I told Phil that I had to first clarify my position with Province – although I knew they wanted me gone – and I had to know what Phil had planned for me after the Super 12. At the time, Phil was the coach of both the Bulls and the Falcons. If I was contracted to the Bulls for only the Super 12, what would I do for the rest of the year? But Phil said he wanted me to work with the Falcons too, and that was the deal clincher.

My wife and I sat down to discuss the matter, and she agreed that I should go to Gauteng alone. So the decision was made, and I had to leave my family. I was going to a completely different environment from the one I was used to. As my children were happy at the schools they were attending, I didn't want to uproot them, and, after all, in rugby you never know how long a job is going to last. I might have found myself heading back to Paarl within a couple of months.

But my time with the Bulls ended up being a great experience that both benefitted my career and enabled me to expand my outlook on life. It also showed me what made South African rugby players, and South African people, tick.

I made some great friends at the Bulls. They were mostly good people who looked after me very well, and I really warmed to them. For the first time, I was made to feel worthy of being in a first-class rugby environment as coach to a provincial side. The structures at the Bulls were very impressive – everything was done extremely professionally. It was an eye-opener for me. The players were well looked after, as were the coaches.

But I did learn a few things about Phil during that Super 12 season. Although he gave me a few responsibilities, he seemed to think that I would be an easy guy to bend to his will. James Stofberg and I were the assistant coaches. James would later become a top rugby administrator and be present at some of the arguments I had with SARU during my tenure as Springbok coach.

He didn't stick around for long at the Bulls, though. I think he was offered the job of coaching Russia round about then, and he left to take up that appointment. His departure didn't surprise me, as he never seemed very comfortable with or confident in Phil's coaching style.

So they brought in a guy from Pumas, Chris Grobbelaar, but he didn't get along with Phil either, as he couldn't cope with how demonstrative Phil could be. Phil would get so worked up during a game that wasn't going his way that he would start smashing up the coaching box. He would get into such a mood that he couldn't even give the players the information they required on the field.

Phil was a morbid person who easily got depressed. When a player dropped the ball, he would just yank him off the field. He wasn't cool at all, but for me it was an object lesson on how *not* to coach, as it was obvious that his approach was not going down well with the players.

While the union was run very efficiently and there were good structures in place, there wasn't a great deal of planning or structure coming from Phil. Remember, this is the Bulls in the Super 12 we are talking about, and Phil's day job was actually to coach the Falcons. But in that first season I didn't challenge him, even though there were many times I felt I should. It just didn't seem like good manners to take him on.

So after a not particularly successful Super 12 season with the Bulls, off he and I went to the Falcons. Quite early in that season Phil called a meeting with the players and asked them what he could do to help them make the team better. They said that he should give me and fitness advisor Neels Liebel more time with them.

Phil did the exact opposite. He almost completely distanced us from the team. At training sessions, he would leave us on the side of the field to do nothing more than laugh and joke with the onlookers and the media. I was a professional and pitched up for my job each day, but I wasn't utilised at all.

To be honest, I rather enjoyed myself on the sidelines. We had a lot of fun. Then, suddenly, Phil got a bee in his bonnet and called me back onto the field.

That year, the players couldn't handle the coaching situation. There were even fights in the changing room. When Phil sensed that there was a fight brewing, he just wouldn't pitch. So I was left to sort out the mess, which was tough, but it was a good learning experience for me.

But I couldn't carry on like that indefinitely. The prevailing atmosphere wasn't good for anyone. So a board meeting was called, headed by former Springbok prop Guy Kebble. Phil and Rautie Rautenbach, the president, were great friends, so I was blindsided when Rautie asked me if I would accept the head coaching job.

'Now where the hell did this come from?' I wondered.

Kebble said that the players enjoyed the way I worked and stressed that if I didn't take the job, he would appoint another coach – they were not going to stick with Phil. The Falcons were playing Currie Cup rugby at the time, so I would have the opportunity to be a head coach at Currie Cup level. It was a no-brainer, actually, and I accepted the job.

Although it initiated a happy period in my coaching life, it wasn't always plain sailing. I had many fights with Harry Nieuwenhuis, the chief executive, who gave the impression that he never believed in anything I did. If I said something was white, he would say it was black. If I then said it was black, he would say, 'No, on second thoughts, it's white.'

In retrospect I achieved quite a lot at the Falcons, considering the challenges I had to overcome. In 2001 we were in contention for a semi-final spot in the Currie Cup right until the end of the league phase of the competition. We had some notable wins, and were it not for a poor refereeing decision, we would probably have beaten the eventual champions, Western Province, at Newlands.

The players seemed to relate to me and they appeared to play for their coach. Life was good in that respect. I felt as if I had arrived as a coach at that level, as we were now a competitive team in the Currie Cup.

But the board had substantially cut the budget Phil had been given, which was a huge problem. I had been made certain promises that never came to fruition, so we had to work with a budget of under R1 million, which included management salaries.

The team also never had a permanent home ground. We would play one game in Brakpan, then the next one in Kempton Park. In our most successful year, we played most of our games at Kempton Park, which made all the difference. Unfortunately, though, the penny never dropped for the decision-makers, and afterwards we continued to be shunted around between Brakpan, Kempton Park and even Springs.

It's not easy coaching at a smaller union, as you can't really compete against the bigger unions' infrastructures. The union bought us a bus to transport players to games, but, boy, you should have seen it. When it rained, water poured in. The players would ask me, 'How can you expect us to tackle all those expensive players from the other unions when we get paid so little money?' And as their coach, I had to try to explain the situation to them.

So there were a lot of challenges, and these grew even bigger when the administration suddenly decided to stop the players from earning an income outside of rugby. The result was that we lost 31 players in three years. That was the end of the Falcons ever competing successfully again. Because of the board's decision, we lost guys like Braam Els, Adi

Jacobs, Ettienne Botha, Dawie du Toit and Joggie Viljoen – the kind of players you just can't replace. In Joggie Viljoen's case, he'd lost form quite badly, but the CEO demanded that I select the player of *his* choice. That was another stand-off between us.

What they had promised me in terms of my own financial remuneration never materialised, and the support, both in terms of manpower and finance, which was needed for us to be successful on the field, was lacking.

Towards the end of that year, Nieuwenhuis called me in. I can't remember what the argument was about, but I don't think anyone would have liked to be spoken to the way he spoke to me. I chatted with my daughter, Odile, that night. She was only in Grade 6 at the time, and I asked her, 'If a person says this sort of thing, what do you think it means?'

'Ugh, Dad,' she responded, 'that sounds like a person with real issues.'

So, suspecting that perhaps a race issue underpinned his dislike for me, I went back to Nieuwenhuis and told him, 'I am black, and I am proud to be black.'

He went ballistic. I told him that if he and I had the same skin colour, he would never have made it this far. A lot of ugly things were said by both of us. I even threatened to slash his car tyre with a knife, which, in hindsight, was a bit crazy. But I was very angry at the time, and so was he.

It was nasty, and we were probably both in the wrong. The upshot was that my position at the Falcons became untenable. Nieuwenhuis influenced Rautie against me, and eventually Kebble and the board also turned on me, though the amazing thing about Guy Kebble was that when I got the Springbok job, he was the first person to phone and congratulate me. He said he always knew that I would make it big.

So the Falcons thought that I had become too strong for my own good, and they wanted someone more compliant – someone who could be ordered around and told what to do.

Although some of the administrators told me that they knew the players liked me, they and their fellow administrators didn't like my style. It seemed to be the story of my coaching career.

Leaving the Falcons was the start of one of the toughest periods of my life. My departure set in motion a snowball effect, to the extent that I got into so much debt that I had to sell my fully paid-up house in Paarl, as well as my car. I went back to the Western Cape with no job and not even a brass farthing to my name.

5

Fighting for justice

When I returned to the Cape from the Falcons in 2002, it wasn't the first time I had been relieved of a coaching job, as you could say that that had also been the case in 1997, following my stint as a Springbok assistant coach. Apart from the meetings I had with Rian Oberholzer and Sas Bailey, when they tried to extract information from me about Nick Mallett and Alan Solomons's management style, nothing further was said. So although I wasn't asked to leave, it just seemed to be accepted that I was no longer the Springbok assistant coach.

Perhaps I was asked to coach the South African under-19 team in 1998 because SARFU didn't know what to do with me. It was a tough job to start with, because when I took up the position, I had not followed any rugby at under-18 level, nor had I attended Craven Week the previous year. As Craven Week is the senior schools' provincial tournament, played annually in July, much of the provinces' recruiting is done there, as the scouts get a chance to assess the cream of South Africa's young talent.

So I was thrown in at the deep end, as there would have been quite a few coaches who would have known a lot more about the young talent than I did. It was going to be a steep learning curve for me, but it was a challenge I relished. Life is all about challenges, and I love embracing them.

As always seemed to be the case, the challenges seemed even tougher for me, perhaps due to the perception that I had not got the job on merit alone. Perhaps I was expected to hide in the background while someone else did the work? Considering that I had not worked in the schools system, it was somewhat understandable that my assistant coach, Dries van Heerden, seemed to think that I didn't know what was going on. Perhaps Dries would have preferred me to coach in a way familiar to him and the players, but he also seemed to want to think and speak on my behalf, which I found highly irritating.

He did not appear to understand that, in my view, I had been appointed because I was the best man for the job and that I had my own way of doing things. For me, the important thing was to advance the development of young players who, in the future, would play a big role in the Springbok team.

It was odd, as I had as many coaching qualifications as any of them, but there were often times when the white coaches treated me as if I needed my hand held. It was a recurring theme throughout my rugby career.

The bottom line for me was that I would stand and fall on the decisions *I* made. I also resolved that I would open the eyes of the assistant coach to the fact that there is more than just one way to coach a rugby team. Coaching is not only about paying attention to the technical aspects of the game, nor does it revolve only around coaching techniques. Although those two components are important, just as important is the ability and willingness to understand the players and what makes them tick so that you can get the best out of them.

I was lucky enough to work with many talented players at under-19 level. Adi Jacobs and Jean de Villiers would later combine as centres for the Springboks when I was coaching the Boks, while Joe van Niekerk was another youngster who showed his potential at under-19 level.

The under-19 guys seemed to enjoy my coaching style, and it seemed as if most of the support staff eventually liked it too. When the wins came, we thus enjoyed them so much more.

An incident that may explain my coaching philosophy occurred during one of my early under-19 tournaments, in France. We had won a game comfortably, by more than 70 points, and afterwards some of the boys ignored the curfew and slipped out to go to a disco.

I was woken up in my hotel room by the manager, Ronald Bantam, to be told that some of the players had gone out. The way everyone was behaving you would have thought they had just received news that an aeroplane had crashed into the building.

I volunteered to go down to the disco to pick the boys up. Looking very sheepish, they came back with me to the hotel and went to bed. They had been told that we would be conducting a disciplinary hearing the next morning, which would involve the entire squad, to get to the bottom of the incident, and they were left in no doubt that there might be some form of sanction taken against them.

Hell, I struggled to fall asleep again after all that drama. I understood the challenges players faced when they were on tour. Although France is a great place, you do not know the language, and it's hard for some of the guys to get used to the food. In addition, on this tour there were several good players in the group who had not made the starting line-up in the early games and did not get the amount of game time they probably felt they deserved. All of these factors suggested we could be in for some trouble during the rest of the tournament if we didn't treat the nightclub misdemeanour sensitively.

Boys will be boys, after all, and there hadn't really been a plane crash. I had this in mind the next morning, and before we'd even had breakfast, we gathered all the boys together for the disciplinary hearing. Even those who had not gone to the disco were made to sit through the proceedings, which just seemed to go on forever. All the guys' heads were drooping.

As I listened to my fellow management members chastising the players and behaving as if this were the sinking of the *Titanic*, I kept thinking that I must save the tour; I had to lift the spirits of the boys or they would not retain their hunger to destroy their opponents.

I asked the management and SARFU representatives to leave the room so that I could speak to the team alone. I even asked the assistant coaches to leave too.

After everyone had left, I said to the team, 'Guys, you are supposed to be future Springboks. You are supposed to be the cream of South Africa's rugby future. So how damn stupid are you that you get caught sneaking out to a disco? Surely you are cleverer than that? Surely you should *know* how to slip out without getting caught?'

I continued in this vein, saying that a Springbok is supposed to be good at *everything* he does, and that that should include being good at sneaking out. I said it was completely unacceptable for a Springbok to get caught.

The relief on their faces spoke volumes and confirmed that I had followed the right approach, but I asked them not to look too satisfied when they left the room. I wanted them to give the impression that I had given them a proper bollocking.

That helped save the tour for us and we didn't lose another game until the semi-final, where we drew the match and then lost in a penalty shoot-out. I had taken Conrad Jantjes off the field after officials informed me that anyone in the squad of 22 could kick in the shoot-out. But when I wanted to use Conrad for a kick, I was told it wasn't allowed.

But for the next three years, we were successful in all the tournaments we competed in. We played with the necessary passion and really enjoyed our rugby. I had by then got myself up to speed on the young talent that was available, and spent a lot of time at youth tournaments assessing the players coming through. I was a rather good talent-spotter, as many of the guys I brought in later went on to play for their country at senior level.

As I said, I believe the players liked the way I coached and managed them, and some even told me that should they not make it as professional rugby players, they would make it in life because of the valuable life lessons they had learnt. That was, and is, an important part of my job to me, even when it involves senior international players. There is always room for personal growth, and a player should never have the attitude that rugby is the only thing there is to him as a person. In my view, a strong, well-rounded person makes for a better rugby player, as he is better equipped to deal with the challenges on the field if he can confront those he faces off the field head-on.

In 1998, 1999 and 2000, the under-19 team enjoyed a very successful run, and I had high hopes of being appointed as the national under-21 coach the following year. It seemed like a natural progression. But in 2001 SARFU appointed Swys de Bruin from Griquas as the coach of the under-21s. I was disappointed. It didn't seem fair, but when Sammy Paulse and I were appointed as assistant coaches to Swys, my professional instinct told me to work with him to try to help him be successful.

Although Swys was a nice enough guy, he allowed his assistant coaches very little responsibility. He would coach the forwards, and then he would coach the backs. He gave me very little to do, so there was also no accountability. That's not how I wanted it to be – you didn't become an assistant coach so that you could go on holiday. So once again I refused to just go with the flow.

This was in an era when SARFU had taken over the Super 12 franchises and had a big say in the appointment of coaches. Several black coaches had been dispatched to the Super 12 franchises to learn the ropes. I had heard complaints, though, that none of these guys was given a hands-on role to play.

I was working with the Bulls then, but I hadn't yet had that problem with Phil Pretorius. In the early days he had allowed me to be involved; it was only later that I had problems with him. Some of those other black coaches came to me and complained that they weren't being given any responsibilities, and I told them to stand up for themselves.

And that was what I was determined to do when I felt as if I were being sidelined. Swys and I had a chat, and he agreed that I should take on more responsibilities. He said he would coach the forwards and I the backs.

But when it came to preparing for the IRB tournament, which that year was to be held in Australia, no one ever discussed strategy with either me or Sammy Paulse. Swys would draw up his plans and then bring them to the training field.

So I said to him, 'Listen, Swys, you must make up your mind what you want from me. If you don't want me to be accountable for anything, then I would much rather just stay at home.'

I again asked him to give me more responsibility, with the proviso that if we weren't successful, I would take the blame for it. He agreed and said he would give me what I wanted, but he nevertheless continued to blow hot and cold. I made it clear to him that I was not going to allow him to do to me what other coaches were doing to their black assistants in the Super 12.

'I don't want to let my people down,' I said, 'because they are depending on me and want me to progress as a coach.'

The team doctor from the Free State, who had been involved with the Cats in the Super 12, chimed in to announce that there had been no coaches sidelined at that franchise. I cut him short.

'Doc,' I said, 'I don't see any sick people around me at the moment. I am fighting for a much bigger cause here. It's about accountability, but you won't understand that. Please excuse us, because this issue cuts much deeper than you can see.'

The result of it all was that Swys again agreed that I would coach the backs and he the forwards, but the next day, when I went to the SARFU offices, I heard all about the fight there. I couldn't understand it, as I had thought the debate would remain within the inner circle.

I was called in to explain myself, and I stated my case very clearly: 'Swys is the coach, I know that, but I want some responsibility and want to be accountable for something, otherwise I am wasting my time.'

The next week we were in Johannesburg, where we trained at the school opposite the old Grayston Drive Holiday Inn, where we were staying. Again Swys took the backs, and this time I just lost it. I made it clear that there was no point in me continuing. I couldn't go on tour with him, and I would tell people why I refused to travel overseas with the team.

Swys must have panicked, because he said I could take over the backs, which he then allowed me to do, just as we'd initially planned. It was a very strange situation; I couldn't understand why he didn't just let me take the backs in the first place. Nevertheless, it was an important victory not just for me, but for black coaches in general. Other black coaches weren't making it in the system at that time because when players who went on tours with national teams returned to their provincial unions, they were asked what value the black coaches had added. They would then report that the black coaches had made no contribution. I couldn't afford such a negative report myself, as it would be imprinted on my CV forever.

Swys and I had a long chat after the practice, and I told him that this was the last time I would be sidelined. Next time, I would not come back. After that there were no more hiccups and we successfully completed our preparations for Sydney.

In the meantime, Sammy Paulse continued to be sidelined, but he

I became an educator later
in life, but first I had to get
an education

In action on the rugby field

With my brother Joseph
(on the right) and my
regular halfback partner
Eddie Adams (middle)
showing off another haul
of trophies won for
Young Gardens

A proud Young Gardens team was victorious again at the
annual Easter club tournament at City Park in 1985

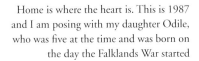

Home is where the heart is. This is 1987
and I am posing with my daughter Odile,
who was five at the time and was born on
the day the Falklands War started

Andrew Koopman

My first taste of the Springboks was as one of the assistant coaches to Nick Mallett on the 1997 tour to Italy, France and the UK

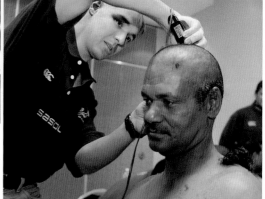

My forfeit to the players after we won the 2005 IRB Under-21 World Championship semi-final against New Zealand in Argentina was to have my hair shorn off

Paths that were to cross again later – here I am working with a young Morné Steyn at the 2005 IRB Under-21 World Championship

Chris Schoeman

Gallo Images

Coach of the Falcons in 2002

Under-21 coach at the 2006 IRB Under-21 Rugby
World Championship in Clermont-Ferrand, France

Gallo Images / AFP

All smiles, but I don't think either of us was that happy, given what had transpired – shaking hands with
Oregan Hoskins after being announced as Bok coach in 2008

Gallo Images / You and Huisgenoot / Corrie Hansen

The new Bok coach at home, January 2008

Fronting a press conference in Wellington, New Zealand, in my first season with the Boks, along with Andy Marinos, who was then both the manager of national teams and acting CEO of SARU

Gallo Images / Getty Images

Gallo Images / Getty Images

Seriousness etches my face and those of my two assistants, Gary Gold (left) and Dick Muir as we watch the team play the All Blacks from the coaches' box in Dunedin in 2008. The sombre looks were replaced with elation after the final whistle

Meeting Prince William in the Twickenham changing room after our record victory against England in 2008

The calm before the storm – in conversation with Schalk Burger before the fateful Loftus test match against the British & Irish Lions, after which all hell broke loose

All is fair in love and war – posing with Lions coach Ian McGeechan before the final test in Johannesburg. The way the Lions carried on after that game, you would have thought they had won the series

Wearing the white armband in protest at Bakkies Botha's suspension

The sheer bliss of knowing you are the best in the world. Bakkies Botha, Bismarck du Plessis and Victor Matfield celebrate after winning the Tri Nations title in Hamilton in 2009

A happy management team, with kicking coach Percy Montgomery joining Gary, Dick and me to celebrate the Tri Nations series win in the changing room

President Jacob Zuma welcomes back the Springboks after our Tri Nations series victory in New Zealand

The 2009 end-of-year-tour – training at the Old Albanian RFC in St Albans

Os du Randt made a big contribution as scrumming consultant in 2010. It was because I felt his work had been done that I did not continue with him in that role the following year

Blowing a vuvuzela with Bryan Habana in Green Point, Cape Town, during the 2010 FIFA World Cup

Gallo Images/ Foto24 / Denzil Maregele

Chatting to Fourie du Preez prior to the match against Australia at Vodacom Park, Bloemfontein, on 4 September 2010

Gallo Images

Gallo Images

Comrades in arms – the two big men, Bakkies and Victor, and I share a moment prior to the team photo in Edinburgh in 2010. The result of the game against Scotland wiped the smiles off our faces

seemed completely unconcerned about it. He would lie on the tackle bags watching the training sessions. I argued with him about his attitude: 'What are you doing here?' I asked. 'Please stand up for yourself!' But he seemed quite happy with the *status quo*.

Once in Australia, Swys and I had massive disagreements. My strength lay in identifying talent, but as soon as we got to the tournament, I saw the roles changing. At a tournament, you do everything possible to enable the players you have identified to deliver their best performances. But Swys was determined to bring in a new game plan that we hadn't practised at home. I felt there wasn't enough time for the players to familiarise themselves with the style of rugby he wanted them to play, and I told him so. Swys also had the old military drill-sergeant approach to coaching, and I suggested to him that he might get more out of the players if he placed more emphasis on enjoyment.

We ended up getting a fearful hiding from Australia's under-21 team, with Mark Gerrard scoring four tries against us. I remember Joe van Niekerk, whom I had coached in the successful under-19 team, coming to my room and lying on my bed, looking extremely unhappy.

'Coach, why can't we just go back to the days when we enjoyed ourselves?' he asked.

When we got back to South Africa, we were summoned to see SARFU president Silas Nkanunu and chief executive Rian Oberholzer. They gave us a lot of flak. Silas even harangued us for not wearing ties, and asked us why he should bother organising free clothing for us if we weren't going to wear it.

Silas and Rian wanted to get to the bottom of our failure in Australia, and I recalled how I had been asked to snitch on Nick Mallett and Alan Solomons after the 1997 Springbok tour. Like then, I couldn't see the point of playing the man and not the ball. Swys had not asked to be appointed; in fact, I thought we were the victims of SARFU's poor decision-making. To appoint a coach who had no national experience at all to coach the under-21s just seemed stupid to me. If you coach a provincial side in South Africa, you deal with the culture of one area, which is not too difficult. If you go to the Bulls after coaching Western Province, it is easy to integrate yourself, as you are the newcomer and just have to adapt.

But when you coach a national side, cliques will form because of the different cultures, and most new coaches at that level take a while to understand that. I didn't want to burn Swys, but the result was that they sacked the whole lot of us, the entire management.

Well, maybe I should rephrase that. They didn't officially sack us. They just never reappointed any of us the following year. It was a similar ending to the one I had after my brief sojourn with the Springboks on the end-of-year tour – nobody said anything, you just knew you were on your own again. It was the first time since the end of 1997 that I had no involvement with SARFU, and this would continue until 2004, by which time I was facing my own massive challenges, counting the cost of my fall-out with the Falcons.

Apart from my family, I really did have nothing when I returned from the Falcons, and it is embarrassing when your daughter, who is still at school, offers to lend you money.

But then my luck changed. It was 2004, and SARU were looking for a new Bok coach. My decision to apply for that position resulted in another job: I was appointed as the SA under-21 coach. Of course Jake White got the top job, but Arthob Petersen told me later that I had done really well in my presentation and had impressed the selection committee, on which basis I was then given the under-21 job.

You learn a lot about yourself when you have nothing to your name, and I was tested in a way that proved I had no price, even at my lowest ebb. When I first got the under-21 job, I was still feeling the financial pinch. Then a guy from Springs phoned and offered me a BMW 5 Series on condition that I invite his brother's son to the under-21 trials, which I had the power to do, as the coach calls up the players for a trial game.

This man said that not only would the car be mine, he would also throw in R500 for petrol every month. That payment would stop after a year, but the car would be mine.

It didn't take me long to make up my mind. I told the man that there is a place in Paarl called Chicago, and that living there is a guy who can't give me an eraser, let alone a car, and yet his kid is so much more talented than this guy's. How can I live with myself if I sell myself to the highest bidder?

But he was very persistent and wouldn't take no for an answer. So I told the guy to meet me at a mine dump near Springs, where we could settle the matter once and for all.

'Bring whatever you want to bring along. If shooting me will make you feel better, go for it,' I said.

So I drove to the location we had agreed on and waited for a few hours, but the guy didn't pitch. Hell, I was mad. I called him the next day and said that he was all bark and no bite, and that I never wanted to hear from him again.

* * *

But the under-21 job did at least bring some financial relief, and then came the job at the Spears. It was hoped that the Spears – a combined team drawn from Eastern Province, Border and South Western Districts – would be included as one of the Super Rugby franchises.

I was able to do the two jobs concurrently, at least for the brief period that the Spears were in existence, but for now, let's stick to the age-group part of my story. In terms of my growth as a coach, the under-21 job was the biggest one I'd had up till that point, as it is supposed to be a stepping stone to coaching the Springboks.

I didn't find the initial challenge with the under-21s as tough as when I'd started coaching the under-19s in 1998, as by this time I was familiar with the players who were coming through. But we didn't have a good season in my first year, even though we won more games than the previous year. The important thing was, we didn't do well at the international tournament, and I take the blame for that. We had strong leaders in the squad, and I might have allowed them to assume too much control. Some of them weren't ready to handle that much responsibility.

Luke Watson was the captain, and he impressed me hugely. He was one of those special, once-in-a-generation leaders you don't often come across. Had he been there for the entire tournament, we might have done much better … we might even have won it. But I had not anticipated that a bad injury would force Luke to go home early, after which I quickly realised that we had built far too much around his leadership and that the other players were now a bit lost without him.

When I took up the reins of the under-21 team again the following year, I felt a new energy that I had not experienced before. It was as if I had turned off a dirt track and now found myself on a smooth, tarred road again.

That is not to say that the job itself was easy, for preparing a national age-group team for a tournament is never a ride in the park. It's a struggle to get the provinces to release their players for national training camps, particularly the top players who are good enough to play Super Rugby, though I accept that Super Rugby is more important than national age-group rugby.

In addition, the under-19 side, which was being coached by Loffie Eloff, enjoyed a number of training camps and had a bus at their disposal, whereas I had been told that there wasn't enough money for the number of training camps I wanted and the use of a bus was denied us. I felt a bit stupid in the eyes of the players, as to them it must have seemed that nothing was ever delivered on time. But I refused to let these side issues affect the players or drag them down, as we had to perform at a world-class level to do well at the tournament.

At around this time I heard through the grapevine that it was being said within the corridors of SARFU that I was difficult to work with. It probably explains why no one from headquarters ever pitched up at a training camp to wish my team luck or see how we were progressing. Luckily we had great support from the staff at Brandvlei Prison just outside Worcester, where we were preparing for the tournament.

By the time we had our final training camp, word had filtered down from the SARFU offices that my job was on the line and that promises had been made to other coaches that they would succeed me. But the three major factors that have always kept me going served as motivators and kept me level-headed: first, be yourself and don't compromise your principles; second, don't ever forget that you are there only to serve the players; and, third, make very sure that your game plan and man-management skills are in place. I made a decision to only react to something if my input could improve a situation. If it couldn't, then it was better not to react at all.

I had many talented players to choose from, but after much soul-searching, some of it done in church in the build-up to our departure for Argentina, I finally settled on a squad that I thought could win us the IRB Junior World Cup. The squad was a good representation of our country's different race groups, but this had not been my intention during the selection process. It just so happened that 2005 saw some brilliant black players coming through.

By the time we reached the semi-final against the All Blacks, we had nine black players in the team. I had not selected them because I was trying to make any kind of point, or because I was aggressively following any transformation policy. They were all selected on merit and were genuinely the best players on tour.

But, unbeknown to me, a team-management meeting was held to which I was not invited, and afterwards I was told that the team would have to be changed, as it excessively favoured one race group.

I did some digging and questioned my management team about the decision, and was told that the message had come from South Africa. Ian Schwartz, our manager, was adamant that we must change the team, and he told me that people back home were not going to support me if I persisted with the selection.

'This is your last chance to make it big in South African rugby,' he said. 'If you lose this game, nobody is ever going to give you a job again.'

Ian told me that I had better include several white players in the team, as they would strengthen it to the point where we could win the tournament. I told Ian that I couldn't change the team, as I believed it was the best one we had. I added that I, too, wanted to win the tournament. I really believed that the players I had selected would win it for us.

Many of the black guys had been stand-out players at the tournament. Thabang Molefe, for instance – although he never achieved anything else in rugby after the competition, and I would love to know why – was the best under-21 centre in the world at the time. He proved it at the tournament. We also had Mzwandile Stick, Chiliboy Ralepelle and prop Sangoni Mxoli, not to mention Earl Rose and Paul Delport. Morné Steyn was the flyhalf.

But my management team was adamant. They were determined to dig their heels in, to the point where we had an open mutiny. The guys threatened to boycott both me and the team.

The only exception was Neels Liebel, the fitness trainer, who did not go along with the rest of management. 'The coach brought me here, and no matter what he does, my loyalty is to him,' Neels said.

I told management that if the team I had selected lost the game, they could rejoice, and I would be happy to let them celebrate. But I told them that if we won the game, then I didn't want to see any of them anywhere near the team, or in the changing room, for the rest of the tournament.

Hell, what a drama it all was. The upshot of what I said was that the management guys changed their minds and decided not to implement a boycott, and the match went off well. In fact, we won that game, and we won the final too. So everyone was happy, and by the time we celebrated the win, it seemed that most people had forgotten that the argument had ever happened.

But of course some negative stories had been relayed back to South Africa, in particular the management stand-off. I remain convinced that there are more black players who are capable of playing for South Africa than most people think.

I don't know what causes this situation, but too many promising young players don't progress any further than under-21 level. The issue is not really about development, but about trust. It seems as if the coaches don't have sufficient trust in the players to pick them, the aforementioned Thabang Molefe being a good example of someone who was the best in the world in his age group, but was never given an opportunity at provincial level.

Some people will probably say that I am out of line in saying this, as I didn't exactly select an army of black players when I was Springbok coach. But they are missing the point, which is that more should be done to keep these young black players in the game from age-group level on so that they can be developed towards a standard where they can play international rugby. As the Springbok coach, you need to be able to select players who have at least gained some experience at provincial and Super Rugby level, but before then many talented young players have already fallen through the cracks in the system.

Unfortunately I got labelled as someone who fights for black rights, but the reality is that I fight for justice. I know I tend to alienate people simply because I cannot easily be persuaded to behave in a certain way just for the purposes of being 'polite'. What is the point if it compromises what you believe in? It just makes you a dishonest person.

At times I was penalised for having the guts to stand up for what I believed in, but I can't agree with everything just so that I can have a job in rugby. The bottom line is, if you can't persuade me with a good argument, I'm not going to adjust my viewpoint in an attempt to be nice. Many of my critics in rugby thought I should be eternally grateful to them for giving me a job, but that is not how I saw it. As far as I was concerned, whether or not I continued in a position should always have been based on how well or how badly I did the job.

I will probably be accused of being paranoid for thinking that some people in SA Rugby zealously tried to get rid of me, but perhaps the fact that I had to reapply for the position of under-21 coach in 2006 will go some way to proving my point. And this was the year after we had won the IRB Junior World Cup! We were the reigning champions, but there were people who thought the team should go forward with a different coach.

But despite all the behind-the-scenes machinations, I managed to keep the job, and we left for France for the annual IRB tournament. It's difficult to play France in France, regardless of whether you are playing at under-21 level or for the senior side, and we lost in the final in Clermont, where the French team had a stadium packed with 12 000 fans to cheer them on.

But in progressing to the final, we had played some great rugby and beaten some good teams. There was a great spirit in the camp, and a number of players, many of whom went on to become top players at national level, later wrote me some really emotional messages thanking me for my contribution. That, more than any praise from an administrator, is what a coach really thrives on. Coaching is all about improving the players and creating the best environment for them to achieve their full potential. When they thank you for it afterwards, you feel as if you have done what you set out to do.

6

Into the belly of the beast

When the opportunity to coach the Spears came up in 2005, I was already coaching the South African under-21s. The Spears stint was quite an experience. The idea was to get some semblance of a team up and running in preparation for the region's anticipated inclusion in an expanded Super Rugby competition. Border, Eastern Province and South Western Districts were the three unions that combined under the Spears masthead and, as one can imagine, the geography was a challenge in itself.

George and East London are between six and seven hours apart by road, and East London and George are each about three hours' drive from Port Elizabeth. So the team would have to congregate in a central location, with many of the players living away from their homes.

If the region was ever going to be competitive in Super Rugby, we would also need to bring in new players to extend the talent pool. I like telling people that I started the Spears by hiring a minibus kombi. I picked up six players in Cape Town, we jumped into a minibus and off we drove to the Eastern Cape to start the new franchise.

I was given four weeks to pull a team together that would play preseason friendlies against other Super 12 franchises. South Western Districts coach Johan Lerm was appointed to assist me.

Despite the Spears being the brainchild of SARU, there wasn't much money available to us. I negotiated rates at self-catering places for the management and players, and they were all paid a fixed salary. One of the two locks I had recruited approached me one day and pointed out that in no other region was everyone paid the same amount of money. I had to tell him that this was the way it had to be at the Spears for the time being, and if he didn't like it he should leave.

My plan was to form a squad of 26 players who lived and played together, hoping that they would bond and learn enough so that they could progress to a higher level the following year. And although we didn't win any games against the Super 12 sides, I thought that we had succeeded in our mission to improve the standard of the players' game. I promised most of the 26 guys only good things for the following season.

But behind the scenes there was a nasty fight going on between the Spears' chief executive Tony McKeever and SARU president Oregan Hoskins and the SARU board. Tony wanted greater clarity on when the Spears would enter the Super 12 and also more financial backing. I was always loyal to the person I worked for, so that was probably why Oregan took a dislike to me at this point. I find it odd that, to this day, not one SARU official has ever asked me for feedback on the rugby the Spears played. They just seemed to write off the entire experience as a complete waste of time and money.

But I put a lot of emotion and effort into it, as did Tony McKeever. Tony left all rugby-related matters to me, trusting me to get on with the job of coaching. I am not sure what he said in meetings that might have irritated the SA Rugby officials, but I thought he was a good administrator – he just needed stronger financial backing.

Sometimes Tony did go a bit overboard in his desire to sell the Spears brand, but to him the brand was *the* most important factor. He believed that we needed to establish the brand before we could attract the level of players that would make us competitive. So he branded virtually everything he could lay his hands on, including the bus, and he went out of his way to get the players kitted out in all sorts of branded clothing. I understood that this approach was necessary when you have virtually no money and are up against competitors with a R30-million marketing budget.

From my side, I made promises to players based on what SARU had promised us. I told them that they must tolerate the hardships now because the next year would be better. I asked them to stick with the Spears, even though some of them were struggling to put food on the table.

The players formed a strong bond among themselves due to the sacrifices they were all making, but everyone was living for the next year. Then the rug was pulled out from under my feet when SARU decided that they would not continue with the franchise. I cannot remember when I felt more miserable and depressed about what I had directly been responsible for doing to people. I had taken some of those players out of their jobs and had made them promises I could not keep. Some of them had given up everything to throw their lot in with the Spears. And while a few of them went on to bigger and better things, for many of them it was their only chance to make it big.

Agh, it's very hard to feel like you have failed people, and I really felt I had failed them. I took up the issue with Oregan, but he didn't want to know about it.

'I can't promise you anything,' he said, 'because I have to look after other people first.'

I lost my cool completely. I told him I didn't need people who couldn't honour their promises. I might even have threatened him a bit, which I felt bad about afterwards, but it was as if no one cared about the people involved, which frustrated me terribly.

I suppose after my 'discussion' with Oregan it wasn't that surprising that I had to reapply for my position as coach of the national under-21 team the next year. It seemed as if I was being viewed as a bit of a nuisance, which I could sense in the body language of someone like Andy Marinos, the manager of national teams, whenever I spoke to him. Johan Prinsloo, the SARU chief executive, said as much to my face in 2005. I went to see Prinsloo after I'd heard that the under-19 coach, Loffie Eloff, had been given a car in addition to the big bus and minibus his team had access to.

'Why is there such disparity [between what my team gets and what Loffie's gets]?' I asked.

'Ja,' Prinsloo said, 'you squeal about everything.'

When Loffie won the under-19 competition in 2005, Prinsloo called me and told me to stop complaining. He said that if my team did not win the under-21 competition, I would be out. We did win it, but it didn't bring about a change in SARU's attitude. In 2008, when I was Bok coach, Marinos would tell me that he found me extremely easy to work with, and yet in 2006 I had a reputation for being damn difficult.

After winning the 2005 under-21 tournament and making it to the final in 2006, I felt I had earned the privilege to ask for certain concessions. Even before that, my under-19 teams had hardly lost a game in three years. As far as I was concerned, my results suggested that I also had every right to want to be promoted up the coaching ranks. But in 2007, when the Emerging Boks were due to play in the IRB tournament in Romania, I asked the guys at SARU if I would be involved. They said, 'No, probably not.' They couldn't tell me why not.

SARU intended for the Emerging Bok coach to become the next Springbok coach, so they initially offered the position to Heyneke Meyer, the Bulls coach who had just won the Super 14. But he turned it down, as he would have only one week to prepare the team before the tournament. They then approached Dick Muir, who I understand turned them down for the same reason.

In the end, just two weeks before the Emerging Boks were due to fly out, they gave me the job. Before we left, I was at the SARU offices, where I bumped into Jonathan Stones, the newly appointed managing director of the organisation. I didn't know him from a bar of soap.

'And who are you?' I asked.

'I'm the new MD,' Stones said.

'So you know who I am and I guess you've heard a lot of bad things about me,' I said.

He basically said, 'Go on the tour and if you're successful, we'll talk again.'

I said, 'That's not a problem. I will be successful, I will come back and we will talk again.'

But he never spoke to me when we got back, despite the fact that we'd had a successful tournament, so it seemed to me that I had buggered up their plan, which was that I would fail and thus be ruled out of the running for the Springbok job. My mistrust of SARU and the discord between us had therefore started long before they announced me as the new Springbok coach.

If SARU did not want me to be in the running for the job of Springbok coach, I suppose to some degree they had wanted me to fail with the Emerging Boks. But they underestimated the ability I have to work with people, and particularly players. I knew that most of the guys in the Emerging Springbok team had just been through a really tough Super 14 season, so to try new tactics and techniques with them would have been plain stupid and would not have served any purpose. On the contrary, it would probably just have tripped us up. Most of them were disappointed for not making the Bok squad, so I had to pick them up.

I concentrated on melding the players into a team in the truest sense – I wanted to build them into a unit so that they would want to play for each other. We did fun team-building exercises instead of concentrating on technical aspects, and perhaps that's where the rumours that I am not technically sound originated. There were times, such as on this occasion, when I didn't pay much attention to technical and tactical facets, simply because it was better for the team at the time. And of course the players weren't inexperienced guys who had just come out of school and needed to be taught ball-presentation techniques, for example.

I made Schalk Brits the captain, which proved a masterstroke, as the players responded very positively to him. He inspired his teammates and made them spark – they were prepared to follow him through a brick wall.

The upshot was that we won the tournament quite easily. And our success gained me some surprising supporters, among them Cheeky Watson, who would become a major player in the campaign to have me appointed as Jake White's successor.

I think Dale Granger's story in the *Weekend Argus*, when I was quoted as saying that there were 60 black players who could play for the Springboks, got Cheeky behind me. My words were misinterpreted a bit, and helped fuel the enmity towards me of those who thought I had a political agenda. But I hadn't said that there were 60 players who *would* or *should* play for South Africa, which could have been considered contentious, but only who *could*. (After all, a significant number of those 60 black players were wings, and you can only have so many wings in a squad!) But although it was read the wrong way, the story inspired Cheeky.

Some people thought that Cheeky and I went back a long way, as we had both played for SARU when the sport was still divided in the bad old days of apartheid. But this was not the case.

I first phoned Cheeky at the start of 2004. His son, Luke, was playing for the Sharks at the time, and I had decided that Luke would be my team leader in the South African under-21 team. I wanted to ask Cheeky for a bit of background information on Luke so that I could gain some insight into what made him tick.

Our conversation turned to the Springbok job only in 2007. To be honest, it was not a subject I often spoke or thought about, which was why I was blindsided when Granger phoned me in Bucharest, where I was with the Emerging Springboks, and asked what I would do if I became the national coach. Although I had always been a big Springbok supporter, I had not followed them that closely and didn't have any big ideas to share with him.

As far as my relationship with the incumbent Springbok coach, Jake White, was concerned, to say that we hardly communicated would have been an understatement. Communication between us was, in fact, non-existent. When I was coaching the national under-21 team, Jake and I worked in the same offices at SA Rugby headquarters in Newlands, but we saw little of each other and never traded information or ideas.

The only interaction I had with Jake that I can recall happened some time in 2007, after he had hosted a coaching seminar at a hotel in Paarl. He'd invited former England World Cup–winning coach Clive Woodward to be one of the speakers. I bumped into Jake as he was walking down a passage at SA Rugby and told him that I would really have loved to have been invited to the conference so that I could learn what makes someone like Woodward tick. But Jake didn't even show me the courtesy of stopping to have a conversation with me. He just marched on.

I was hurt by his apparant lack of respect, and that was the first and last time Jake and I said anything to each other while I was coaching the under-21s and the Emerging Boks. Of course, I had known Jake when I was an assistant coach with the Springboks under Nick Mallett in Europe in 1997. I helped show him how to turn the computer on. But not once in the three years that we worked in the same building and shared a corridor did he come to me and say something along the lines of, 'I am thinking of playing Meyer Bosman. What can you tell me about him? Is there anything in particular I should know about him?'

Because I believed Jake and John Smit, his captain in the Springbok team, were extremely tight, I couldn't see how I would work with John should I ever become the Bok coach. So I mentioned players like Luke Watson when Granger asked me about possible candidates for the captaincy.

But hell, I didn't even have the job! Nor had I recently given it much thought, so nothing I said about the Springboks at that time should have been cast in stone. At that stage I hadn't even worked with the senior players, so I would only figure out how to manage them if I ever got the job.

Neil de Beer and I decided together that I would apply for the Springbok job. Neil had been a close friend for a long time and had also been a very good aide and team manager during my stint with the under-21 team. But I actually sacked Neil in the wake of the under-21 2005 tournament win in Argentina. After our return to South Africa, he was a guest speaker at a couple of events where he told people that he had run the team by himself. Naturally I wasn't happy about that, so I told him I couldn't work with him any more.

I told Neil that we could still be friends, but that his opportunism made it impossible for us to work together. The weird part was that I had had a hell of a fight to get him accepted in the first place, as he was *persona non grata* with some rugby officials.

Neil has a great nature and is really good at public relations. He was always a tremendous help when it came to dealing with the media. Many a time when I was doing the Springbok job I wished that he was around to help me. Also, I am not always comfortable in social situations; I don't really know how to make small talk. When Neil was around, he did all that for me, as he's very socially adept.

In the end Neil and I hit an impasse when I realised his loyalties lay with Cheeky Watson rather than me, but that happened much later.

By the time I was considering whether or not to apply for the Bok job, Neil and I had made up after our fall-out in 2005. He, probably more than anyone else, was instrumental in starting the groundwork to get me appointed. So my initial supporters were Neil, Cheeky, Koos Rossouw, who ran two companies and provided finance, and the radio journalist JP Naude, who enjoyed respect among the communities in Cape Town and whose programme I listened to a lot. JP had a good understanding of the socio-political aspects of the job and was an excellent sounding board. Those were the people in Cape Town. I also had people in Joburg working on my campaign, like Theuns du Toit and Wanda Henning, who worked for a marketing company. They assessed my presentation and changed it where necessary.

I was very thorough in the way I went about drawing up my presentation. I showed it to a few people, some of whom were sceptical and said, 'Hell, don't say that' and 'Maybe you should leave this bit out'. There are therefore probably quite a few people who can claim that they had some input in my presentation and helped with my campaign. (As journalist Mark Keohane has, indeed, done. Mark was close to my manager, Rian Oberholzer, and no doubt he would have given Rian advice to impart to me.) But not all the people who worked on my presentation would have known about each other and the roles they played.

Of course, I started the presentation by extolling my virtues, and then went on to list the top 14 Springboks I had coached. Then I set out my vision for the Boks, starting with the four core values that we'd need to succeed in attaining the goal, which was to win the World Cup in 2011. Those values were trust, fair play, an open mind and team spirit. I then stressed the importance of consistency in behaviour and the need to empower the players. I also prioritised benchmarking ourselves against the best, managing our environment well, and always looking at the next level and being prepared to progress and improve further.

I know it has been said that I did not do well in the technical tests – some reports even claimed I had come last. But in 2004 I was told that I had done well in the technical tests, and I knew from then that SARU didn't really know how to interview a coach about that aspect of rugby. In my view, there shouldn't even be a technical component to the interview process at all. Surely if a coach makes the shortlist, he knows his way around the technical side of rugby? Or otherwise what is he doing there? A coach is on the shortlist in the first place because of his technical ability, not because he is a good Christian and wants to be the pastor of the rugby union.

And this so-called technical component of the interview process is actually quite bizarre. It consists of the selection committee showing you video clips of rugby matches and asking you how you would respond to certain incidents in a game. As a funny aside, Jake White did well in the technical tests in 2004, which was hardly surprising, as he was an employee of SARU at the time and had had a hand in drawing up the tests. At the time I thought it was rather unfair, but I didn't make a big fuss about it. I didn't want people to think I had sour grapes about Jake's appointment. It was a bit of a joke, though. To some extent, the entire selection process for the Springbok coach is a bit of a joke. Or it was at the time I went through it.

It was important for me to know who would be on the technical committee. If Ian McIntosh was going to be on the committee, then it would be important to know your way around scrums, but if Dawie Snyman was going to be there, you needed to be smart about backline play. But again I must stress that all the technical test consisted of was the playing of a video clip, nothing more. And you knew that the committee members had preconceived ideas on what your answer should be.

If I did come last in that test, I wonder how the technical committee could have voted for me to become the new Bok coach by 7 votes to 1. The only person who didn't vote for me was Brian van Zyl, the Sharks chief executive. Although I was later told that he had recused himself from the process, apparently that hadn't been the case – he was on the committee but just didn't vote for me.

Having now done the job for four years, I am convinced that SARU get it completely wrong in the selection and interview process. Given how important these issues are when you are the Springbok coach, SARU should be spending more time interviewing the prospective coaches on how they will handle the media – public relations is a massive part of the job.

Obviously it's important to be strong technically – that should be the bottom line when you are appointed as coach. But you can always appoint specialists to work with you and take charge of that particular field of expertise. When I became Springbok coach, I quickly learnt that the technical side of coaching is but a small part of the job, particularly when compared to communicating with the public and the media and dealing with the pressures the various stakeholders are applying.

But this was all in the future. At the time, it was more important for me that I concluded the interviewing process confident that I had put in a strong bid to be the next Springbok coach.

7

The contract

If what happened on my first day in the job was odd, what followed next was even odder – and confirmed how reluctant the South African administrators were to have me as the Springbok coach.

Not only did they not have a contract drawn up for me when I was appointed, it seemed as if they hadn't even thought through its terms or what I was going to be offered. It's hard to imagine that when Heyneke Meyer was appointed in 2012, there hadn't been a discussion with him before the announcement was made on what the job would entail and what he would be paid.

So I had them over a barrel, although for me, it wasn't about the money. I didn't want to drive a hard bargain just so that I could enrich myself. Money has never meant much to me. After becoming Springbok coach, I continued to live in the same area and followed the same lifestyle as before. In my opinion, all people are equal, and you should not use money to try to set yourself apart from others.

I fought the package they offered as a matter of principle, as it was just ridiculous. It was significantly less than Jake White had been paid, and it made me feel as if they thought that with me coaching the Springboks, the standards would drop. If you were offered the position of CEO at a top company and you learnt that you were going to get paid only a portion of what the previous CEO was getting, you'd think that too.

Surely if you wanted the company to continue at or exceed the previous level, you would pay the new CEO the same as his predecessor? That old saying that if you pay peanuts, you get monkeys, crossed my mind. Perhaps they thought they were getting a monkey.

I was determined that the Springboks' game would remain at the same high level. It made no sense to allow standards to drop – as coach, I didn't want that to happen. But I wanted to be paid what the coach of a world-champion team should get paid, not only because that was the right thing to do, but also because it would impel me to produce the goods.

So I called Rian Oberholzer to negotiate the contract on my behalf. Rian, of course, was a former chief executive of SARFU and SA Rugby, so he knew his way around the contracts of national coaches. When he saw what I had been offered, he wasn't happy. He didn't like the package as a whole and, like me, didn't think I was being paid according to the status South African rugby was enjoying as world champions.

Another cause for concern was that the contract did not include a performance clause. Why the hell not? Did they perhaps want some lee-way so that they could get rid of me for something inconsequential? So I fought for a performance clause, and it is a good thing I did, for in 2010 it would save me my job.

I wanted a performance clause in my contract because, if they were going to fire me, I wanted to know why; I wanted to know the reason for it. Also, the initial contract was for only two years, which meant that regardless of my results, once the two years were up, they could just send me on my way. I wanted a four-year contract. Most of all, I wanted all the finer points included in the contract so that I could be judged the same way all the other coaches had been judged.

Unfortunately, SARU landed a few low blows in the Battle of the Contract. They leaked information to the media that gave a false impression of the money I would be earning. They claimed that I could earn as much as R14 million. Yes, I could possibly have earned that much, but I could also have won the lottery. I would have made R14 million if I won every tournament and every match over a period of several years. Which team wins *every* game?

This misleading information would make people think that I was just in it for the money. If SARU wanted to turn people against me and make me look greedy, they were doing a good job of it. They were certainly painting an ugly picture of their coach.

In the end, both sides made compromises, but I basically got what

I wanted. Although I can't recall exactly what part of the deal Rian compromised on, I know it involved the issue of money, which was of less importance to me than some of the other issues.

Most crucially, I was given the right to have the last say in selection. I had no problem working with selectors, as you can't be everywhere at once and you need experts to help you identify talent and tap the country's playing resources, but if I was going to take the rap as the coach when things went wrong, then I wanted to have selected the team. So I had to have the final say.

I was quite unexpectedly also given something I hadn't even asked for. The previous year, controversy had surrounded Oregan Hoskins's decision to add Luke Watson as player number 46 to Jake White's World Cup training squad. As the president of SARU, he had the right to do so, as he signed off the team. So it came as a surprise when Regan publicly stated that he would no longer do so. I was now in total control of selection, which was a privilege not even my predecessors had enjoyed. And I hadn't even asked for it.

Perhaps I am being unkind to Oregan, and if I am, I am sorry, but it crossed my mind that his decision to no longer sign off the team was motivated by a hidden agenda. As I was most emphatically not Oregan's choice as coach, he didn't want to be held accountable if anything went wrong under my auspices.

Another oddity was SARU's decision not to link the rest of the Bok management contracts to mine, as is normally done in international rugby. In other words, the futures of the assistant coaches were not dependent on my results. Were SARU waiting for me to fail so that they could replace me with one of the assistant coaches, Dick Muir or Gary Gold? To his credit, Dick opted to throw in his lot with me and demanded that his contract be linked to mine. So if I was fired, he would be fired too.

At the time of my appointment, several negative stories that were never properly verified did the rounds. For instance, Jake White was quoted in the media as saying that none of the Springboks wanted to play for me, and one newspaper even conducted a poll. And on the day I was appointed, one story even alleged that the South African Rugby Players Association (SARPA) was against my appointment.

Of course the rumours made me very uncomfortable. How was I going to coach the players if they didn't want or support me? When the newspaper announced the result of its poll, it did not state what number of players in the country had been canvassed, but they still came up with a percentage. How did they measure that?

So I went to see the guys at SARPA, who couldn't enlighten me. Piet Heymans, the CEO, told me that Hennie le Roux had been against the appointment and he might have spoken to a couple of people and drawn some assumptions. The identity of the players was irrelevant, and it was not my mission to find out who they were. My concern was what level of support and cooperation I was going to get.

The combination of the above factors made me feel very alone and prompted me to look for allies outside of SA Rugby. I needed someone to talk to – I wanted a sounding board I could rely on, which I could not find at SARU.

It was against this background, and with the knowledge that I had lots of enemies within SARU, that I assembled a reference or support group that I could use as my sounding board. But in choosing Cheeky Watson as leader of the group, I would once again expose my naivety.

Cheeky, the Eastern Cape activist who had turned his back on white rugby in the seventies, seemed to be driven by both a political and a personal agenda – he and his supporters wanted the Springbok emblem removed and Luke Watson included in the Springbok team.

Just a couple of months after my appointment, Hoskins had fought off a challenge by his vice-president, Mike Stofile, for the presidency of SARU. Mike, who had been one of my big supporters at SARU, subsequently turned his back on rugby.

I went to Cheeky and said, 'What is going to happen now? I feel all alone here.'

Cheeky responded by suggesting that we set up a committee that would help me make the right decisions. Included on his list were the names of quite a few guys who were high up in government. I thought the support group was a great idea, as were the names Cheeky suggested, as having such powerful backing would obviously put me in a much stronger position.

Besides himself, the committee Cheeky suggested included Butana

Komphela, the chairperson of the Parliamentary Portfolio Committee on Sport and Recreation, Cedric Frolick, the deputy chairperson of the same committee, Dr Asad Bhorat, the secretary of the Transformation and Anti-Racism Rugby Committee, Mike Stofile, the former rugby administrator, Neil de Beer, the manager of the age-group rugby teams when I coached them, and a few others. Because we were anticipating that Neil would be on my management team, he would be the direct link between me and the committee members.

I thought things were suddenly looking up for me, as I now had access to some wise counsel. These people would be able to help me with the thorny issue of transformation, a very important factor in South African rugby, and they would act in my best interests. Well, if it all seemed too good to be true, it's probably because it was.

There were many occasions in my four-year tenure as coach when perception did not correspond to fact. Looking back, I was stupid. Of course the situation would be manipulated; I was so naive in my assumption that everyone would act for the good of South African rugby.

I knew as much almost immediately when I informed the committee that I intended bringing back John Smit and Victor Matfield. Cheeky reacted as if I had told him I was going to take an aircraft and crop-spray everyone in the Eastern Cape with deadly poison.

Neil summoned me to a meeting with Cheeky at the Dros restaurant in Paarl. When I got there, I could see Cheeky's face was like thunder. It was one hell of a thing.

'What the bloody hell do you think you are doing?' he demanded. 'Don't you know the damn Afrikaners don't support you? They never have and they never will!'

He was very angry. And I got angry too. In fact, I lost my temper. I tore into him. I asked him if he thought I was just a black man who he could manipulate, and if this was why he had helped me get the job – so that he could treat me like a puppet that he could control from behind the scenes. It galled me that he had perhaps backed me not because I was the best man for the job, but for reasons of his own.

'If you're so damn good and know everything, why don't *you* do the job?' I asked him. 'Why didn't you just apply for the Springbok coaching position yourself?'

I told him to go back to the support group and to SARU and to tell them that he would take over the Springbok job.

That was my first fight with Cheeky, and my strong reaction must have had an effect because he backed off. I think he realised then that I had a mind of my own, and that I knew where I wanted to go and what I wanted to accomplish. My relationship with Cheeky would come to a head during that year's Tri Nations, when he travelled to New Zealand bearing a bizarre message, but, in the meantime, it all calmed down after our argument.

I had a few meetings with the support committee, where I revealed some of my plans. I told the members that while I had reappointed John Smit, I thought my next captain should be Luke Watson, and that he might take us to the 2011 World Cup. At that stage I couldn't see John going beyond the 2009 British & Irish Lions series. My intention with John was for him to bring some continuity to the team, and that he would make way for someone else once we had laid the foundations and stabilised the ship.

At the time, there were a lot of misconceptions about my intentions with Luke Watson and my attitude towards transformation. Let's deal with transformation first.

At the press conference during which my appointment was announced, I said that transformation was a bit of a swear word to me, and I still feel exactly the same about it – at least, in the sense that most people understand transformation. To me, transformation is about attitude and not skin colour.

Some of my critics have claimed that I neglected transformation during my tenure, as I did not include enough black players in the Springbok team. I disagree. If you were to ask me if I thought I had transformed the Springboks, I would say yes. The Springboks were more a people's team at the end of my stint than it had been when I took over. The players were often out among the people, signing autographs, clearly representing all their countrymen in this great land of ours. They became more accessible to their supporters across all race groups.

To me, the word 'transform' means you progress from what you were to what you can be. If it becomes an accepted fact that you can only transform society in South Africa through skin colour, then we are all in big trouble. If that is indeed the case, then we are setting ourselves up to fail.

You will always find good black people, you will find bad black people; there are good white people and there are bad white people. You can't change that. What you can change is the respect people have for one another. And that is what I am talking about – the colour of a person's skin can never be more important than the basic respect we should have for each other.

If we can transform the way we think about races and cultures different from our own and learn to respect people for their abilities, then we are winning. That is why Oregan Hoskins's statement that I had not been appointed for rugby reasons alone was such a massive insult. It was an attack on my character. He was judging me on my skin colour, not on my abilities.

The Dale Granger newspaper article that was written when I was in Romania with the Emerging Springboks, and which I have mentioned before, also created a misconception about me in the general public. When Granger phoned me from Cape Town, I wasn't quite sure what he was after, but he asked me about transformation, Luke Watson and the Springbok job.

I told him that there were plenty of good black players in the country, and I knew this because I had coached most of them. In my opinion, I said, there were about 60 black players who were capable of playing at the top level, and I could easily identify them. Unfortunately the story implied that I was saying we had 60 black players in the country who could play international rugby and there was no place for any white players. Yes, there may have been 60 black players, and I still believe that, but at the same time there were also more than 60 white players who were good enough to play for South Africa.

When I won the Junior World Cup in 2005 with nine black players in the starting line-up, I made it known that in other years we would be lucky to have nine black players in the team. That was just the way it had worked out that particular season; it just so happened that there were nine black players who were the best in their positions.

Conversely, there were only six white players that year who were good enough to start for the South African under-21 team, but other years have been different. Ultimately you have to choose the players that fit the combinations that you require for the team to be successful. And sometimes that will mean more of a certain type of player and fewer of another.

People are forever coming up with lists of names that they throw at you: Elton Jantjies, Earl Rose ... It makes you think, 'Phew, we have a lot of talent! Why aren't all these guys playing?' But that is to completely misunderstand the team environment and what constitutes a good rugby team. If you are talking about the number of players that are available, the list is almost endless, but when it comes to finding places in a 15-man team, then it's a very short list.

I was successful in putting teams together because, before I was appointed as national under-21 coach, I took the time to study the different cultures that make up our country. I spent time with black people and coloured people, and I sought out Afrikaans people and English-speaking white people. What I found was that an Afrikaans person who lives in the centre of Cape Town thinks quite differently from one who lives in the suburbs. And the Afrikaans person in Pretoria is different from the one in Johannesburg, yet those cities are only 60 kilometres apart.

Based on those findings, I decided that every team I coached in future would have to have a culture that excluded skin colour. Instead, I would emphasise the importance of open-mindedness and fair play. I built that culture into every team I coached, and I think all the players I've worked with enjoyed living by those principles.

'In this team, we live according to the team culture, not the culture you live by at home,' I told them. 'And you can do whatever you want within the parameters of the team culture. You are welcome to return to your own culture when you leave the team.'

I broadcast the message that a team functions not according to a specific social culture but according to strong principles, like fair play, which made it easier for them to accept. From what I heard said by some of the players, I got the impression that other coaches didn't always manage to create a unified team culture.

Obviously this philosophy wasn't something that could really be put across in a newspaper story in those early days, and some people thought I had taken the Springbok job just so I could ruin South African rugby. I remember reading stories that claimed radio stations and websites had been swamped with comments about my appointment, among them: 'SARU has shot rugby in the head' and 'We will never be a force in world rugby again'.

These allegations were very hurtful, and also wrong. My agenda was no different from that of previous coaches – I wanted the Springboks to win and I wanted to be a successful coach. Unfortunately, even my support committee seemed to be affected by the stories, for they now made suggestions about team selections, among other things.

I didn't have a team in mind when I was appointed for the simple reason that I didn't know who was going to carry on playing after the World Cup in 2007. Some of the players were planning on going overseas to continue their careers and others might decide not to play under me.

That newspaper article also sparked the perception that I was going to bring Luke Watson into the Springbok fold and make him my captain. When Granger asked me about Luke, I said that Luke had captained my national under-21 team in Scotland and that I had never worked with a more dynamic person. Luke had been prepared to put his body on the line for the team and his teammates, he understood the game really well and he was a motivator with extraordinary gifts.

One of the things that made me believe that Luke was an excellent leader was an incident that occurred while we were in a team huddle after winning one of our games. A supporter approached us waving an old South African flag. Luke politely and respectfully told him that the country had changed and that there was no place for someone who thought like he did. That was enough to chase the man away.

I really respected Luke as a young leader, so I could see him as a future Springbok captain. When he was injured and had to leave the tournament, it became even more obvious what he'd brought to the team. Without him, the team's performance hit a downward curve. I realised then that perhaps I had relied on him too much, and I had to work really hard to motivate the guys again.

When you come across someone like Luke, he obviously stays in your mind, especially because I truly thought he had the potential to make a great Springbok captain. But that did not mean he *would* be my Springbok captain. Although I envisaged Luke taking over the captaincy after John, sadly other events that occurred prevented this from happening.

When I did bring Luke into the team at the start of my stint as Springbok coach, a lot of water had already flowed under the bridge. Luke was at a disadvantage because of what had happened in the Jake era, as the players knew that he had been forced upon the squad as player number 46. Naturally, they weren't happy about that. Luke was subsequently quoted as saying he hadn't been happy with the situation either. I gather that since his stint playing for the English club, Bath, he has matured a great deal and what had held true for him then may not hold true for him now.

But I was disappointed with Luke when he refused to cooperate with some of the senior players when they did open themselves to him. On a few occasions, Victor Matfield and John Smit tried to involve Luke in their team discussions.

'What do you think about that idea, Luke? Do you think it will work?' they would ask him.

Luke would say, 'I am just here to observe.'

Later in my first year as coach, Luke made some comments about the Springbok emblem that further estranged him from most of the players. His attitude made me change my mind about him, though, as I've said, I hear he has changed a lot since his return from England. If that is the case, I wish him well, as I have no doubt that he is a good man. But the bottom line was that I couldn't appoint Luke as my captain, as he would not have been accepted by his teammates.

You wonder why I am spending so much time discussing Luke Watson? It's because the Luke issue was to play a big role in fomenting some of the controversy I was to be embroiled in later, and it was to lead to the dissolution of my support group.

8

Rounding up the leaders

After my battle to be given the contract I reckoned the job merited, everything was finally settled and I was able to start planning my first international season in charge of the Springboks.

I can't tell you how excited I was. This was what I had dreamt about; the opportunity I had thought about but never really believed would come my way. Ever since that furtive and ill-fated first taste of being Springbok assistant coach in 1997, it had been my ambition to nail down the top job in coaching in South African rugby.

But thinking about it and actually doing it are two different things. Although I had made a presentation to SARU in the application and selection process and had set out my blueprint, the details of the job were not something I had considered all that much. I was adamant that I didn't want to arrive with any preconceived ideas.

That was why all the speculation about me wanting to appoint Luke Watson as my captain and sweep out all the elder statesmen from the team made me so cross. I wasn't sure about the senior players for one reason, and one reason only: I wasn't sure where I stood with them.

I suppose it was understandable that some people thought I would bring Luke in because of my relationship with Cheeky, but it was only after I had selected John as my captain that Cheeky and I ever really discussed the captaincy issue. As I've mentioned, he was mad at me not only for that, but also because I was bringing back Victor Matfield. Cheeky was quick to tell me that the Afrikaners would never support me, and that I must just accept as much.

But I was determined to let people know that I was everyman's

Springbok coach; I wasn't just the coach for the blacks, or for the English-speakers or the Afrikaans-speakers. The challenge I faced was no different from the one that Jake White had faced before me, when he appointed John Smit as captain in 2004 – I needed a leader who would be accepted by everyone and who would be respected by all the players, regardless of race or culture.

Maybe I would have chosen Luke as my captain if he had been a veteran of 10 tests by then and was more popular among the players. Perhaps then I would have left John in France. But that wasn't the case. As I said to Cheeky and my support group when they quizzed me on the subject, Luke was a potential leader only once John retired. He was not a consideration during my first season in charge.

The appointment of a captain might have been extremely important, but so was appointing my management team. And here I needed to do some smart thinking if I was going to convey the right message about who I was and what I stood for. I had to make appointments that would be 'politically correct' in the sense of surrounding myself with people who would support me, while at the same time indicating that I was aware of the diversity of my country; I didn't want to exclude any group.

Initially I was keen on appointing Cheetahs coach Naka Drotské, an Afrikaans guy, as the forwards coach, with Dick Muir, an English-speaker, as the backline coach. We would then have a black coach working with an Afrikaans person and an English-speaker, which would make everyone feel included.

But while I rated Naka as a forwards coach, he did not want to be an assistant coach. That set me on the path of bringing Gary Gold in as my forwards coach, with Loffie Eloff, the former under-19 coach who had taken over at the Lions, as my backline coach. Like Naka, though, Loffie didn't want the job, which I later understood when I heard that the SARU bosses were considering him as my replacement should I not make the grade.

SARU board member Jannie Ferreira, then the Lions president, had let slip that there were plans afoot to set some form of succession plan in place, where the under-19 coach would become the under-21 coach and the under-21 coach the national coach.

The two coaches who remained after that were Dick and Gary, and to my mind they were ideal assistant coaches in that they had markedly different philosophies. I have always encouraged healthy debate within a management team about rugby issues; I have never seen the point of having people who are too like-minded on my team. A team consisting of clones is never going to win a tournament.

Dick likes to run the ball, so he was a bit like me in that sense, while Gary is the conservative guy whose philosophy centres around structure. He had done sterling work at WP in this regard. I didn't know Gary personally and had had only brief dealings with Dick when he was a player, so I relied heavily on my support group's advice in choosing my assistant coaches.

Cheeky strongly recommended Gary, mentioning time and again how solid he was technically. But I didn't need Gary as my technical advisor. I needed him as my assistant coach, which was a different thing. So, in the end, I had to make up my own mind. I eventually made my decision when people I had asked for advice assured me about Gary's technical strengths in forward play.

Although my assistant coaches were to be the subject of much debate during my four years as coach, they were nearly unfortunate victims when I compromised my principles in 2010 for the only time in my tenure. But in 2008, their appointments went largely unremarked. It was the reappointment of John Smit as captain and Victor Matfield as vice-captain that got everyone talking and raised the hackles of those who supported me.

I have subsequently heard that some people said John's reappointment had been suggested by Rian Oberholzer. This is not quite true, though I had run the idea past him. I said: 'Maybe it will be a good thing if I bring John back.' And Rian said, 'Ja, that sounds like a great idea.'

I respected Rian, whom I had worked for as South Africa under-19 coach and who had also 'fired' me as assistant coach of the Boks in 1997. Above all, he certainly knew what to look out for in a contract. In my opinion, he was one of the very best CEOs ever employed by our national rugby body.

Rian never really advised me, though; he managed me, and he was a great manager. I still have enormous respect for him, but two factors eventually caused us to part ways: first, his other business commitments, which meant he couldn't give his full attention to my concerns. He was a very busy man who spent a lot of time in the UK. The second was his relationship with the rugby writer, Mark Keohane.

Rian and Mark were close, which put Rian in a compromising position. I was worried that he would tell Mark things he and I discussed in private. And even if Rian was never guilty of doing that, I knew Mark was a damn good journalist who was well connected. He might well come across information that I might incorrectly assume had come from Rian. So, in my second year as Bok coach, Rian and I parted ways.

It was Rian, though, who facilitated my first meeting with John Smit. I met John in South Africa, and then I flew to France to see him again. John had built up so much intellectual capital in his years as Bok captain that it was just too valuable to throw away. However, I assumed that he and Jake White had become inseparable by then – a mistake I think a lot of people made at the time. Of course I suspected that Jake didn't have much respect for me, as he had made obvious both in the way he behaved towards me and in what he had said to the media. So why would John want to work with me? I needed to find out from him if he would.

Andy Marinos accompanied me on a trip to France and England. We went to England at the start of our trip and meant to see Butch James at Bath, but it turned out that he was unavailable. Then we went to France to meet with John, Victor Matfield and Percy Montgomery. Andy was a great help at this time, a consummate professional who knew his way around the business and how to put structures in place. A lot that was established then might not have happened without his input. The trip also gave us the opportunity to do a lot of talking.

I am not quite sure how it happened, but we ended up not meeting with Victor. I think it can be attributed to a miscommunication; I suspect that former All Black captain Tana Umaga, who was then coaching Toulon, wasn't keen on letting Victor go. The message he conveyed to us was that Victor didn't want to see us. So any meeting with the man had to wait until later on, when we were back in South Africa.

Percy, who was playing for Perpignan, had been one of the stars of the Springbok World Cup victory the year before. It had been a masterstroke on Jake White's part to get Percy involved with the Springboks again when he was playing club rugby in Wales. Percy was a great servant of the game in South Africa, and had been a great Springbok, but he was nearing the end of his career, and many might have wondered why I wanted to keep him involved.

The answer lay in the number of test caps he had. I attach a lot of importance to how many test caps players accumulate, as players with that kind of experience can play a huge role in ensuring that new-comers have an easy transition into the major leagues. I also think it is a huge source of a nation's rugby pride when a player reaches his 100 mark in test caps. I thought it was important for South Africa to have a centurion, so this factor, as well as Percy's mentoring potential, was why I very much wanted him to be part of the team.

At the time, Percy stood on 94 caps. I told him that although I didn't think he would play at international level for much longer, he had six more games to reach the magical three-figure mark. Then we would reassess his future. I just felt that in South Africa we don't respect ourselves and our heroes enough. If you look back now, we actually wrote the perfect script for Percy, who played his 100th test match at his beloved Newlands.

But back to our trip to France: I met with John and his wife, Roxy, in Clermont. I got the impression that she wasn't enjoying herself in France – it's hard to live overseas with a young family. I thought she might have some influence on the decision John had to make.

John immediately wanted to know whether it was true that I had said I didn't want him as my captain, and that I wanted to make wholesale changes to the team. This had all been reported in the media. I told him that this wasn't the case at all and that my words had been taken out of context. I was being misrepresented by the media – they were painting a picture of me that I had not intended creating.

I told John that while I may have said that there were 60 black players in the country capable of playing for the national team, I also knew of more than 60 white players who were good enough to be Springboks. I said that I wanted to select the team on merit, and while

I did feel a responsibility to bring talented black players through the system, my chief objective was to ensure that the Springboks kept on winning.

John immediately impressed me; I liked the way he conducted himself. I said that I needed him as my captain for two years, and that if he still had the passion and urge to continue after that, we could discuss a possible continuation up to and including the 2011 World Cup. I told him that it was imperative that, in return, he helped me keep the Springboks' game at the highest possible level. At that stage, of course, we were the world champions.

John is a man of great integrity. He never said a bad word about Jake at that meeting, and I never heard him say anything negative about him subsequently. I value loyalty and honesty, and John struck me as a person I could trust and depend upon. I thought straight away, 'Hell, I must make this guy my captain. He's the right man for the job.'

But I must stress that, at the time, I also thought that John was the best hooker in South Africa. I did not agree with anyone who said he wasn't – not in 2008. Bismarck du Plessis was still a baby then, plus John had played extremely well in the 2007 World Cup. It was important that I establish a personal relationship with him, as his history with Jake might have prevented him from playing for the Springboks again. At the same time, John had thought that because of his closeness with Jake, the next Bok coach would be wary of using him. It had been one of the main reasons why he had decided to go to France.

And he was probably right about that. If Heyneke Meyer had been appointed, I don't think he would have chosen John as his captain. He had, in fact, promised Victor the captaincy if he got the job – there would have been no place for John.

I quickly realised that John and I could discuss issues relating to players and the team that I couldn't discuss with anyone else. He appeared to have special insight – a way of simply understanding people. I liked that about him. It also became apparent that we shared the same interests, which was to put the Springboks before anything else, including ourselves. John has never had any ambitions for himself – all of his ambitions revolved around the team. He always wanted the team, and not himself personally, to do well.

I knew from the beginning that I would have to earn John's trust. And I think that I got that right just by being honest with him and by being prepared to listen to the senior players' input. I wanted to ensure that the environment in my first season as coach was the same environment players like John were used to, as it made them feel comfortable.

It was a pleasant surprise for John when I came to see him in France. He told me that he wanted to come back to South Africa. He had a small child and Roxy was struggling to adapt to a new life in a foreign country. For me it was a no-brainer – he deserved his place in the side and, as the recognised leader in the team, it was only right to bring him back.

If Victor had been in South Africa at the time and not playing for Toulon, I might not have called up John. I would have gone for the leader who was based at home. But because they were both playing overseas, it made sense to bring them both back. Without John or Victor, we would have struggled to find a respected and recognised captain to step into the leadership void, particularly as Luke Watson was inexperienced at international level. And because of the other factors already mentioned, he would just have been too risky a choice. I even thought of Fourie du Preez as a possible alternative, but he was injured.

After the miscommunication with Victor in France, Andy Marinos and I resolved to try to get him to come to South Africa so that he could speak to us here. We decided not to intrude on his privacy if he wasn't interested, as we didn't want to put him in a difficult position with Toulon. So we sent him an email asking him whether he was interested. We stressed that if he didn't want to play for the Boks, that would be fine and we would move on without him.

I was going to attend the Varsity Cup rugby tournament in George, and as Victor said he was off that weekend, we arranged to meet then. It was going to be an important meeting, as I had read media reports in which Victor had apparently said that he would only play for the Springboks again if Heyneke Meyer was the coach.

Of course Heyneke had coached Victor for a long time at the Bulls and they had achieved some amazing successes together. In fact, Heyneke had been instrumental in making Victor the player he was, so I completely understood his loyalty to the man. But I wanted to know if Victor would be prepared to play for me; I wanted him to tell me how he felt face to face.

Jake's comment that the players were not prepared to play for a black coach was still fresh in my memory, and Victor's name was always mentioned whenever that story came up. So I wanted to get that out of the way too. I had heard stories about the Bulls players' attitude, and I wanted to know if the rumours were true. I didn't know where those stories had come from – perhaps they had originated in Jake White's insecurities about anything related to me. Through no doing of my own, I had become a threat to Jake in 2005, when my name kept on cropping up every time it seemed that he might lose his job. As Jake himself has written, he was told that he had to win the Port Elizabeth test against France in 2005 or he could face dismissal. South Africa beat France that day, but on the same weekend my team won the international under-21 tournament in Argentina. So I suppose that kind of pressure caused him to be wary of me.

So there was a lot of straight talking when Victor and I met. I asked him frankly: 'Victor, are you a racist?' He said that I could ask his friends and they would tell me whether he was or not. I said that none of his friends were there, that no one else would be privy to our conversation, so he could be honest with me. He looked quite taken aback, but I could immediately gauge the honesty in his appearance and approach. Once I was reassured, I was true to my word – Victor and I moved on and never looked back.

I was honest with Victor from the start. Andries Bekker was just starting to come through at the Stormers, and I saw him as an awesome prospect as a future Springbok No. 5. I wasn't at all sure how long Victor would go on playing, so I was open with him. I told him that if he came back, he would not immediately be part of my starting team.

However, when we gathered for our first training camp, in Stellenbosch, I immediately knew that I had made a mistake. Victor had such an aura about him and was just so professional about everything he did that I realised I should perhaps not have talked so soon or have had too many preconceived ideas. Victor showed me how committed he was simply by spending hours running on the treadmill when I hadn't asked him or expected him to do so; he soon impressed me with his extraordinary work ethic and total professionalism.

But it was still unfair for a man to come back from France and walk straight into the team ahead of someone like Bekker, who had played superbly in the Super 14. So I kept my word to Andries and named him in the team for the first test against Wales, in Bloemfontein.

So, after meeting with John and Victor, my mind was at rest on the issue of leadership. So much had been said and so many rumours had circulated that I'd had to establish the truth by getting it straight from the guys themselves. When I didn't hear any negativity from them, I knew I could build the Springbok team around them.

Not only did John and Victor enjoy the respect of the other players in the team, they were also strongly identified with the culture of the Springboks. Having them in the squad was important in retaining the team's character. In spite of what others might have said at the time, I knew I was taking over a winning team and I had no intention of changing things just for the sake of it. Once that message was put across to the players, they supported me.

The only two guys who took a long time to win over were Juan Smith and Fourie du Preez, but there was a reason for that. Both Juan and Fourie are highly principled guys, and they had been told that I wasn't good enough to do the job. They wanted to assess me themselves before making up their own minds.

I must have done something right, for today I can't find two players who are more loyal to me than those two. And that loyalty stemmed from the knowledge that I cared about the person and not just the player; I didn't see them as just cogs in a machine.

It's important to stress my philosophy, which I also imparted to the players: while rugby will never become my whole life, it is an integral part of it, and I want to make a success of every part of my life. Also, if you don't understand the personality of the person you are working with, you can forget about successfully working with that player. You don't get loyal rugby players – you only get loyal people. The person inside the player must be prepared to die for you, so that the rugby player will follow suit.

It has always been a crucial component of my coaching philosophy.

9

My coaching philosophy

When Joel Stransky interviewed me on television in my first season as coach, he and I had a bit of a disagreement. He told me that he didn't understand my game plan or my philosophy or what I was trying to accomplish. I told him that he didn't need to understand, as it was his job to sit in the stands and commentate as he watched my game plan unfold. The players were the ones who needed to understand it.

There was a lot of debate about my philosophy in those early months of 2008, in the build-up to the Boks' first series with me as coach. Unfortunately, this was one of the many instances where what I was trying to say probably got lost in translation. I had no plans to radically change the Springbok game – it would have been a stupid thing to do.

While I come from a running rugby background, which was the style of play of most of the teams I'd played for, you just had to look at my track record at national age-group level to know that it wasn't as if I believed only in Barbarians-style rugby. I had never coached a team to just run the ball willy-nilly from all over the field.

When the under-21 team won the IRB tournament in Argentina in 2005, their approach had been close to the traditional Springbok game, with strong forward play and an emphasis on a physical, in-your-face defensive effort. And it was the same in 2006, when we made the final and lost to France. I also wasn't 'anti-structure', as some put it, although I did say that with the amount of talent we have available to us in South Africa, we should be less reliant on structure than a nation like Australia, where there just isn't the same depth of talent.

I am a man for total rugby, and by that I mean the rugby the Springboks played in the pool-phase games at the 2011 World Cup. In those matches, we ran beautifully when it was appropriate to do so, and then, at other times, when the opportunities weren't presenting themselves, we played a more structured kind of game.

For instance, we couldn't run the ball in our opening game against Wales; we had to maintain our patterns, as conceding a turnover would have been costly. We weren't turning the Welsh ball over easily, so we had to keep it tight. But later on in the tournament, we made some easy turnovers in other games and could then play the ball wide.

It all comes down to decision-making. When I took over at the Springboks, from what I had seen of them, I thought they were a bit too rigid in their approach. In fact, they were rigid to the point where they sometimes neglected the decision-making aspect and just blindly followed the structure that had been drilled into them at training.

If you go into a ruck and the ball is loose, why would you still want to go and clean out the ball and set it up rather than just picking the thing up? This was why Ruan Pienaar impressed me so much. He was one of the few South African players who seemed able to make instinctive decisions and, more often than not, he was right. But I got the impression that some of the coaches Ruan had played for didn't like that about him.

From watching and coaching South African rugby players, I had come to realise that where overseas players see gaps, our players tend to see a wall of defenders. Instead of finding gaps in the wall to run through, they tend to want to bash down the wall.

To my mind, that is the biggest problem our so-called top rugby schools present us with. The drive to win motivates most of the schools to coach the same way, and by the time the players come through to play senior rugby, most of them have been coached in this pattern from the ages of 15 or 16. Sometimes, when I was coaching the national under-19 and under-21 teams, I wanted to tear my hair out because of the number of times players would do something but then, when I asked them why they had done it, they couldn't tell me. It was just what they had been coached to do.

I never wanted to change the South African game significantly, but

I could see the benefits of having players who could think on their feet and make their own decisions. It was only much later, when I carried out psychological tests on the players in the build-up to the following year's series against the British & Irish Lions, that I realised that if I wanted to try to change the way they played, I would have to change the whole team.

For us to have a different type of player at international level, we would have to break down and reinvent the whole system from the bottom up. So it was impossible to make radical changes at international level; the players' psyches just wouldn't allow it.

Unfortunately, even some of my supporters exaggerated what I was trying to accomplish. They made it seem as if I was making much bigger changes than I actually was, and confusion reigned as a result. The common perception was that I wanted the players to run from all over the place, which was not the case at all. I may act like it occasionally, but I'm not really crazy.

But I was fully aware that the top players were probably thinking that I was a bit mad. They had been hearing and reading what the media were saying about me. One of the allegations was that I thought the players were all robots! As if it is not intimidating enough coaching the Springboks without having to do so against the background of so much misinformation. While quite a few of the players had played under me before, I would be completely new to many others, so I knew that all these misperceptions about my intentions could come back to haunt me. I therefore needed to get all the players together so that I could explain what I wanted to do and allay any fears they might have.

To make sure that the message was conveyed as far and wide as possible, I called together 47 guys for my first training camp, in Stellenbosch. I wanted as many players as possible at the camp, as I didn't know how things were going to pan out. The SARPA poll had, after all, suggested that I had next to no support from the top players, so of course I was worried.

I thought that if the top guys decided they didn't want to play for me, perhaps the next level of players would be ready to step in as their replacements.

I was extremely nervous when I drove to Somerset West for the start of the camp. We stayed at the Lord Charles Hotel, which was conveniently located for our training in Stellenbosch. The reason I wanted to train at Stellenbosch was that I had coached there before and knew the lay of the land. I felt comfortable there, and would not have wanted my first training camp to take place in a location I was not familiar with.

All the top players attended, and most of the players who had won the World Cup the year before were recalled. That should have put a few minds at rest, but there were also some newcomers I wanted to assess. The young Western Province flyhalf, Isma-eel Dollie, was one of the players who attended my first camp, but unfortunately he didn't make the cut and never featured again.

Duane Vermeulen, then in great form for the Cheetahs, was also part of the group, but his medical assessment showed up a serious injury that demanded either an operation or a lot of rest, and he was forced out of the camp early. He was not to feature again in my plans until the World Cup season four years later, when he was unfortunately struck by another injury. He really was one of the unluckiest players.

Reserve lock Johann Muller was one of the 2007 World Cup winners I did not select for that first camp, but he was called up much later in my stint as coach, and ended up travelling with us to the World Cup in 2011, where his experience was invaluable.

Many critics saw Adrian 'Adi' Jacobs as a surprise inclusion, but he had played for me in my South Africa under-19 team, where he and Jean de Villiers had been an excellent combination, and he had also played for me at the Falcons. He could deliver what I wanted, and although he was not the most popular choice among the rugby media, he ended up being one of the Springbok stars of 2008. He certainly never let me down.

Adi has the ability to run off players around him, as he instinctively knows where the spaces are. Funnily enough, when he and Jean played together in my under-19 team, Adi was at inside centre and Jean at out-side centre, and I remain convinced that those could still be the best positions for them both. As well as being good at playing off others, Adi is also a good player to play off. I think Adi was set back a bit playing for coaches at the Sharks who didn't appear to rate him. The way he was treated gave rise to the perception that he was no more than an impact player, which was unfair.

Victor Matfield also attended the first camp, but, as I said earlier, Andries Bekker was the rising star at the time. However, Victor then earned my respect with his work ethic and the way he conducted himself. He had a bit of catching up to do on his conditioning at that stage, as not only had he been injured, but he had been playing flank for Toulon. However, had Andries not been available, I would have had no problem starting with Victor in the first test against Wales.

At the time, an injury to Schalk Burger allowed me to spread my net wider at loose forward and look at other options. Thus Luke Watson became part of the initial team, and he got to start in the first test against Wales. But it quickly became apparent to me that he wasn't a good team man when he wasn't playing as the captain – at least not at that stage of his career.

We had several meetings during the initial stages of the training camp, as we had much ground to cover. I know it's been said that I changed my game plan for the Springboks only later in the season, and that the so-called 'player-driven system' was introduced when we struggled in that year's Tri Nations, but that is simply not true. The player-driven system actually started in that very first week!

At the same time, I tore up all the plans I had made before and buried any preconceived ideas with which I had arrived. I was at a completely different level from where I had coached before, which was obvious from the first day at the camp. When I compared my knowledge to that of the experienced players, there was simply no comparison. I knew I had to start from scratch.

And not just me. My one assistant coach, Gary Gold, had arrived with a huge file that he had compiled on the art of the line-out. I don't think that file ever saw the light of day – Victor knew exactly what he wanted to do. It was a real eye-opener for me. As it was the first time I had worked at that level as coach, I had had no idea that the players were as clued-up as they were.

From that first week, I knew that if I was going to produce results as a Springbok coach, I was going to have to evolve with the players. It quickly became apparent to me that they believed in the tried-and-tested strategies that had worked in the past. My resolve was that henceforth the players and I would work as a collective and produce results together.

The most pleasing aspect of the camp was that it was clear from the start that I had made the right decision regarding the leadership of the team. The leaders had an unbelievably strong influence on the rest of the players, which was a crucial component to any future success we would achieve. People who haven't worked at the highest level in rugby will never understand how important it is to have strong leaders. As a coach, you need the backing of the top guys if you are going to get buy-in from the rest of the players. It seemed that even brilliant senior players, and leaders in their own right, like Schalk Burger and Juan Smith, were prepared to follow John Smit anywhere.

We had a lot of work to do, but even in those early days it was obvious that some division had existed in the squad during the Jake White era. It soon became apparent to me that the Bulls players had never really believed in Jake and his methods. During Jake's time in charge, John had been the middleman between him and the players. It was now up to me to show the players that I saw everyone in the squad as equals.

I made it known to the guys that they could wear their hair long if they wanted to – all that mattered to me was the person's performance and that he produced when and where needed. I also conveyed the same message about the wives. I made it clear that I had no problem with partners coming on tour, but the quid pro quo was that the players must produce on the field. Most of the players were mature adults, so I had to treat them like the grown-ups they were and not like schoolboys.

Another coach may have done things differently, and in another era of Springbok rugby a coach might face different challenges – I fully accept that there are times when a strong disciplinary hand is necessary. But for me, family life is important. I believe players draw their energy and strength from their loved ones. They have to break away from rugby routine at times, which is when their wives and family are really important. Players can end up calling time on their careers early if the importance of their families is not taken into enough account. When pushed to make a choice, a player will always put his family first.

Of course, I had an ulterior motive in giving the players so much so soon: I know very well that you can't take anything away from a player if he has nothing. But if you give players a lot of privileges, they have more to lose if they don't produce what you expect of them. I have always believed in this form of personal motivation.

In that first week, I told the players how important it was to create a team culture. It had to differ from the attitudes of the rest of the country and from what they experienced at home. I told them about the surprising insights I had gained when I had conducted my own study of the make-up of our country – that the Afrikaner in Pretoria differs significantly from the Afrikaner in Johannesburg; I said to them, let's not even start on the differences between Englishman and Afrikaner, black and white, Christian and Muslim! The players seemed to buy into the philosophy of breaking down cultural boundaries in order to create a new, unique team culture.

Before I met with the players, I had my first meeting with the management team, during which I made the following statement: 'We're only here because of the players. If there were no players, there would be no coaches. So whatever you do, you do on behalf of the players. You are secondary in importance to them.'

When I then told the players that we must all be honest with one another, it wasn't difficult for them to buy into the concept. In fact, that part of my job turned out to be really easy, ironically precisely because of some of the preconceptions they'd had about me. What they had heard about me and what they experienced first hand were completely at odds with each other.

But I knew that my toughest test still lay ahead. If they were going to forget what the SARU president had said about me being an affirmative-action appointment, I would have to prove myself on the training field. It was my biggest challenge. Initially, though, everything went off really well, so I relaxed a bit.

I'd arrived with some ideas on how to motivate the players, but I quickly gathered that the team thrived on internal factors. Statistics seemed to be a big motivating factor, and analysing those got them going for the next game. For example, the players would be motivated by an analysis of the weaknesses in an opposing team, or, conversely, from stats that showed where their own game fell short. Remember, we are talking about a highly experienced group of players in this case. External or artificial methods of motivation, like asking them to compete against one another while completing an obstacle course, didn't have the desired effects – they'd done it all before.

I also quickly caught on that Victor and John had different styles of leadership. Whereas Victor exuded calmness, John's passion could sometimes explode, especially when he felt that some players were not 100 per cent committed. For example, on one occasion he even smashed a glass against the wall in a fit of temper. But that was his way of pulling the team together. Nevertheless, I sometimes had to gently chide him about his approach and encourage him to be a little more subdued.

10

The first tests

When I assembled the squad for my first series, against Wales in June 2008, I might have surprised some people with how much I based my selections on the players who had won the World Cup a few months earlier under Jake White. But although Jake never showed much respect for me, I had a lot of respect for him and what he had accomplished.

Apart from Victor Matfield, whom I had not selected for the opening match of my tenure, and Schalk Burger, who was injured, the one other player missing from my first Bok team was Fourie du Preez. The scrumhalf was injured, and according to a medical assessment, he would require some time to fully recover. I knew how important Fourie was as a player, so I flew him down to meet with me in Somerset West. I informed him that I would not select him for the first part of the season, because I wanted to allow him enough time to make a full recovery.

I think my decision was misinterpreted, as I then started hearing that I didn't want Fourie in my team. Nothing could have been further from the truth. I rated him highly as a scrumhalf and fully understood the massive role he had played in helping to orchestrate the game plan that had won the 2007 World Cup. Even back then, I knew that Springbok success in my four-year spell would depend heavily on this world-class player being able to reproduce his form of 2007.

But where does one draw the line between having just enough World Cup veterans and having too many? The media speculated that I wasn't sold on Butch James and that he wasn't part of my initial plans, and they were right on that one.

Butch was getting on a bit, he had struggled with several serious knee injuries throughout his career and, to make matters worse, he was leaving South Africa to continue his rugby career with the English club, Bath. It was reasonable for me to assume that here was a player who would not be around for much longer and, if I did select him, it would be for the short term only.

But my antipathy towards Butch did not just stem from the fact that he seemed to be nearing the end of his career. I had always seen him as a bit of a liability. When I say that, I mean it in the way in which Schalk Burger is often seen as a liability too. Referees and citing commissioners love to punish him. To me, he was a walking yellow card.

During the training camp in Stellenbosch, Butch, along with Victor Matfield, would remind me that I should always assess players first hand before passing judgement on them. Butch so impressed me on the training field that he forced me to change my plan, which had been to play Ruan Pienaar at flyhalf.

Ruan had actually not played at flyhalf much, so my intention was to ease him in gradually, with Peter Grant starting against Wales. Peter had played well for the Stormers in the Super 14, but I noticed that it was whenever Butch was at flyhalf during the training sessions that the backline really started to fire. I had to weigh up the possibility that Butch might be a liability, as he was so prone to being carded, against the knowledge that he was clearly the best flyhalf we had. I thought he would give the team an edge they wouldn't get from any other No. 10.

What swayed me in the end was that I realised if I expected Jean de Villiers to play the game I wanted him to play at inside centre, I had to have Butch in the team. I had to have someone who was strong at the gain line. Throughout my coaching career with the Springboks, the backs were always at their best when a player like Butch or Ruan was at flyhalf. It was only much later that Morné Steyn began to play nearer the gain line.

Peter Grant may be considered unlucky not to have played for the Springboks during my tenure, but he had two shortcomings that kept him from being considered: he didn't have the speed required from an international rugby player (he couldn't run in a try, even if he did make a break), and he couldn't kick equally well with both feet. These limitations would have put his teammates under more pressure. Perhaps

Peter would be better at No. 12, where kicking would not be such an important factor in his game. But I suspect his lack of speed would be a drawback at inside centre too.

With Fourie du Preez unavailable, I was starting with Ricky Januarie, who wasn't a great tactical kicker. As Ruan's tactical-kicking game was also flawed, and Jean could hardly kick at all, it became imperative that Butch continued in the role he had performed at the World Cup in order to maintain a good balance in the team.

Speaking of Ricky Januarie, whenever his name was mentioned in the same breath as mine during my four years in charge, it seemed to lead to controversial headlines. This pattern started just a few days before the first test against Wales. It was the Wednesday before the game in Bloemfontein, to be precise.

The players had been given the day off, but they were to attend the weekly team dinner that evening. Some friends of Ricky's picked him up from the hotel and they went out for the day. Unfortunately he went a bit overboard, for when he came to the team dinner that night, you could tell that he wasn't in a fit state. I was very disappointed and also a bit disconcerted, as I knew that I couldn't just let it go unnoticed. Ricky was an important part of the team.

Remember, we didn't even have Fourie du Preez there as a back-up; Bolla Conradie, who hadn't played test rugby for quite some time, was the back-up scrumhalf. I was faced with a dilemma. It was my first test in charge, and obviously I was really desperate for us to win, and win well, but would dropping Ricky as a punishment for his indiscretion scupper our chances of making a solid start to the season?

In the end I decided that it was important that I lay down boundaries the players could not overstep. I had told them during the training camp that they were going to be treated like adults – on condition that there was mutual trust and respect between us. Ricky had clearly invalidated this agreement with his behaviour.

So I called John to my room after dinner. Ricky had been part of the World Cup squad the previous year and involved with the Springboks since 2004, and I knew he was a popular member of the group. However, I told John that I had to be firm in this case.

'Listen, mate,' I said, 'Ricky has overstepped the mark and his behaviour is unacceptable. I am going to drop him from the squad in order to make a point.'

It was a bold but important move to make. As a result, a lot of people who suspected that I may be too soft suddenly had newfound respect for me. And there was also no denying that the players respected my decision, as no other incidents of a similar nature occurred during the remainder of my tenure. Had I allowed Ricky to get away with his behaviour, it would have created enormous problems going forward.

But while I was doing the right thing, it was still disruptive to our plans. Ricky was in good form at the time and had been one of the star Stormers players in the Super 14. Not many people recognised how good Ricky was at putting his opponents under pressure around the fringes.

We expected Wales to be a tough opener to the season. The team was evolving, with Warren Gatland having taken over the coaching during the period following the World Cup. He'd had an immediate positive effect on the team, and they had ended the Six Nations as European champions. Their players had come to believe in one another and were starting to buy into the systems Gatland had introduced. He was the second Kiwi that Wales had had as a coach.

But I think Warren got it wrong when they played against us. He slagged us off both in the media and in his team talks. In fact, he talked the Springboks down at every opportunity, an approach that didn't work with Wales, as they had to believe they were coming up against the number-one team in the world in order to play at their best.

I knew that, so I tried to get into Warren's head. Whenever possible, I lured him into talking us down, into saying things that would motivate my team and perhaps demotivate the Welsh players. He fell into the trap every time. The more he denigrated us, the more motivated our players became. At every turn, I told the media that I rated Warren Gatland as one of the best international rugby coaches in the world and said that I agreed with most of what he said.

In the end, we won the first test quite comfortably. We played a very structured game to start with, with Butch performing particularly well at flyhalf, and then we attacked with telling effect later on, after we had worn them down. By then, we had earned the right to run the ball wide. In the second half, when we were throwing the ball around, Adi Jacobs and Luke Watson really came into their own.

But while it was a satisfying victory and a good feeling to have won my first test, the moment was overshadowed by the ugly reception I had been given before the start of the game. The stadium in Bloemfontein was being revamped at the time in preparation for the FIFA World Cup, and before the kick-off the coaching staff and the players had to mingle with the spectators, who were close to the field of play.

I couldn't believe the ugly things some of the crowd said to me and the racial insults I had to listen to. I had invited my mother and father to be with me for my first game in charge of the Springboks, and I was really disgusted that they had to experience what they did.

There was so much animosity that I knew then that I was going to have to keep my head together and my spirit intact if I was going to survive the four years. It wasn't pleasant to listen to the abuse they shouted at me as I walked across the field, the terrible words they used when the team was warming up, and then the taunts while the game was being played. It certainly was not a pleasant way in which to start the journey.

Nevertheless, as I've said, we played good, structured rugby in Bloemfontein and won the game 43-17. Afterwards I was criticised because we hadn't run the ball as much as the critics had hoped, and some newspapers pointed out that we had played 'Jake White rugby'. But I always knew that we wouldn't have the opportunity in international rugby to run every ball.

A week later, in Pretoria, our victory was a lot less emphatic, and several reasons for this were bandied about afterwards. One of them was that we had tried to run the ball *too* much – that the players had been instructed to play 'Peter de Villiers rugby'. However, I think that what had happened was a repeat of what always appeared to happen to the Springboks after a good win – even before my time – and it would continue to be a pattern throughout my four-year tenure. To put it simply, we were just too complacent, as it had been too easy for us the week before. Conversely, Wales, after having been outplayed, were determined to make up for their loss.

We made a few bad mistakes and were too individualistic, and this allowed the Welsh back into the game every time we looked like we were about to take control and go well ahead. We didn't protect the ball enough and opened ourselves up to turnovers, which the Welsh capitalised on.

So, although we won the game 37-21, which looked comfortable enough on the scoreboard, and thus completed a 2-0 series win, we weren't entirely happy. If you look at how we struggled in that Loftus game and then at how we played in the Tri Nations series that followed, you will notice one common denominator – we simply couldn't get through our phases to gain any momentum in our game. Even in the opening win in Bloemfontein, we hadn't got onto the front foot to the extent that we'd wanted to.

In retrospect, I think we can blame our shortcomings on the structural imbalances in the team. We had too many ball carriers and not enough cleaners, but at that stage, we didn't have *big* ball carriers in the backline, as Jaque Fourie was out with an injury. Changes in the rugby laws were also forcing us to play a bit wider than we'd previously played, so Adi Jacobs was the logical selection for that particular period in our rugby. He and Conrad Jantjes made the magic in the backline, while Bryan Habana and JP Pietersen were the finishers.

But we hadn't got the balance quite right, which was how it stayed for much of that season. If we'd had a big ball runner at No. 12, it might have been different. Luke Watson was also not playing to the ball at the time, and he had Joe van Niekerk and Juan Smith with him, so our loosies, too, were mostly ball carriers and not cleaners. In fact, Bakkies Botha was the only guy in the forward unit who could clean.

Brian Mujati couldn't get across the field, Beast Mtawarira was new to international rugby and John Smit liked to play it tight. This mix negatively impacted on our performance.

The most notable feature of the next test, which was against Italy in Cape Town, was the selection of Frans Steyn at flyhalf. After saying earlier that we had never had a big ball carrier at inside centre, you might well ask why I didn't try Frans in that position against Wales. It would be a good question.

My problem with Frans was that he was just too individualistic. Everything was about him; he was always shooting from the hip. If he scored a try in the 17th minute, then you could forget about him for the rest of the game. He would have achieved what he had set out to do.

Maybe Frans had come too far at too young an age. How many players win a World Cup when they are still only 19? We will return to the subject of Frans Steyn later, for he would cause a big media controversy in 2010; at the time a lot was said that I would like to set straight in this book.

But in June 2008, I felt I owed it to Frans to give him a chance at flyhalf, because that was where he wanted to play. I just never factored in the possibility that it would rain in that match, which changed everything. Frans didn't play well in the prevailing conditions, and he was also trying to do *too* much. As a result, the team struggled. It was one of those underwhelming wins (26-0) that did nothing to boost our confidence ahead of a difficult away leg of the Tri Nations.

I suspected that things would not get any better overseas.

11

One triumph and many tribulations

When we left for New Zealand for the away leg of the Tri Nations, I knew the pressure was on. We had won three games – the two tests against Wales and the one against Italy – but we had not always been that convincing. Oregan Hoskins's words still hung over me: *not for rugby reasons only*. I knew it was at the heart of the vitriol that had been sent my way in Bloemfontein.

Two years later, in the final game of the 2010 Tri Nations, I would be back in Bloemfontein, where I faced even more aggression, but on that occasion, it was different. The abuse wasn't racially motivated this time – the fans were just fed up with our below-par performances. I could understand that and didn't shy away from it. When you are the Springbok coach, you are expected to win.

After the home tests, I wasn't feeling very confident. Apart from the imbalance within the team set-up, confusion also reigned in the team itself because of the conflicting messages the players were getting. This confusion was to manifest itself during the Tri Nations tournament and led to a meeting in Durban, where we cleared the air and decided on a common purpose in charting the way forward.

The confusion was rooted in the different philosophies of the assistant coaches, Gary Gold and Dick Muir. Ironically, I had chosen them because of their divergent approaches to the game, but when we got down to work, I was amazed at just *how* much their philosophies differed. Gary was conservative in outlook and had a rigidly structured approach, but he had coached Western Province and they had never had a problem with that. Dick was more like me – he wanted to play the situation. What I didn't understand at the time – and Dick wouldn't have understood – was the psyche of the players. You can't force players to do something they are not comfortable doing. It's a recipe for disaster.

But fortunately Dick was not as set on his running philosophy as one might have thought, nor was Gary as rigid about his structured approach. The problem lay in the process of relaying the game plan to the team. Management would sit down with the senior players to determine how we were going to play a specific game, a decision would be made, but then there would be different interpretations of what Dick or Gary had said.

Dick never instructed a player to go onto the field and run from all over the place. What he was trying to say was, within the structure we'd set in place, when it was viable to run, they should give it their all and play their best running rugby. It took us a while to figure out that we had got the idea right but the instructions wrong. Dick never said that the players could just go mad on the field, but unfortunately that was how some of them interpreted his words.

Matters eventually came to a head and we had a meeting in Durban before the first home game against Australia, where we clarified the issue. Unfortunately, by then we had lost 0-19 to New Zealand in Cape Town and were heading for a crisis. However, I had known long before then that we were in trouble, as the South African teams hadn't done well in the away games in the Super 14 that season. That certainly didn't boost the players' confidence levels.

And, of course, you don't just go to New Zealand and expect to win. I tried to convince the players that they had won under-21 and under-19 games against New Zealand and that they could beat them at this level too, but the reality was that the Springboks had not beaten the All Blacks in New Zealand since winning in Wellington in 1998.

That 10-year drought needed breaking, but the fact that we were going to New Zealand as the world champions did not help our cause. I knew from playing for a top club for so many years in the Boland how your champion status always makes your opponents more determined to beat you. At press conferences, I was being honest when I said that there was never an easy test match for the Springboks.

I so badly wanted to win the first match, in Wellington, given the circumstances under which my appointment had been announced. Before the first test against Wales it had been said that I wasn't good enough and that we would struggle. Then, when we won that game quite comfortably, the goalposts shifted. I knew the players read the newspapers, and the trust I had started to build with them would be on shaky ground if we did badly in the Tri Nations.

Before the test against Italy in Cape Town, we suffered a small disruption when John Smit had to return to France to play in some knockout matches for his French club, Clermont. It was only right that we released John, as Clermont had accommodated us by agreeing to release him early from his contract. So, in the week before the Wellington game, John had to fly halfway across the world, and he missed most of the team's Tri Nations preparations.

But it was only a minor disruption, which I didn't think would hamper our chances of winning. And we could well have won the Wellington game. We were treated very unfairly when the referee didn't red-card Brad Thorn for the ridiculously dangerous way he had spear-tackled John early in the match. The injury John sustained as a result forced him out of the rest of the tour.

Nevertheless, we thought we were in with a chance for most of the game, and were only really out of it towards the end. However, we did slip up once or twice, and whenever we did, the Kiwi crowd really got behind their team. It made it difficult for us to recover, and we lost 8-19.

Seldom in my four years as Springbok coach did we ever use the words 'winning' and 'losing' before a game. Everyone understood what was expected of them, so all we did was set achievable goals. If you didn't win, then you just didn't achieve your goal.

In those early days I had to withstand a bit of pressure from some players who were in favour of employing a team psychologist. They had used a psychologist at the 2007 World Cup and had become comfortable with having one around. But I was against it, and I had my reasons. One of them was that the players share their feelings with the psychologist and not the coach. I preferred to hear first hand how my players were feeling without a psychologist operating as the middleman between us.

Also, when players start seeing a lot of a psychologist, they start to depend on him or her. The psychologist becomes a comfort zone. I wanted the players to develop their own mechanisms to cope with the pressure and the hard times.

But while I liked relating to the players, I shied away from having one-on-one conversations. Both parties tend to prepare themselves before having a one-on-one, and whenever one prepares for a meeting, you are immediately creating an artificial environment. You can't just be natural with each other. But if you surprise a player by saying, 'Wow, that was a great scrum', or, 'Goodness, you struggled in those line-outs', it's more spontaneous and more meaningful and opens the floor to further discussion. However, I eventually had to adjust my view on having one-on-ones, because I realised I wasn't getting to speak to everyone, and sometimes players need that contact and reassurance.

At the same time, I liked to promote the idea that we were all there for rugby, and if you did everything that was expected of you, then I didn't need to talk to you. When I did call you in, that was when you knew there was trouble. When the occasion called for it, I sometimes told a player that I wanted to see him later in the day. It took him out of his comfort zone and made him think a bit.

In order to be accepted by the players, I had to have respect for them first. So if the players did something wrong, I had to decide whether to confront the issue or turn a blind eye to it. That was why I never socialised with the guys – I didn't want to know what they got up to in their downtime, as I felt I needed to keep a distance. If something did happen, I would be able to look at the incident dispassionately, whereas if you are part of something then it is so much harder to retain your objectivity.

Many of the older players didn't buy into my way of doing things at first. They demanded that I appoint a psychologist. But I wasn't going to give in on that one and told them I wasn't going to get them a shrink. The guy might tell them that they weren't that bad when, in fact, they may have been terrible. I told them that inner motivation was now what would drive them.

But after that loss in Wellington, I wondered whether we didn't all need to see a psychologist. Hell, it was a heck of a week for us after that game, and I felt rotten. I had known ahead of time what would happen after the match. Whereas a loss for any other coach would have been regarded as just another beating in New Zealand, with me it would mean that I was incapable of doing the job.

I knew about the negative reactions in the press back home. It certainly wasn't unexpected. But fortunately I didn't have much time to worry about it – we had to get the tour back on track. One bit of criticism did sting me, though, and it turned into an international incident. The New Zealand media reported that former All Black prop Craig Dowd had called me a puppet – I understand that friends of his back in South Africa had urged him to say that. I won't name names, because it could just be gossip, but that was the information I was given. I heard what Dowd had said just before I went into a press conference, and it touched a nerve. I considered what he'd said to be a racist comment. It would be seen as such in a South African context, as the subtext was that although I was a black face coaching the team, I didn't really have any power.

And Dowd was a Maori. I couldn't understand it. But I must say, I did pick up a strange attitude in the Antipodes. For example, it was as if many Maoris were no longer proud of their heritage and had instead embraced a more Western way of life. I also recalled how Makhaya Ntini had been racially abused when the Proteas toured in Australia and can easily understand that it happened.

The problem was, if Dowd didn't respect his heritage, how could I expect him to understand that what he had said about me was gravely and deeply insulting? I didn't want to fight with him, as he was just a former rugby player. At the presser, the first question I was asked was about what Dowd had said. I responded, 'How the devil does he know me if I don't know him?' I haven't met the man to this day, but within two hours I received a phone call from Dowd and he apologised.

I suppose what he'd said boomeranged quite badly, considering that subsequent to that tour I often got into trouble for *not* toeing the line. My actions were the antithesis of those of a puppet.

It was a tough time for me; in fact, it was a tough time for all of us.

I travelled to Dunedin for the next game thinking that we weren't going to win on tour, as I was convinced that the All Blacks would draw confidence from their victory in Wellington. They had been under heaps of pressure going into that match and their media was giving them plenty of stick. In fact, we were under the impression that everyone expected us to win, so I thought their victory would be a sort of ice-breaker for them.

John's absence didn't make the week any easier. Although Victor had taken over as captain, Bismarck, John's replacement, was struggling with an injury. The pressure was so great that I decided I had to release some of it. I told the guys that the All Blacks had never lost to the Springboks in Dunedin, so we weren't going to set ourselves the goal of winning the match. I told them I just wanted everyone to go out there and enjoy the game. I told the guys that I wanted each of them to finish the match feeling good about themselves, regardless of whether we'd won or lost.

By then I had started to think that I wouldn't be coaching the team after the tour. I reckoned that I would be relieved of my position when we got home. Everyone just seemed so divided over me as the coach. The way I saw it, 50 per cent of South Africa wanted me to win because I was a black coach, but at the same time they wanted the team to lose because it consisted mostly of white players; and for the other 50 per cent of the population the reverse was true.

I was also getting sick and tired of having to prove myself to the world. As a result, my attitude started to change. I became more insular and started cutting myself off from people. I also assumed a more fatalistic approach – I told myself that I had a job to do and, if I wasn't good enough to do it, then I wasn't good enough; I wouldn't fight it.

But at the same time I was very aware of my responsibilities as South Africa's first black rugby coach. I was always conscious of the fact that I was breaking the mould, that perhaps I was a beacon of hope for black people, who had always thought that the position of Springbok coach was out of their reach. I agonised over the boy in the township, the youngster who had been given a glimpse of what was possible. I knew people would think, 'If he can do it, then so can I.' And that knowledge directed much of my behaviour. If I failed and was forced out of my job at that point, there was a possibility that my appointment would be perceived as having been a failure – not only for me, but for *all* black coaches. When would they be prepared to appoint a black coach again?

I had to do something that would inspire my people first, particularly the coloured people. They had never really had a public figure to look up to. Allan Boesak, the cleric who had been a leader in the struggle against apartheid and who had the potential to become a respected figurehead of the coloured community, had let the people down when he was jailed for misappropriating funds meant for development projects, and the people turned against him. His actions seemed to confirm the old myth that you can't trust coloured people.

If I failed at this job, I knew some would see it as an indication that coloured people can't be successful. I really didn't want to return to South Africa with that hanging over me.

But the hours in the day were short. I had to think hard – was less perhaps more in this case? Should we ease off on training after a long Super 14 season? In the back of my head, I was imagining what the players might be saying: 'What does this little coach know? *We* have won a World Cup.'

I tried to take the pressure off the players whenever I spoke to them in the build-up to the Dunedin test match, but they were well aware of how desperate I was to win, as I kept on going on about how we had beaten the All Blacks at junior levels and there really wasn't anything that special about them, regardless of where we played them.

We felt we could beat them if we could get them to trail in the first part of the game, as we reckoned that would make them fall apart psychologically. This was a time when they had only a handful of really experienced players, and Richie McCaw, their captain, was injured. We figured that if we took the lead at the right time, they would have too few big-name players to take control and keep the rest calm.

That was why I was so furious when Victor was yellow-carded straight after we went ahead late in the game. It was a bad refereeing call – it was never close to a yellow card, and yet it could so easily have lost us the game.

In many ways, it had been a lonely week for me. I spent a great deal of time trying to get into the All Blacks' heads, into the players' heads, and even into my own head. I realised that it was not necessarily the best players that were needed on the field, but the right ones. The player's self-belief and the trust others placed in him were the most important factors in this game. If they believed Percy Montgomery could win the match for them, then he had to be on the pitch. So I left Conrad Jantjes out.

Bismarck du Plessis started the game but then had to come off, and there were a few other changes too. Joe van Niekerk played at No. 8 and vindicated his selection with a brilliant try. He was my first-choice No. 8 back then. I reckoned he was in the same mould as Bob Skinstad, a guy whom the smashers and bashers had to have in a team to complete the balance. Nobody at Western Province appeared to believe in Joe, but I did.

But when Joe left the country, I could no longer select him. I didn't want to go against the policy on overseas players, which dictated that we would only call up overseas-based players in an emergency, or when there was no one else who was good enough to play in that position. We had Pierre Spies, who was also an excellent No. 8.

But even after Joe left, I was in constant touch with him, trying to lure him back to South Africa, right up until the June test against Wales in 2010. Had he played in that game, he might have featured in my World Cup plans, but unfortunately he was injured.

We were very close to winning in Dunedin, and then Ricky Januarie made a decision that could easily have gone wrong for us. We were in an attacking position when Ricky got the ball, and it looked like the right option would have been for him to keep the ball in hand. He had a lot of guys in support, we were in a favourable field position and at a stage of the game where we had to keep the pressure on the New Zealanders by carrying the ball forward.

But instead of passing or carrying the ball up into the tackle, Ricky chipped it over the advancing defenders. Fortunately, it dropped right into his hands and he scored a memorable try. I am sure Ricky will remember it for the rest of his days!

Before the game, I had said to the guys that this was a day when structure would keep us in the game, but that our talent and natural skill would do the talking at the decisive moment. I assure you, I wasn't thinking of Ricky when I said that. Once the ball bounced back into Ricky's hands and he went over for his try, I knew it would be difficult for the All Blacks to come back, but there were still some minutes to go. With Victor off and only 14 men on the field, we had to dig deep.

My heart sunk into my shoes on several occasions as the match looked as if it would be stolen from us in the last minutes. Fortunately, though, the guys were steadfast. The clock was counted down without the All Blacks scoring, and then we erupted into the most joyous celebration.

Although I'd had some belief in our chances beforehand, I hadn't thought I could inspire the players with the same optimism. But our preparation had been good, and that had given us a real chance.

The fact that we had won that particular game was not only important to me, but had other significant consequences. By winning in New Zealand for the first time in 10 years, and in Dunedin for the first time ever, we had laid the foundation to come back and do it again. If you can face the All Blacks with 14 men, and without John Smit, and still win, it proves that banishing self-doubt and finding some self-belief is the overriding requirement in beating your nemesis.

Winning in New Zealand had suddenly become a more attainable goal for other players watching back home, particularly the Super 14 guys. I think that our win, though only by two points (30-28), was a watershed moment for us, and that South African teams will in future not struggle as much in New Zealand as they had before Dunedin.

But of course it was also an important win for me personally, as it helped change a lot of people's perceptions about me. Although the Hoskins statement would never go away, at least by beating the All Blacks in New Zealand the Springboks had achieved something under my leadership, which surely indicated that I wasn't completely useless.

By now I had accepted that I would always be targeted for criticism and subjected to controversy, and I realised that I would have to grow a really thick skin so that I would not be harmed by it. If I was affected by the criticism, it would impact on how I managed the team, which would then negatively impact on the players. So I had to erect a protective shield around me.

Whenever I was publicly criticised, it affected the players. I saw how they looked at me. There was a lot of sympathy in their eyes. But I always tried to make light of it. I just deflected whatever was thrown at me in the interests of creating positive energy around the team. I realised that if I were just in the job to fulfil Peter de Villiers's dreams, then I would risk hurting the many people for whom the success of the Springboks was a matter of life and death. If I could subjugate Peter de Villiers's dreams to those of the country as a whole, then I would make more people happy. That's what I wanted to do.

The Dunedin game will always be one of the highlights of my four years as coach, and the team thoroughly enjoyed celebrating afterwards. Such an experience within a team environment really draws everyone together. You all become part of a close-knit circle, and you can draw on its support whenever necessary. I usually avoided going onto the field after a win, but on this occasion I was pulled into the team huddle.

Trust me, the one place you don't want to be as a new coach is in the changing room when the Springboks win. It took me a while to become familiar with the culture. For instance, when everyone yells, 'Bokke, Bokke, Bokke!' how many times are you supposed to repeat it? I admit I often felt like a bit of a spare wheel at those moments.

It took me a while before I understood how the rituals worked, but I still couldn't relate to certain of their aspects. Where did I draw the line with those traditions I didn't agree with, particularly as many of the players had been adhering to them for years? For example, I had a problem with corporal punishment as part of the initiation process, during which a player was caned. But later on, during the 2010 end-of-year tour, scrumhalf Charl McLeod said that he had felt like a Springbok and a part of the team only through experiencing the initiation, so I guess it serves its purpose.

The Dunedin win was unfortunately not the end of the tour for us. We still had to go to Perth to play Australia, and the one thing I could never figure out in my four years as coach was our habit of being really good one week and then, the next, not being able to follow that up with another excellent performance.

Remember that we were on a three-week tour, and this was the last week. So I wanted to make everyone on tour feel a part of it. However, while you may believe that everyone in the team can stand up for themselves, this is often not the case. In fact, the reserves on that tour had a bit of an inferiority complex. It was only much later, at the 2011 World Cup, that the guys not in the starting line-up started to assert themselves.

I never substituted a player with one who wasn't up to making a telling contribution, but too often I detected a feeling of inferiority among the players who were on the bench. And frequently that was bigger than their desire to fit in with the team culture. Even Danie Rossouw saw himself only as an impact player, so his attitude was not the same as that of the players who were regularly starting.

I couldn't understand this mindset. Eventually I deduced that because most of the reserves had been part of the squad at the previous World Cup, they probably now felt that they deserved better and should start a game.

Anyway, these considerations played a big part in my selections for the Perth game. I really believed we would beat Australia, as the Wallabies weren't a very good team, so I picked players in order to make them feel part of the team.

There were no issues concerning the game plan, but perhaps in the end we just made too many changes and we lacked cohesion as a result. I also didn't realise before I made my selections that a lot of the players would play to impress me. That resulted in far too much individualism in the game. Obviously the guys didn't know me very well yet. The upshot was that we lost the game 9-16 and had to return to South Africa having won only one of our three overseas matches.

It was a disappointing end to the tour.

12

You can't make a round world flat

When we arrived back in South Africa, there was a massive debate going on about the Springbok emblem at a sports indaba in Durban, and it was all very emotional.

Some interested parties thought they could use me to help them get rid of the Springbok emblem, but, as I said at the beginning of this book, when I applied for the position of coach, I applied for the *Springbok* job. I had always supported the emblem.

I think my support group also wanted me to lobby for the removal of the emblem, but I had made it clear to them that this was not part of my agenda, which further diminished the support they lent me. My relationship with the support group had started coming to a head when I was in New Zealand with the Springboks, when Cheeky Watson had arrived with a message from the sports minister and said he had instructed him to tell me to put Luke Watson in the team.

I will go into this story in greater detail in the next chapter, but it led me to conclude that there was little difference between what Oregan Hoskins's words had done to me at the press conference and Cheeky's modus operandi.

So why didn't I want to get rid of the Springbok emblem? Frankly, I just didn't see the point of all the fuss. You can see it as a symbol of the old apartheid regime, but was it the Springbok emblem that had suppressed people? I saw it as a South African rugby symbol rather than as a political symbol. So far from being against it, I would enhance its importance during my time as coach. For example, I made the Springbok blazer more exclusive by insisting that it only be worn as ceremonial attire and stopped the team from travelling overseas in it. Of course the World Cup was a different situation, as that was a special occasion.

While I was coach, the team travelled in the black suits I had brought in. I wanted everyone to be dressed identically, but I didn't want them to always be wearing their Springbok blazer, as I thought it undermined how special it was.

Cheeky's visit to New Zealand made me ponder the future of my support group. I had leant on these guys for support and treated them as my advisors. The question was: Did I want the support group to make the team selections, or did I just want them to support me? Of course the answer was the latter, but they didn't seem to understand that.

It was clear that they weren't there for me any more, and I felt very isolated. The people I had thought I could open my heart to were now turning against me. For instance, when I said in a newspaper interview that Victor Matfield was a rugby genius, Cheeky took issue with it. I tried to stay out of their reach, as I had no answers for them whenever they confronted me.

I had grown up believing that you have to stand up for what you believe in. You were obliged to speak your mind when the occasion called for it. Surely it wasn't possible that seven guys could always be in agreement with one another, as was the case with my support group? I have a problem with my advisor if he and I always agree on everything. If that is the case, why would I need him, as I am always right!

Chris Hewitt, who had been the Springbok media man at the start of my tenure, was close to both Cheeky and the politicians in my support group. Not long after we had arrived back in South Africa, he approached me with a message from the ANC MP Cedric Frolick. Chris told me that Cedric had said he would rather have a white coach that he could control than a black coach that wouldn't listen to him.

And Cedric publicly slammed me when I made my selections for the first home Tri Nations match, against the All Blacks at Newlands. I had recalled Fourie du Preez to the team according to the agreement we had reached right at the beginning of my tenure. But Ricky Januarie had scored the winning try in Dunedin and was being fêted as a hero. In my opinion, though, Fourie was the best scrumhalf in the world, and he was always going to be my first choice once he was available for selection.

Cedric and some other politicians, like Dr Asad Bhorat, tore into me in the media, and not just about omitting Ricky from the team but also because I had decided to start with Percy Montgomery ahead of Conrad Jantjes. I was always going to select Percy for that match, as the plan was to let him play his 100th game for the Springboks at Newlands. That decision had been made when I'd met with Percy earlier in the year in France to discuss his return to South Africa.

Replacing Ricky with Fourie had been discussed with both players at the outset. Ricky knew where he stood. I couldn't go back on my word. And neither could I go back on my word with Percy.

There was a lot of drama going on behind the scenes, with Cedric attacking me on transformation numbers, but the ANC never approached me directly. If they had just set down some guidelines I would have conformed to them, because I would have had to adhere to what the government directed. But they never set out a clear policy, and Butana Komphela of the Parliamentary Portfolio Committee on Sport and Recreation never came to speak to me.

I later worked out that it was because Komphela reported to Cheeky Watson, and he would have struggled to make Cheeky happy had I given him good reasons for my decisions. Whenever I asked for a meeting with the committee, they never seemed to have the time. Anyway, when Cedric attacked me about racial representation, he also mentioned Luke Watson in the same story, and Luke, as we know, isn't a black player. That told me – as it should have told any other person reading that report – that it was all about someone's personal agenda.

In the end, we probably lost the Newlands match because of all the fuss that had been made about Percy's milestone. There was just too much hype preceding the game, and you had to be part of the squad to understand the sentiment involved in that game. In retrospect, it was just too much for the players to handle.

The All Blacks started at pace and we found ourselves behind early on when they scored a try. By the time we woke up, we were running out of time. We made too many mistakes in our attempt to chase the game, such as the intercept try that Jean de Villiers gave away in front of our posts. The 0-19 defeat was a rare whitewash, something that isn't supposed to happen on home soil, and naturally the media went ballistic.

Perhaps the communication breakdown I discussed in the previous chapter, between the assistant coaches and the players, had contributed to the loss, but I think it was more a case of the occasion of Percy's 100th cap just being too overwhelming.

I put a lot of stock in players achieving personal milestones and felt it was important to have a centurion in South African rugby, and it was great to see Percy celebrate. He had played much of his career at Newlands, so it was the perfect venue for him to play his 100th game. But we all knew his game wasn't as sharp as it had been, and rugby is a game for a team and not an individual.

However, his selection for that match may still have been the right thing to do for South African rugby, as we now have three centurions. John and Victor joined Percy on the magical three-figure mark within a week of each other in 2010. And giving Percy his 100th cap by making him come off the bench would not have been right.

Conrad was my man to play fullback at the next World Cup, which I told Percy at the outset. He was never going to play much beyond that Newlands game, and in the end he announced his retirement after the last Tri Nations game, in Johannesburg. Sadly, the horrible broken leg Conrad suffered at the start of 2009 meant he had to drop out of my plans, but he was very good in 2008.

After the Newlands game, we travelled to Durban to play Australia, and we lost that game too. That was the worst low of my first season, and I really struggled to handle that defeat. The Wallabies won quite easily (27-15) and the crowd booed me afterwards. It was ugly, and I was incensed. I detest that people can be so cowardly. They don't usually have the guts to tell you to your face what they think of you; they just boo you from a safe distance

After the Cape Town defeat, the letters I had received in the week prior to the next game had been terribly accusatory and nasty, and the booing was just the cherry on top ... or, in this case, the rotten lemon on top.

As mentioned, the players and management had met at the start of the week to try to eliminate the mixed coaching messages that were confusing the players, and although there were signs of improvement in the Durban game, we were still well beaten. Afterwards the media reported that the players had been given two different game plans. It was not a good time for me, and I feared for my future as Springbok coach. My chances of making it to the 2011 World Cup seemed zero.

I knew, too, that I had reached a crossroads with the players. It was clear to me that they weren't playing to their true potential and were not doing what I wanted them to do. The number of missed tackles and lack of real hardness in contact indicated that we weren't playing with enough passion. Normally our guys get really physical in contact with the opposition, but now it was as if we weren't fully on the field.

I thought that if I was to achieve my goals in the long term, I might have to sustain some knocks in the short term by changing the team and losing a few games. I called the players in and told them that I would rather lose with a bunch of no-names than continue with a team of big-name players who were not prepared to take the team to the next level. When the guys realised that their careers were on the line, my job suddenly became a lot easier.

But at the same time, I knew I had to keep the morale of the team up. I didn't want the players spending the week before the final Tri Nations match, against the Wallabies at Coca-Cola Park in Johannesburg, feeling personally aggrieved and down in the dumps about what I'd said. If they did, it might be my last game as Springbok coach. I could see that they felt insecure because they weren't sure what I wanted from them.

The Durban game had been Fourie du Preez's second since returning from injury, and he wasn't himself. I knew that Fourie and Victor Matfield, who was captaining the side in the absence of the injured John Smit, were great mates. So I told Fourie that he wasn't supporting Victor by playing the situation as he should; he wasn't taking charge. I told him to stop trying to impress me and that he should realise that I knew he was the right man for the job. There was no question of me not wanting him in the team.

It proved a wise thing to say, for Fourie was brilliant in the final Tri Nations game, where we smashed the Wallabies 53-8. Some people said we won that game because we were more direct than we'd been before, which was true, but, more to the point, the guys were on the same page at last and made the right decisions. Although they weren't doing much different to what they had done before, they now knew that they had been misinterpreting me; they now knew that I believed in them and that they didn't need to impress me as individuals on the field.

I would detect the same problem in the England team when they played us in London later that year. Martin Johnson was their new coach, and we thrashed them because they played like individuals in an effort to impress him and stay in the mix.

Those little things I did wrong as a coach bit me in my first season. Not knowing the Springbok song and the rituals of the dressing room may seem inconsequential to outsiders, but everything has an effect in that closed environment. Off-the-field traditions play a huge role in the Bok set-up, and I also soon came to realise that I had to get to know the players better.

So although Victor Matfield had captained the side in five of the six Tri Nations games following John Smit's injury in the first game of the competition, I kept John with the side for the entire home leg. In fact, I called him in before the one-off test against Argentina, which we'd played the week before the Cape Town game and won convincingly (63-9).

I told John that even though he was injured, I still needed his input. He knew the Springbok culture inside out, and I realised how important it was for me not to take the players too far out of their comfort zones. John played a part in all the big team decisions that were taken during that home leg of the Tri Nations.

It is important to stress that it wasn't John alone whom I asked for input. Whenever we debated a game plan or a tactic, Victor would also contribute, as would other senior players who'd assumed leadership roles. Fourie du Preez, for example, was the one who would say, 'No, that won't work', or, 'Yes, I think that will do it.' Jean de Villiers, in turn, was good at explaining his ideas on the blackboard. And then, whenever I was getting too far ahead of myself and becoming overly ambitious, a voice would pipe up from somewhere in the room and say, 'Hey, Pete, don't try and change the world.'

Although the players' committee was founded on day one, the players' input became even more important to me when I found I no longer had any support elsewhere. I couldn't approach the SARU board for advice, as I knew I had no support there. And my support group, far from supporting me, was now my sworn enemy.

Up till the end of that Tri Nations season, I had relied a lot on my assistant coaches, much in the same way as I had relied on the support group. But later that year I got the impression that Gary and Dick considered my inclusive approach and willingness to take advice as a sign of weakness. It was as if they, too, had started to believe what Oregan Hoskins had said and had become too eager to hold my hand.

Also, when some players suffered injuries in New Zealand, I had been disappointed in their inability to make the right call on who should come in as replacements. For example, when we needed a prop or a hooker, Gary and Dick suggested players who weren't even the first-choice prop or hooker at the provinces where they had coached before. I thought they were too confined in their thinking regarding the available talent.

I decided from that point on that I would have to rely more on the experienced players in the squad than on my assistants. However, I knew I could only do so if we shared a mutual trust, and I thought John and Victor were the two guys I could trust the most. I called a meeting with the two of them and we discussed the situation at length. We agreed that we would need each other's support going forward, and that we had to trust one another. I asked them to accept that not all the decisions I made would go their way, but that even if we disagreed on something, we should support each other. I said, 'We are the only ones who can make it happen [for the Boks].'

This is probably where the story originated that the players had taken over the team. In truth, the players' committee had been there from the first day. But I had come to understand an important feature in rugby, which had further motivated me to approach John and Victor. I don't think my assistant coaches were even aware of this, but I discovered that the technical component of coaching becomes a less important factor at the highest level of rugby.

Of course, that is not to say the technical side of the game is not important. Far from it – a lot of the detail of rugby coaching lies right there. But while Gary's attention to detail was excellent, I sometimes thought he was wasted at Springbok level, as he covered the basics far too much. It bored the players, as they had heard it all before at many different levels of the game. Players at the highest level don't want to be told again and again how to set up a ball.

Just think about it: if a Springbok had played in all the Super 15 games for his franchise and was taught the basics before each game, he would have heard it many times over. And if he was coached to repeat something five times before each game, it would mean that he had to repeat it 70 times in one season. To me, that's a recipe for boredom. The Bok players knew what to do and what was expected of them.

(Having said that, I don't think South African rugby values Gary's talents enough. He would make an outstanding high-performance director and would be great at creating Springboks from under-19 level upwards.)

Another factor that made me decide to count on the support of some of the senior players was the extent of their experience. The management group only had experience of national age-group, provincial and Super 14 rugby, which was a relatively limited world in comparison to the experience of a guy who had played in 70 test matches and won a World Cup.

Then there was the psyche of the team, which I quickly got to grips with, but which I don't think Gary and Dick understood very well. They kept pushing for the kind of game that did not match the team's capabilities. Juan Smith, for instance, can really play only one way. If you play too wide, you lose him. It's the same with Victor Matfield.

This is why Jean de Villiers has lost some of his individual brilliance. As a senior player in the team, he started to become involved in setting up structures, and as a result he became reluctant to do anything that didn't fit in with the game plan. Because he was so aware of the structures that had been put in place, he lost some of his intuitiveness and, hence, some of his potency on attack.

Among the senior players who had excellent spatial awareness were Fourie du Preez and, to some extent, Butch James. Because of that gift, they could read the game better than anyone else. But as most of the other guys were very structure bound, how could you play outside of what they understood?

I certainly hadn't wanted that situation when I started coaching the Boks. I'd wanted to change a lot of things. But in those first few months of 2008, I reconciled myself to the fact that you cannot make the world flat if it is round.

And I had to impress upon my assistant coaches that it wasn't a case of not wanting our rugby to be played a certain way, but rather understanding what style of rugby the players were capable of playing.

Although I'd wanted a more creative style of rugby, I soon came to realise that I couldn't have it.

13

The sex tape

A week after the big win over Australia, which some felt saved me my job, the sex-tape scandal broke. All I can say from the outset is that I couldn't believe how low my enemies would stoop to discredit me. You ask me if there was such a tape? No, there wasn't.

The first time I heard about the so-called sex tape was the weekend of the Tri Nations test against the All Blacks in Cape Town. Chris Hewitt, the SARU media manager who was later killed in a light-aircraft crash, informed me about it. We had just had a training run at Newlands when Chris said he wanted to see me privately. I told him to come and see me in my hotel room.

That was when he told me of the existence of the tape. Apparently Cheeky Watson and Cedric Frolick were going to reveal a sex tape that they had obtained of me in a compromising position with a woman in a car park during a trip to the Eastern Cape. As I later told the newspapers, it amazed me that people thought I had the time for such things.

By then Chris had already informed me that Cedric, who as an ANC MP was involved with the Parliamentary Portfolio Committee on Sport and Recreation, had told him that he would rather have a white coach that would listen to him than a black coach who did his own thing. Chris had been the middleman between Cheeky and the politicians. He was the one who conveyed to me their unhappiness that I was not toeing their line.

I was very naive. I knew no such thing as a sex tape existed, though I would have loved to have had a look at whatever tape was supposedly around. Hell, it would have made interesting viewing. So I told Chris that they must produce a sex tape if they so wished. I was pretty flippant about it and not thinking about the consequences. So I said to Chris, 'Tell them to bring it, man. I'm looking forward to seeing this.' I was actually laughing when I said it. It seemed like a big joke at the time.

Once there is even an allegation of a sex tape out there, it is hard to shake it off, regardless of whether it exists or not. But this didn't really cross my mind right then. I just thought it was a ridiculous story. I called Oregan Hoskins, something Chris was adamant I shouldn't do.

'Let's just keep this between us,' he pleaded.

'No,' I said. 'This is a serious allegation, and if there is a sex tape involved, then the president of the union needs to know about it.'

I could tell that Chris was mortified that I was making the call. Oregan asked to speak to Chris. Chris was very polite and almost fawning when he spoke to Oregan. You could tell he didn't want him or anyone else involved. Someone had obviously miscalculated my reaction – perhaps they had hoped that I would just meet whatever demands they were going to make without involving SARU or any other authority figure.

At the time, Chris was facing a disciplinary hearing for transgressions relating to team protocol. Chris loved being around the players, but for some reason he didn't understand that he had to attend team meetings when required to do so. He was subsequently killed in that tragic accident, and no sex tape was ever produced. However, SARU did nothing to clear my name. There was never an official inquiry or a hearing. It was almost as if they didn't know whether to believe me or not.

Either SARU were worried that if they pursued the matter, they would discover that such a tape existed, or they wanted to leave a question mark hanging over my behaviour. I suspected that they could find the incident useful if they ever wanted to get rid of me, using the so-called sex tape to prove that I had brought the Springboks or the game into disrepute.

However, the 'sex tape' wasn't a problem at first because I just laughed it off, and it wasn't made public at the time but handled internally – Oregan dealt with Chris. But then a week after the end of the Tri Nations, I received a call from Neil de Beer saying that a newspaper was going to run a story about the sex tape the next day, a Sunday.

Neil had remained one of my confidants, even though I knew he was also close to Cheeky. Neil told me that even the rugby administrators, who had so many contacts in the media, couldn't stop the story from appearing. But to me, it looked like they didn't want to stop it. So the story ran. Before that happened, though, a couple of other newspapers also got wind of it.

I had been totally unprepared for the media reaction. I told the newspapers that no such tape existed and denied that I would ever have been involved in such an incident. But that didn't stop the story from gaining momentum and becoming big.

I was in Stellenbosch the next day watching the national club championship, and it wasn't a pleasant place to be, as everyone was staring at me and it was all anybody wanted to talk about. It is one hell of a thing to have hanging over you.

It also had a really negative effect on my family. When you see your 80-year-old mother in tears, you can't help but wonder whether being Springbok coach is all it's made out to be if this is the price you pay. My daughter Odile, who was in Grade 11 that year, went from being a B-candidate for matric to a D-average. People taunted her about the 'sex tape' at school.

It was against this background of bitter disappointment and frustration that I made the comment about giving rugby back to the whites, which SARU heavily objected to at the time.

'I knew there were still people who do not want a black coach,' I told the *Sunday Times*. 'I just never knew the extent people would go to [to] discredit me. My biggest problem is [that] I've now got to sit down with my wife and two daughters. People will stop them and ask them [about the tape] and that is why I think I should walk away from this job and give it back to the whites.'

I was referring to the faction that was working against me, the writer of the article and people like Mark Keohane, who I knew was trying to get Jake White reinstated. I had been told of a conversation Mark had had with Rian Oberholzer during which he'd said that SARU must reappoint Jake. Apparently Mark had said, 'We want to get rid of this guy, because we want Jake back.' Rian's response had been: 'Are you mad? SA Rugby won't bring Jake or any other white coach back.'

People were saying that rugby was in the 'wrong hands'. But they just didn't want to give me a chance because of the colour of my skin and my strong character. I thought to myself, why give my life for my country when everyone is against me? If people won't respect me, I would rather just hand the job back to the people who had been in control before. I now realise I was wrong to make that comment, as it blanketed all whites together. That was a generalisation, as I knew there were a lot of good white people and just a minority was working against me.

I couldn't understand why no pressure was applied on those involved to produce the tape. Only the allegation existed. I asked Oregan to get to the bottom of it, and said that he owed it to me to conduct a full investigation so that my name could be cleared. But that never happened. As with the Schalk Burger incident during the British & Irish Lions series and the Bees Roux comments I made two years thereafter, SARU would not defend me. And I thought they should have helped me. Instead, I was being hung out to dry.

This was SARU's public statement: 'SARU can confirm that a company employee did approach Mr de Villiers on August 15 in Cape Town. The employee made certain extraordinary claims which SARU has since looked into but has been unable to find any basis to support in fact.'

However, if I had indeed committed such a bad deed, I should surely not have been allowed to remain in the Springbok job, which was why I urged Oregan to get to the bottom of the matter. To this day, this has not been done. The whole tape saga was just left hanging in the air.

But at least I knew why my enemies had chosen that moment to 'reveal' the tape's existence and why the story appeared in the newspapers at that particular time. I didn't have to be a rocket scientist to figure it out. I had lost four matches in the Tri Nations, which had led to the assumption that I was on my way out, but when the team triumphed in the last Tri Nations game against Australia, it made it more difficult for them to get rid of me.

So the way I see it, Cheeky and Cedric wanted me suspended, and if that was the plan – and I did only have Chris's word linking them to the tape – then it didn't work. Eventually the writer of the story (Dale Granger) emigrated to Perth and Chris was killed.

I have to explain what had happened between me and Cheeky Watson in the early part of the Tri Nations series and up until the time the sex-tape story broke. As I've mentioned, Cheeky was in New Zealand for the first Tri Nations test in Wellington and took a room on the opposite side of mine at the Duxton Hotel. Not long after he arrived, he called my room to tell me that he had been sent to New Zealand to pass on a message from the minister of sport. Apparently Makhenkesi Stofile was very unhappy with the way I was treating Cheeky's son Luke, as were other politicians back home, who were incensed because I wasn't starting with him (Luke was on the bench).

I told Cheeky that I would not make political decisions, but my own. It did not necessarily mean that Luke would not play, but that I would be guided only by rugby decisions only when I selected my team.

Cheeky then talked to quite a few people involved with the team, including Gary Gold, and they related to me what he'd said. When it became clear to Cheeky that I wasn't going to bow to his pressure, he packed up and flew home.

But once back in South Africa, Cheeky started campaigning against me behind the scenes and it appeared as if Cedric was his trusted foot soldier. In no time at all, Butana Komphela and Asad Bhorat were criticising me in the newspapers. So I was left in little doubt that my 'friends' were now my enemies and were out to get me.

When I got back to South Africa, I was summoned to the minister of sport's house for a meeting, but I couldn't make it, as we were already in Durban. Butana then got on my case in a big way, saying that I had no respect for the minister. They took me on publicly about the selection of Fourie du Preez ahead of Ricky Januarie, which appeared to be their main complaint, but I knew it was only a smokescreen.

So then I was summoned to meet with the minister in Cape Town, where Stofile duly scolded me. But after he finished, I had my turn. I told the minister that I was really disappointed in him: Why would he send a white guy to New Zealand to express his fury that I hadn't selected a white player? Why, I asked, was he supporting a white player when there were so many black players struggling to make it through the system? It came as no surprise to me when Stofile then told me that he hadn't spoken to Cheeky in over a year. He seemed genuinely surprised at my allegation.

So had Cheeky been using the minister as leverage to get his way, and all for the purpose of getting his son into the team? After the incident with Cheeky in New Zealand and with the support group distancing itself from me, I suspected that they would use any angle they could to discredit me.

I have already described how I had phoned Cheeky years earlier to obtain information on Luke when I had first taken over as the national under-21 coach. We'd started having regular contact after that conversation, but I was aware of his reputation and knew he could turn on you in an instant. That's what happened in his relationship with Mike Stofile, the former SARU vice-president, to whom he'd been close. So I was ready for him when he turned against me.

I actually laughed out loud when Cedric Frolick circulated the story that Cheeky had helped me financially. He had, in fact, given me R400. Cheeky and I had been watching the Stormers play Boland in a friendly game in Paarl when he invited me to go and have something to eat with him. I had just got back from the Falcons with nothing to my name, so I said no. As my family had no food at home, it would have been wrong of me to go and treat myself at a restaurant.

Cheeky then offered me R400 as a gift. I didn't like it, but I was desperate, so I asked him if he was sure. He insisted. So I was pretty amazed when the story came out that I had been given financial help. I hadn't asked for the money – it had been given to me as a gift, and you don't return gifts.

Cheeky was supposedly a good Christian, but he reminded me of what Gandhi had meant when he said he could easily be a Christian if it weren't for the Christians. When Cheeky discovered that he couldn't control me, he dug up everything that had passed between us and tried to use it against me.

I will never feel the same way about Cheeky again, as I gave him my trust, which I feel he abused. That's why I don't have any respect left for him. When I bump into him now, I greet him, because I feel it is polite to do so, but I am not friendly with him. It's a real shame, because that's not how we're really supposed to live.

The whole sex-tape saga left a bitter taste in my mouth. I just couldn't believe that some of my fellow South Africans could sink so low as to try to destroy a person's reputation in such an evil way. We prosecute people for committing other crimes in our country, but when someone damages your reputation, it seems you cannot expect justice to be done. I will say again what I said then – rugby really isn't worth the kind of sacrifice I was being asked to make.

And I sincerely hope no other Springbok coach has to endure something similar in future.

14

Ugly takes us forward

Before the final Tri Nations test against Australia in Johannesburg, I was asked in possibly the worst television interview of my tenure what it would feel like to lose four in a row. My strategies were under fire, and the negative questions were merely an indication of the mood before that game, as we had lost one too many matches. But after the game, which we won well, everyone completely changed their tune.

It was an important moment in my development as a Bok coach, as it made me realise that most people who support the Springboks live in the moment; they don't care about structures and how a game plan is put together. They just want us to win.

So, with the view that winning was everything, no matter how it was achieved, I started planning for the 2008 end-of-year tour, which was to feature matches against Wales, Scotland and England. For most fans, rugby is more than just a game, and the Springboks are more than just a team. As the coach, it really sinks in how many Bok fans plan their whole lives around one Saturday afternoon and live from Sunday to Saturday waiting for the game. Everything seems to revolve around the result of that weekend's rugby match.

So, on this basis, I decided that we must forget about debating our game plan and set aside our differences of opinion on rugby philosophies. I was moving further and further away from what some people called my 'romantic rugby philosophy', and I stopped worrying about whether we could make any big changes to the Springbok game, though in reality that had probably already happened after my first meeting with the players in Somerset West. Henceforth it was going to be about winning at all costs; we would do it for our supporters and for the people who paid our salaries.

By then, I was also getting to know the players better. Most of them would never be ready for the changes to the game I had envisaged when I first took up the position as Springbok coach. Most importantly, though, I felt I had a better understanding of what satisfied the important stakeholders, like the media and the supporters. As Nick Mallett had found in 1998, you could win 17 matches in a row and then lose one and suddenly you are no longer considered a good coach. For South African supporters, the scoreboard is the most important thing, finish and *klaar*.

So when we went to Cardiff for the first match of the tour, we knew it was imperative that we get a good result. We started the match against Wales playing the sort of rugby I had never appreciated. Everything we did was very basic and dour; we were just intent on strangling them with our defensive and kicking game. There was no flair.

Ruan Pienaar was at flyhalf, and we all know what an exciting player he can be. But in that match, he kicked the life out of the game. We had come to realise that dominating territory would almost certainly ensure victory at international level. Ruan faced some criticism for his performance afterwards, but he was also praised. He was playing to instructions, though, and generally the team was happy with the way he had performed in his first major test match in that pivotal position.

This was supposed to be the beginning of Ruan's new career as Bok flyhalf. Butch James had played really well in the previous test against Australia in Johannesburg, a game in which we'd got everything spot-on in terms of winning territory and then striking. We had also got the balance right in our selection. But I thought Butch's career as a player was over after that match. Not many people know how much pain Butch had to suffer on an almost daily basis so that he could play rugby. I really don't know any other player with his guts or anyone else who was prepared to suffer so much physical agony for his team.

Butch had his own recovery apparatus that he had to exercise on every day to get his leg right after having had multiple knee operations and other injuries. He had to work through the pain every time he played; one kick at goal and he sometimes couldn't walk the next day.

So because of all of this, I thought it was the end of Butch's rugby career, and I thought his decision to go to Bath indicated as much.

But I was wrong. South Africa still needed him; we struggled to replace him over the following few years. In many ways, he was the Bakkies Botha of the backline, because of his ability to instil fear in the opposition.

Nevertheless, I preferred Ruan back then, and if you recall the games he played and study the nuances he lent the team with his instinctive decision-making ability, you would have to agree with me that he had been brilliant.

I think Ruan has never truly fulfilled his potential, because he is always either very good or very poor; there is never anything in between. And at international level, you can't afford a bad performance from a flyhalf. Ruan's game depends a lot on his confidence on the day. If he succeeds with his first kick at goal, you can bet that he will have a great game. But the opposite is true if he starts badly with his place kicking.

You can't tell Ruan that you don't want him to do the place kicking, because it destroys his self-confidence. And in South Africa, we have a weird and not entirely explicable expectation that the flyhalf should always be the place-kicker. Of course, Percy Montgomery achieved enormous success as a kicker without playing at flyhalf, but he was the exception to the rule.

But I am getting ahead of myself now, because towards the end of 2008, I had not yet discovered that Ruan struggled with big match temperament (BMT). I was determined that he would be my flyhalf against the British & Irish Lions the following year, and I was using the end-of-year tour to build up to that series.

In retrospect, I probably made a mistake not giving Morné Steyn a chance on that tour. I didn't rate him at the time, as I thought he was too limited in his game and not of the same standard as the other players. But I started to value him a lot more when I realised exactly how many test matches were decided by successful kicks at goal. And of course this was particularly so in the World Cup. So Morné never even made the touring party. If people want to say that I made the wrong decision there, I will take it on the chin.

Fourie du Preez was very important in the Cardiff game, as it was his responsibility to look after Ruan. He built on his good performance against Australia in that match. After our meeting during which I'd told him he wasn't supporting Victor as best he could, he started to blossom, as he knew then that he was my first-choice scrumhalf.

Switching Ruan to starting flyhalf was not the only big selection call I made for the Cardiff test. It was also the first game John Smit played for me at tighthead. At that stage, we didn't have many good tightheads in the country, and Bismarck du Plessis was starting to emerge as a potent international-class hooker. He had played well in the home leg of the Tri Nations when John was injured.

I thought having John at tighthead would be a win-win situation; I would have a tighthead I really believed could excel in that position, and I would have Bismarck on the field as well. I assured John that he would make a good tighthead prop, but I gave him time to think about it.

John didn't like the idea at first, because it had been years since he'd last played prop. But I told him that I wouldn't judge him on his play in that position; I wouldn't drop him from the team if my experiment didn't work. He was my captain and he would remain so. So he agreed to do it.

I have a great deal of respect for the way John always put the team before his personal concerns. It was one of the many attributes that made him such an outstanding leader. But in hindsight, I messed him around and caused him more discomfort and unhappiness than joy.

When John agreed to play tighthead, I told him to pick up some weight, which he did. But the next year, when it became apparent that he was struggling to make the adjustment and we got a few other good tightheads, like BJ Botha and CJ van der Linde, back, with Jannie du Plessis starting to find form again, I had to sit John down and ask him to go back to hooker. And that required him to lose a lot of weight. I moved him from one position to another and expected a different player each time, which wasn't really on. I hope South African rugby remembers John kindly for the huge sacrifices he made.

As it turned out, John produced a solid performance against Wales, who had the experienced and respected Gethin Jenkins at loosehead. It was a good start, but props need to grow into the position. To be a good prop, you have to go through a long learning curve, and time wasn't on John's side. Whereas he had a wealth of experience to draw from playing at hooker, that wasn't the case when he was playing prop.

John's progress in the No. 3 jersey was not helped by Bismarck du Plessis suffering an injury in the early minutes of the next game, against Scotland, which forced him to fly home. John had to move back to hooker, which is where he remained for the rest of the tour. It seemed the right thing to do, as we wanted to win the games, but it probably wasn't wise considering the upcoming series against the British & Irish Lions.

So that was another mistake I made. I should have called for a replacement hooker from South Africa and played him in that position and left John at tighthead. It might have been a risky move, but we would have gained more in the build-up to the Lions series. With John continuing at hooker on that tour, he had to go into the Lions games with little experience at tighthead. But winning was everything at the time.

We moved on from Cardiff to play against Scotland in Edinburgh, and we managed to beat them, but it was a close affair. Perhaps we had underestimated their team, and no matter how much we tried to convince ourselves otherwise, we just couldn't believe that they would be strong opposition. Playing against Scotland at Murrayfield taught me a lot about rugby at the highest level and a great deal about the Springbok team's psyche. I had been with the team for several months by then, but I had never seen them play so poorly. Absolutely nothing worked for us. We tried all kinds of tactics, and we didn't play badly because we weren't trying.

Before half-time, I walked down to the touchline to prepare myself to address the players during the break, and I was furious. I normally spoke to the assistant coaches first and then allowed them to address the players before I said anything, but this time I told them I would do all the talking.

I had some harsh words for the players – I was livid. But when they came into the changing room, where I was sitting in the corner, waiting for them, I abruptly changed my mind. I might have been wrong, but for the first time since I'd started working with him, I thought I saw genuine fear in John Smit's eyes. And all the other players were looking at me as if they were schoolboys seeking direction from somewhere. So I changed my mind. I just knew I couldn't go hard on them. Instead, I told them that they were playing well! I am sure my assistants, Gary Gold and Dick Muir, were as surprised as I was at the unbelievable rubbish that was suddenly coming out of my mouth.

'Guys,' I said, 'hell, we are playing such good rugby, the only place we are struggling is on the scoreboard. Just go back out there and round off the moves and score the points. We are playing really well today.'

Then John stood up, and I saw the belief flooding back into the team. I really think that my little half-time speech won that game for us. As a coach, you sometimes have to improvise. You have to understand that what motivates one player won't necessarily work for another. But I think I read the mood correctly that day; the players didn't need to be brought down any further than they already were.

We started playing better after half-time, and Jaque Fourie, who had been out for the entire season and was now just coming back into the game, scored a try after replacing Bryan Habana on the wing as we scraped to a 14-10 win. Bryan was not in good form at that time. I actually had to come down quite hard on him. After the game I called him in and read him the riot act, which helped get him back to his best form the next week, when we played England.

I didn't think we were under as much pressure to win as was being made out in some quarters before the match at Twickenham. We had won two games out of three on tour, and while not everyone will agree with me, I thought two wins in three starts was a passable record for a tour. But the way we stood up against England that day was big. In fact, it was huge!

We took a different approach to our training before the game by hardly training at all. Before the Scotland game I had worked the players really hard, but I didn't take into consideration the soft underfoot conditions one encounters on Scotland's training fields. Although the actual playing fields are great, the training fields are awful. And if you think you can and must train in the rain, you are making a big mistake, as the fields are just too heavy. If you have to train in the rain, do so on Astroturf, or else it just takes too much out of the legs.

We decided that we couldn't add anything to our game for the test against England, so instead of training physically, we had planning sessions. We did all our preparations in the boardroom apart from one session on the field, as I knew I had to motivate the players psychologically.

We decided not to specifically target any of the English players we thought would try to pressurise us, but Gary Gold, who had coached in England, went a bit over the top before the match, as he had enormous respect for their players. His feelings weren't shared by any of the Springboks. On one occasion, after Gary had said a few words, one of the Boks came to me and said, 'This is *England* we're talking about. We don't even get this worked up when we're playing the All Blacks!'

The Springboks don't need any extra motivation when they play England. 'Hate' might be too strong a word to use, so let's just say that the guys love competing against and beating England. I'm not sure whether this attitude will continue into the future, as the youngsters coming through are perhaps not as aware of the legacy of colonialism as those of us who were told about it by our parents and grandparents. This was probably the last generation of players who had been influenced by it. You didn't have to say too much to a player like Juan Smith, for example, before a game against England for him to be up in arms and super-motivated.

So we just concentrated on what we needed to do to beat them. It had been a long year, and the players appreciated that I had not asked them to put in more training. They liked being trusted with the task at hand.

At a press conference in the week preceding the game, I confused England flyhalf Danny Cipriani's name with that of the former woman tennis player Jennifer Capriati. The English press, and even some of our newspapers back home, kicked up quite a fuss about it. Perhaps it was a good thing that they focused on that *faux pas*, as I might have been trying to be too clever. I was, in fact, saying that Cipriani would lose the game for England because he would be too individualistic and try to do too much on his own. It was an attempt to break his confidence. I was being very sarcastic, so had the press picked up on it, it might have come across badly.

I was also encouraged by my suspicion that the England players would try too hard to impress their new coach, Martin Johnson. If too many individuals try to stake their claim for a place in the team, it can spell disaster for their game plan.

And it turned out that I was right about Cipriani. On the day, he was way too individualistic. Ruan Pienaar charged down Cipriani's first kick to score the opening try, which was the result of some solid planning on our part. We had worked out that Cipriani took way too long over his kicks. After Ruan scored that try, Cipriani was all over the place and never featured in the game again.

But I could never have imagined that the game would be as one-sided as it turned out. We won 42-6, which was a record defeat for England at Twickenham. For those who remembered that game, it was sweet revenge for the 3-53 defeat the Springboks had suffered under Corné Krige as captain and Rudolf Straeuli as coach at Twickenham six years previously.

I thought Adi Jacobs had played particularly well. Though not every-one rated him, he never let me down. In fact, when I coached him, he was often our match winner. Some of his critics don't seem to under-stand that he possesses the most wonderful BMT.

Although Adi did well in an era when he was a groundbreaker for black rugby players, I don't think the contribution he made to the game in our country has ever been properly acknowledged. His critics said that he couldn't defend, but it depended on who his support players were. He struggled when Joe Esterhuizen was on his inside, because Joe wasn't a good tackler. But in 2008, when Adi had Jean de Villiers and Butch James on his inside for much of the season, he played very well.

On our arrival back in South Africa after the tour, we had a great response from our supporters. So while it hadn't been a terrific Tri Nations for us, we seemed to have salvaged some pride with our results on the end-of-year tour.

It was a great confidence-booster for what lay ahead in 2009.

15

A once-in-12-years' opportunity

As well as a Springbok series against the British & Irish Lions in 2009, there was also a general election. Trust me to get embroiled somehow, although through no fault of my own. The election was to take place a month or so before the start of the international rugby season, and in the run-up to the election I managed to invoke the ire of the SA Rugby bosses for allegedly 'publicly endorsing' the ANC.

According to SARU, the Springbok coach should be seen to be politically neutral – he should not support or endorse any political party – at least not publicly. I actually agree with their view. I never had any intention of backing a political party, but I got 'hijacked' and didn't know how to extricate myself from the situation. I suspect that Chris Nissen, who was vying for the leadership of the ANC in the Western Cape, had used me to further his own personal agenda.

Here's what happened: I was invited to a cocktail party in Cape Town, which I knew would also be attended by Arthob Petersen, the Springbok manager at the time, Jackie Abrahams, the Boland president, and former Springbok selection convener Francois Davids. We all knew each other well – Davids, known as 'Kabalie', is one of my best friends – so they talked me into coming along. None of us was completely sure what the party was about, but we knew that a number of important people were going to be there and thought it a good idea to attend too.

What we didn't know was that the function had been organised by the ANC, and that there would be speeches promoting the governing party. I was also not told beforehand that I would be expected to say something at the function.

When we got there, I remember that I was a bit nervous about the presence of the television cameras and asked why they were present, but was assured that they were there only for private, in-house use. Today, I can't believe how damn stupid I was. Of course I supported the ANC in some way, as I could hardly be against the organisation after the contribution it had made to the struggle. But I have never attended ANC meetings and certainly was not attending the cocktail party with a political agenda.

Because I believed the cameras present were not those of the media but the ANC, I felt a bit better about making a speech when asked. What I went on to say was not supposed to be an endorsement of the ANC in any way – I didn't believe it was my business to be telling people which party to vote for – but the media interpreted it differently. I said the following: '[The] ANC [made it possible for me to] become coach of this country. So I will never go against them. They are doing a lot of things wrong, but so is my church, and I have never left my church.'

I was basically saying that I would always be grateful to the ANC because it had been instrumental in bringing about democracy. I was never asked whether or not I endorsed the ANC – I just said I couldn't go against it.

When the story appeared in the media, I thought about telling the newspapers that I had been manipulated, but I couldn't without damaging the ANC in some way. And that I didn't want to do. At the time, Chris Nissen was embroiled in a big fight within the ANC structures. My guess is that he probably thought that it would help his personal cause if he could get a well-known public figure, like me, to lend public support to the party. If so, what he did was wrong. I never heard from Chris Nissen again, so I only ever got to meet the man at the party itself. But I would never have attended if I had known what the intention was that night.

* * *

My year had got off to a disappointing start when my bosses didn't approve my plan to travel to Britain to watch some of the Six Nations matches. I wanted to see what we could expect in anticipation of the Lions' arrival, but SARU wouldn't give me the money to go.

Why could I not just watch the games on television, you ask? Well, if you are going to make a proper and comprehensive analysis of a game, you need to see the defensive alignment and the running lines, which you can't do when you are limited by the camera angles on television.

I wanted assistant coach Dick Muir to accompany me, so when SA Rugby wouldn't give us the funding, Dick managed to secure us private sponsorship. Hell, it made me mad. The administrators were always going overseas, often at the drop of a hat, and a lot of the executive committee and board members used to travel to watch our test matches, even though it was really quite unnecessary for them to be there. So I wasn't sympathetic to the excuse that SA Rugby was cash-strapped.

It was important for us to see first hand how the British teams played; we wanted to observe Wales in particular, as we knew that their coach, Warren Gatland, who was also the Lions' assistant coach, was going to play a big part in determining the touring team's strategy.

Nevertheless, despite SARU, off we went to watch the Welsh play England and then Ireland. We learnt a lot from those games, so it had been well worth our while to make the journey. The eventual results proved it. But because of SARU's attitude, I look back at that time as a low point in my tenure.

One good thing, though, was the amount of time we were given for our preparation. At last we had a really good gap between the end of the Super 14 series and the beginning of the international season, and while the Lions were touring the rest of the country, we enjoyed three weeks of good preparation. Indeed, except for the time we had for training just before the 2011 World Cup, that was the only proper preparation period we ever had, as all our international engagements usually occurred shortly after the conclusion of provincial and regional competitions.

We managed to get a lot of work done in those three weeks, including focusing on the players' conditioning, which in other years just wasn't possible.

A major factor was to get the guys to believe in themselves, and after the big win over England during the previous end-of-year tour, they were very confident. They also believed in the structures we'd put in place. We suspected that the Lions were likely to follow the Welsh approach in their game plan, and we had beaten Wales three times in my first year in charge.

Nevertheless, we knew we would have to improve our game against the Lions, a composite of all four Home Unions and thus supposedly a lot stronger than just one single nation. It's the reason why beating them is viewed as such an achievement, and it still rankled with South Africans that we had lost the series against them in 1997.

Instead of being afraid of what awaited us, we were excited and well prepared. The Lions were playing in several games before the first test in Durban, which gave us ample opportunity to study their style of play.

I think one of the best decisions I made was to ask the 1997 Springboks to talk to the team before the start of the series. They came in the day before the first test for the jersey presentation and told the team about the disappointment they still felt at having lost the series 12 years earlier. They reminded the players that you only get to play against the Lions once in your career – if you are lucky. If you lose against them, the disappointment lasts a lifetime. It's not like the Tri Nations, where you get a chance to avenge the defeat the following year.

I had to make a couple of tough calls on the selection front, but fortunately one such decision was taken out of my hands, as it was forced by injury. I had not chosen openside flanker Heinrich Brüssow for my initial squad, but after his brilliant performance for the Cheetahs against the Lions in a tour match in Bloemfontein, everyone wanted to know why he wasn't in the team. The truth was that we had assessed him, and although we rated him highly, we had an established back-row combination in Schalk Burger at No. 6, Juan Smith on the other flank and Pierre Spies at No. 8.

I figured that any other flanker would have to be really exceptional to even come into consideration. But then Heinrich showed us that he was indeed a brilliant player, and today he is regarded as one of the best in the world in his position. At the time of the Lions tour, though, he only got called up because Schalk Burger was injured.

So Heinrich was in the starting team for the first test, and what a great debut it was for him. The man is more than just a stealer of the ball – he is also an exceptional carrier, as he cannot be brought to ground easily.

Another player who had not initially been part of my plans but who would have a big say in the series was Morné Steyn. As I wanted a creative player at No. 10, I considered Ruan Pienaar to be the perfect fit. Ruan might not have played at flyhalf much in Super Rugby, but we nevertheless went into the series thinking that he was our man. Morné wasn't even our second or third choice; in fact, he would have missed the cut completely had it not been for his last three games in that year's Super 14. The Bulls had finished the season as if they'd had a train to catch, beating the Crusaders in the semi-finals before smashing the Chiefs to take the series, and Morné had been one of their pivotal players.

I felt a lot of public pressure to pick him, and although I was dead set against his selection at first, he swayed me with his stunning performances. It would have been incredibly stupid of me to leave him out after he'd shown what a match winner he was. As with Butch James the previous year, Morné changed my mind just by playing well. I'd coached him in the under-21 team that won the Junior World Cup in 2005, so I wasn't new to him as a coach. He'd impressed me as a cool customer back then, as even when he was about to kick a really important goal, he would still joke with the guy bringing out the kicking tee. However, I also thought that he had to learn to be more creative if he wanted to play flyhalf at senior international level.

For just a few minutes in every international game, you need a backline player who will use the tiniest of opportunities to ignite the individual brilliance of the inside or outside centre and make the difference between winning and losing. But Morné stands deeper than a lot of modern flyhalves and thus can't deliver that moment, with the result that I always knew if I selected him, the team's backline play might suffer. So whenever the media asked me about Morné's chances of making the team, I couldn't answer them without criticising his game, and while I was coach I tried not to publicly knock players. But later on, when Morné did become our first-choice flyhalf, I felt sorry for Dick Muir, as he had taken a lot of flak on my behalf. Dick was blamed for the backs not playing well, but in selecting Morné, I made it difficult for the backline to click.

Having said all that, I often wish we could combine Morné's head with Ruan Pienaar's talent. What a tremendous player he would be!

But as it happened, I had no reason to be unhappy with Ruan's selection for the first test against the Lions. Along with Beast Mtawarira, who scrummed the life out of the Lions and really put the squeeze on them, Ruan was our match winner in the way he orchestrated matters from the back.

By half-time in the first test, we had established a handy lead. But although we would go on to win the test, it was a tight affair towards the end, and I was slammed afterwards for making the second-half substitutions, which many felt nearly cost us the game.

The critics didn't understand that, although we had been able to prepare really well, unlike the Lions we had not had six games to build up to the first test. In fact, our previous test had taken place the previous November (against England at Twickenham). I worried that if we had a good start, we might struggle to maintain momentum in the second half because we lacked match fitness. I had discussed my concern with the guys on the bench beforehand. I expected them to come onto the field and lift the tempo.

However, if I have to take the blame, it will be for sending the substitutes on too late. We had a big lead but went into defensive mode not long after half-time, and once in that mode, it is hard to get out of it. Had I sent the substitutes on earlier, they would have got into the flow of the match quicker and would have kept the momentum going. So I take the criticism on the chin. I should have made the call earlier, because I knew the Lions were more match-fit than us.

Afterwards I heard rumours that Dick Muir had made the calls. It would have been stupid of me to sit next to international coaches in the coaching box and not listen to their advice, but ultimately the call had been mine to make, just as I had to take the rap when things went wrong.

Yet everything had gone really well and our tactics had worked perfectly almost right up till the end. We were always going to target them in the scrums, as we knew they were expected to be strong in that department. But we knew we really had them when they were forced to run balls that just weren't on to run. We were slowly strangling their game and putting them under constant pressure.

Our defence was not yet as good as it would become later that year, but on the day it wasn't bad at all. We knew that if we did the early running and piled on the points, they might still sneak in a few tries but would not be able to win the game.

One of the changes I made was to replace Fourie du Preez with Ricky Januarie. After the game, Ricky was criticised for being poor and the critics blamed his weight. A lot of malicious things were said and the press got really personal, so when the topic came up at a press conference in Johannesburg on the Monday after the first test, I didn't hold back.

'I am not concerned about Ricky's form,' I told the media. I tried to explain the situation by way of a parable. 'Look, if you go to a black mechanic and he doesn't fix your car, you don't go back [there]. [But] if you go to a white mechanic and he doesn't fix your car, you go back and make sure he fixes the problem. What I am saying is, give Ricky a chance.'

Boy, did I get into trouble with both the South African media and my bosses for that! But should I not have stood up for my player? Ricky might not have been better than Fourie du Preez, but that wasn't why Fourie wasn't in the starting line-up. As the second scrumhalf in the squad, Ricky delivered what I wanted – he could come on and keep the opposition loose forwards busy and thus take the pressure off the other players on attack.

Selection is not always just about choosing the best player in each position. Often you select a player because he fits into a certain combination or is able to execute a specific plan. I didn't want Ricky to run 70 metres to score a try; I wanted him to be a pain in the butt to the opposition defenders so that he could create the space his teammates required to score tries.

Although Dewaldt Duvenage often ran on ahead of Ricky in that year's Super Rugby season, I didn't always agree with that selection. With Dewaldt on the pitch, the Stormers centres got tackled more often and were also made to run into heavier traffic. And even if everyone kept on going on about Ricky's weight, he was not the only player who had ended the Super 14 out of condition.

Which was why I said what I said at the press conference. Why pick on Ricky when there were other Bok players in the same boat? They were being given a chance, so why wasn't Ricky? The All Black scrumhalf Piri Weepu always looks overweight to me, but until recently, you didn't hear the New Zealanders knocking him for it. I thought Ricky should have been given more support and that the media had gone over the top.

I objected to Ricky being judged according to the colour of his skin, if that was the underlying motivation for the criticism against him. Even now I am sometimes judged like that, and it irks me. One thing I had got right by that stage was that I had convinced the players to become the people's team. They were accessible to the public and were not stuck away behind glass barricades. When the Springboks were around, everyone in the country was made to feel that the team represented them, played for them and was accessible to them.

And I never selected any black player just because he was black. It was important to me to be perceived as being honest, and I didn't want the black players to feel they had additional responsibility, that they had to prove themselves extra hard because of the colour of their skin.

Unfortunately, Ricky's performance and the substitutions I'd sent on overshadowed what had essentially been a good win. Mostly the players were happy that we had drawn first blood in the series, but the sideshows deflected attention away from the rugby.

But it was nothing compared to what was to come after we'd clinched the series in Pretoria ...

16

Lions and ... ballet

The big selection poser for the second test against the British & Irish Lions, in Pretoria, centred round Heinrich Brüssow and Schalk Burger. Schalk had recovered from his injury, as had been anticipated, but he hadn't played for a while and Heinrich had been excellent in his debut test.

A lot of rugby journalists and a great many fans wanted me to stick with Brüssow and play Schalk off the bench. But I knew Schalk. He simply wasn't an impact player – for starters, he got too worked up while sitting on the sidelines. In that sense, he is similar to Bakkies Botha – you have to start with Bakkies. And Schalk also manages to instil fear in his opposition, which is a valuable attribute to have when you start a game.

So in the end it wasn't really a difficult decision to make. I had to put Heinrich on the bench. But on this day, Schalk was on the field for only a few seconds before he was off, watching from the stands. He had been yellow-carded for what the media later called an 'eye-gouging incident'.

Fortunately the referee hadn't understood the recommendation of the assistant referee or Schalk would have been red-carded and off the pitch for the rest of the game. The British media made a massive fuss about the incident afterwards, as they did about what I said in Schalk's defence.

But back to the game ... After Schalk was sent off, we were immediately on the back foot; it was as if the guys had been rendered senseless by the incident. The Lions did all the early playing, and our cause wasn't helped when Ruan Pienaar missed some kickable attempts at goal. As

I've said before, his confidence goes for a loop when he doesn't kick well, as it did in this match.

At half-time we were trailing 8-16 and were struggling to keep up with the Lions. But in the second half we made up for the substitution errors of the previous week by getting them spot-on. If the substitutions were the reason why the Lions had staged a comeback in Durban, on this occasion they got us back into the game as the Lions wilted.

It was a really dramatic half, as dramatic as you can get, with tries scored and both teams suffering injuries. Danie Rossouw's injury might have been fortuitous, as Heinrich Brüssow replaced him, and he made a big difference to our game in the final minutes.

The Lions lost both their centres, but Brian O'Driscoll, who was playing well before his injury, looked out of it even before he went off. It seemed like Bryan Habana had gone right through him when we went over for a try. Then substitute centre Jaque Fourie, on for Jean de Villiers, scored an incredible try in the right corner, which put us ahead for the first time. But the Lions struck back with a penalty, and the scores were level at 25-all. Then, with time up on the clock, came the big moment that won us the game. It was, in fact, a moment of madness by Ronan O'Gara. He hoisted a ball onto Fourie du Preez and took out the scrumhalf while he was still in the air.

It was a penalty to South Africa, but just inside our half. The ball was passed to Morné Steyn, who had replaced Pienaar much earlier in the second half. Amid an eerie, tense silence, Morné lined up the deciding kick … I was confident that he would slot the penalty, as he was at Loftus Versfeld, his home ground, and he'd hardly missed a kick all year.

From the moment boot struck ball, you could tell he wasn't going to miss this one either, and as the flags were raised, it sparked a spontaneous outpouring of joy among the Springbok players, who ran onto the field and tearfully embraced one another as the supporters screamed their appreciation. The bedlam even surpassed the ecstatic celebrations in Dunedin the previous year, when we beat the All Blacks.

And understandably so, for many of the players had been building towards a series win against the British & Irish Lions since their World Cup victory 20 months previously; it was the initial reason John Smit and Victor Matfield had come back from France. So it was a case of mission accomplished for those players. We had beaten the Lions for the first time since 1980 and could finally lay to rest the 12 years of dissatisfaction we'd felt since losing the series in 1997.

But the ecstasy of our victory was soon to be dampened by the events that followed. Rugby is not the number-one sport in the UK, and with the Lions now having lost the series, perhaps their rugby writers had to justify staying in the country for another week. They found their reason to stick around in the controversy they helped blow out of all proportion, to the extent that it completely overshadowed our series win.

And one big mistake I made would contribute to the fires that sprung up all around us. During the Monday press conference, I confused the meaning of the word 'condone' with 'condemn'. English is not my first language, and in the heat of the moment I got the words mixed up. So when I was asked whether I condoned what Schalk Burger had done, I thought I was being asked whether I condemned it.

I said yes, and then, as the old saying goes, the canary went into the frying pan.

The judicial officer later found Schalk not guilty of eye gouging but of reckless play instead. I thought that vindicated the stance I had taken after the Loftus test. Although I was deemed to be defending Schalk, I was, in fact, saying that I didn't think he was guilty of eye gouging.

Once again, SA Rugby let me down. SARU could have released a statement after the eye-gouging charge had been dismissed to point out that I had, in fact, been proven right. But that was not done, because they didn't care to. Instead, they seemed preoccupied with constant infighting. The disharmony prevalent among the board members was reflected in the negative comments they made about me in the media, probably in an attempt to score political points. They probably felt they were justified for adopting their stance against me whenever I got into trouble, so why would they defend me? I'm probably wrong, but I felt they had protected and defended my predecessors more than they ever did me.

Later a story appeared in SA Rugby magazine in which I was quoted as saying that I was the 'CEO of South African rugby', and they all went ballistic. But none of them ever approached me to find out what I had really said. They didn't bother to establish the authenticity of the story or hear my side of it before attacking me. Some of the presidents might do good things for their unions, but there are those who are not honourable people, and I didn't enjoy working with them.

Anthony MacKaiser, the third media person who worked with me at the Boks, seemed determined to modify my behaviour, especially towards the press. But that was not who I was. When SARU appointed me in 2008, they appointed Peter de Villiers, not someone by that name who would then behave like a different person once he'd got the job. I had seen a lot of black politicians as well as sports administrators since 1994 changing their behaviour and even their personalities once elected to representative positions, and I didn't want to be like them. You can't represent your community if you distance yourself from your people.

I also didn't like how everyone involved in rugby suddenly had to be so politically correct about everything. Coaches and players from various countries were being trained to answer questions at press conferences in such a way that they said absolutely nothing. I didn't want to be politically correct in that sense – I wanted to say what I felt. What was the point of being asked a question if you were always going to give the expected, predictable and sanitised answer?

The British media were probably so used to watered-down responses to all their questions that they couldn't believe their luck when I came along. Some of the local journalists told me about the glee with which some of the UK writers noted down my comments. They wanted to know whether I was for real. Was I having them on? I gave them good copy. Many of them dined out on the sort of controversy that had been created by the Schalk incident.

I just couldn't understand why so many South Africans were so negative when we had just won a major test series. The muted reaction made me feel incredibly lonely. Fortunately, by this time my defence mechanisms against criticism and media pressure were well developed. I would attend a media conference and not even look at the reporters who were interviewing me. I didn't care what they thought of me – I had to keep my distance or I would never have coped. I used to say to myself, 'You are the only one here' and use that to avoid the anger or discomfort I might otherwise have felt.

I was also very disappointed with the South African rugby media. They had allowed a few negative rugby writers from the UK to dominate the press conferences and decide what should be discussed, when I had expected them to take the lead. Why didn't they rub the visitors' noses in the fact that we had won the series?

At the post-series reception, Lions skipper Paul O'Connell said in his speech that he was talking as the 'winning captain': this on the basis of their victory in the final test! Ian McGeechan behaved as if he was the winning coach. And we let them get away with it. Yes, it had been a close series, decided by a kick, but the 1997 series had ended similarly and yet the British had celebrated like crazy.

On the Tuesday after I'd said that I 'condoned' eye gouging, there was another press conference, and I had to try to douse some of the fires that were raging around the incident. One of the South African journalists asked a question, but a British reporter standing near the window summarily interrupted him to ask a question of his own.

I said, 'Hey, you are rude, man. We have manners in this country.'

They were determined to carry on *ad infinitum* about the Schalk incident. So that was when I mentioned the ballet and tutus and said that, in South Africa, when we want to eye-gouge a lion, we go to the bush to find a real one.

I don't know where that last comment came from. I must have been really worked up. I can assure you that I have never been stupid enough to go to the bush to look for lions to eye-gouge, and I am sure none of my fellow countrymen have either. I was just trying to express my exasperation at the double standards the British press were practising. They seemed determined to undermine our series victory by focusing on this incident.

The last tackle on Fourie du Preez, which got us the penalty kick that won us the series, had been very dangerous. But we never complained about it. And they had done many other things in the games that could also have been construed as dangerous or reckless play. Yet every time Bakkies Botha or Schalk Burger was involved in an incident, it seemed to evoke a massive reaction. What Schalk had done to Luke Fitzgerald, the Lions wing, was not right, but I don't believe that he had tried to eye-gouge him. I just couldn't see how someone like Schalk would have that kind of intent.

As I said to the media, 'If you know Schalk's nature and character, if you know the man as I know him, you would know he would never do this. He [might be] more physical than any other rugby player in the world. But to go to those kind of measures, he would never do it. And I don't think he did it.'

I had started the press conference by saying we would never condone eye gouging.

'We have brilliant players in this country, most of them world-class. We do not prepare them to do things that belong in the bushveld. If you find you want to eye-gouge a lion, there [the bush] is where you go to do it. But we must understand here very, very clearly that rugby is a contact sport – and so is dancing. If we are going to win games in boardrooms and in front of television cameras and in shops, we must say to ourselves, "Do we really respect this game that we honour so much?"

'If that is the case, why don't we all go to the nearest ballet shop, get some nice tutus and get some great dancing going on? No eye gouging, no tackling, no nothing. Then just enjoy [it]. There are no collisions in ballet, but in this game there will be collisions. If people want to make it soft because we won a series, I cannot do anything about it.'

Okay, it was a bit over the top. Perhaps a *lot* over the top ... But that was how I felt. Schalk was (quite rightly) eventually suspended for eight weeks for reckless play. But then we were informed that Bakkies Botha had been cited for what had seemed a perfectly legal clean-out of a Lions player.

Now I was really pissed off. The Lions had perpetrated a fair amount of illegal and dangerous off-the-ball stuff, yet the citing official was just focusing on Bakkies and Schalk. And the South African media just sat there grinning. The Boks are a physical team. When Bakkies runs into you, you will have bruises that you will feel for days afterwards. That is how we play, and win. Why should we allow people to pressure us into taking the physicality out of our game?

I honestly didn't know how I would ever be able to select Bakkies again if he was going to be punished for doing something perfectly legal. In fact, he had done what we had *wanted* him to do. We even congratulated him on doing it so well! In a way, Bakkies had been selected to do *exactly* what he did.

But no one in SA Rugby supported me when I tried to get a fairer deal for our players. In my first year as coach, I pointed out that the All Blacks were scrumming illegally, which was reported by the media. But André Watson, who was then chief of the South African Rugby Referees, didn't back me up. And this when I knew many of our local referees agreed with me.

Our referees are the best in the world, but it doesn't help us much if it means we always have the poor referees taking charge of our games. (I have plenty to say about referees later.) At the time of the Lions series, I didn't have too much to complain about, though; it was just the double standards that irritated me.

My reaction to the pressure that was being applied on me and my team made me a controversial character in the eyes of the world media, but I don't consider myself to be controversial. I am just not like other people. When I feel that someone has been wronged, I am prepared to stand up for them, even if I am the only one to do so. Very few people are prepared to stand alone. They think: 'If people say good things about me, then I am a good person.' Their main goal is to please every-one all the time so they never want to stand up for someone when he or she has been wronged, lest it makes them unpopular.

And so we came to the third and final test of the series. The players were incensed that Bakkies had been suspended for cleaning out Adam Jones. If you look at a video of the incident, it was textbook stuff and proved that Bakkies had done nothing wrong. So at a team meeting the players unanimously decided to stage some sort of protest, and I sup-ported them. They were going to wear armbands with the word 'justice' inscribed on them.

Of course we knew we would get into trouble, but everyone felt that enough was enough. Although Oregan Hoskins (and hence SARU) did support us this time, we still sensed that our administrators were reluctant to risk their chances of advancement within the IRB by stand-ing up for what was right. I remember being angered by a request from

Regan to put out a statement apologising for what I had said. I did it, for I did work for SA Rugby after all and SARU paid my salary, but I did so against my will.

I made 10 changes to the team for the final game, in Johannesburg, and the media and public weren't happy about it. Neither, I suppose, were some of the players. But the fringe players had worked hard in the build-up to the series and I wanted to let them feel part of the series. After all, you only play the Lions once every 12 years – if you're lucky.

But there was more to it than that – the Tri Nations tournament was looming, and I desperately wanted us to win it. The last test, with nothing other than pride at stake and the series already secured, seemed a perfect opportunity to test our player depth. I believe it was a move that paid off in the Tri Nations, but maybe the many changes I made took away the team's momentum, which I take full responsibility for.

However, all the players I selected for the last test were quality Springboks who should have been able to account for themselves. Unfortunately, though, they didn't do justice to their abilities and we lost the game quite badly. It was a bit of an anticlimax to receive the trophy after suffering such a defeat (9-28). The Lions, though, had lost the last game in the 1997 series, but no one remembers that match – they only remember Jeremy Guscott's winning drop goal in the second test in Durban.

So maybe I can be forgiven if I remember the 2009 series only for the winning penalty and the celebrations that followed. We had achieved our objective: mission accomplished.

And it laid the perfect platform for our ascent back to the top of world rugby over the next few months.

17

Ruling the world

After the British & Irish Lions tour, it wasn't just the media who acted like we had lost the series rather than won it. The SARU bosses did the same. According to the rules, the president of SARU has the right to conduct a coach's appraisal twice a year. In other words, Oregan Hoskins was well within his rights to call me in, but then the details were leaked to the press, which made it seem as if I was being rapped over the knuckles.

And I suppose in a way I was, as they came down hard on me in the appraisal. The committee appointed to appraise me consisted of Regan Hoskins, the technical committee head James Stofberg, SARU acting chief executive Andy Marinos and former Springbok coach Ian McIntosh, who was also one of the selectors. They took me on about two issues in particular: how I dealt with the media, and my religion. I told them that I handled the press in my own way, but Regan wasn't happy. I explained that the media were often provocative instead of asking the kind of rugby questions you would expect to answer as a coach. By then I had started suspecting that executive council member Dr Jan Marais, the former Griffons president, and others in the SARU hierarchy were leaking stories to the media so that they could then make a decision based on how the public reacted to the media report.

I wasn't too concerned about what they thought of my relationship with the media – I could sort that out without too much effort. But how they felt about my religion was another story altogether. I had a propensity towards religious allegories and referred to them quite often in public, which irked SARU. So when I was told that I should not mention religion when I spoke to the press or the players, I told them that they could take their job back.

I do live in South Africa and understand the social dynamics. We have many non-Christians in our country and I respect them for their views. I grew up among Muslims, and I have an understanding of their religion. My best friend through most of my youth was a Muslim guy. Because my faith is so deeply embedded in my being, I respect all people's religious beliefs.

Isma-eel Dollie played for me at under-21 level, and when I started with scripture readings, I told Isma-eel that he could read out of the Koran, which he was happy to do. Because none of the other guys understood Arabic, Isma-eel had to translate what he was reading, which was very informative and interesting. The bottom line was that I never forced religion on anyone who played for me. Those who didn't want to participate in the scripture readings didn't have to.

As it happened, I did have a bit of a disagreement with sections of the Muslim community in Cape Town during the 2009 Tri Nations. In January of that year, planning for the season ahead, I went to Schot-schekloof Walmers Rugby Football Club to ask them whether we could use their field for training purposes when the Springboks were in Cape Town for the game against Australia.

I went to assess the facilities with logistics manager Charles Wessels, and we were both happy with the condition of the field. The club people were enthusiastic about hosting us – it doesn't happen often that the Springbok team trains at a club. But it was part of my initiative of taking the Springboks to the communities.

However, there are certain standards that need to be upheld when you host a Springbok team. The last thing the national team needs is for a player to go down injured in the build-up to a major test match because he stepped into a pothole on an uneven field.

So when I went back to the club on the Sunday before the Tri Nations game and saw that the field was now in poor condition, I had to change our plans. It had rained a lot the previous week, and the club had played Maties the day before. The field was a mudbath – there was no other way of describing it. I told the club people that we couldn't train there, and their response was, 'Well, it rained. What do you expect?'

But I explained that the national team needs a field to be in perfect condition for training before a major match. The players would not have been happy if they had been asked to train there. The guys were keen to be seen as the people's team, but they had to be properly prepared for the test match. The club people had known it was raining and should have put measures in place to preserve the condition of the field.

I phoned Peter Jooste, the national selection convener, and asked him if we could train at his club ground at Tygerberg. The Schotschekloof people weren't happy, but what else could I do? This was the first time in 100 years that a national team was coming to their club. They should have gone out of their way to ensure that everything went smoothly.

It erupted into quite a fuss when the club told their story to e.tv, and *Cape Times* rugby writer Ashfak Mohamed, a Muslim, wrote a long story about it on their behalf. The Muslim community then took this opportunity to attack me for having dropped Isma-eel Dollie when he had failed to impress me as a potential international player at my first training camp in 2008. Later on, when I went on a rugby trip to Israel in 2011, the Muslim community in Cape Town made a big deal about that too.

It was a typically South African situation, politicising everything. I was never obligated to go to their club – I just thought I would try to do my bit to take the game to the community. Yet there I was, being cast as the bad guy.

But back to the appraisal after the Lions series: when Oregan Hoskins 'appraised' me, he told me that Trevor Munday, the former deputy CEO of SASOL, who was the sponsor's representative on the SARU board, had instructed him to come down hard on me. But I knew that this was probably just Oregan's way of criticising me without having to take the blame for it. A similar situation would occur a year later, when I landed in hot water after commenting on the arrest of Blue Bulls prop Bees Roux on a murder charge.

But the performance clauses that had been inserted into my contract at the outset saved me at the appraisal, as they would continue to do throughout my four-year tenure. While the committee gave me flak for the issues that had been raised during the British & Irish Lions series, there was one incontrovertible fact that could not be ignored – we had won the series. As long as I was being judged on my performance, I was basically untouchable, and I never scored less than 80 per cent in any of my appraisals.

So I told the committee that as far as religion was concerned, I would continue to do things my way, and that I was just not the politically correct type who always said only what people wanted to hear. I had the opportunity to promote change in our country by expressing my views and I wanted to make use of it.

As far as the media issue was concerned, I wasn't the only one in the firing line. Oregan also chastised Gary Gold for something written by *Sunday Times* journalist Simnikiwe Xabanisa, who had alleged that our media relations weren't up to scratch. Hoskins gave Gary advice on how to deal with the situation, but Gary dug his heels in, as he felt he had handled the media well, which he had.

So after the appraisal I was allowed to resume my main task, which was to prepare the Springboks for the Tri Nations. Although we had beaten the Lions, we were under no illusions. Not everything was going smoothly. The issues we'd had about conflicting coaching messages had resurfaced, and this time they were more serious. Dick Muir wanted the players to give the ball more air and play a running game, which the players were not comfortable with. So we had a meeting to resolve the matter, much like the previous year in Durban during the 2008 Tri Nations. This time the meeting took place in Johannesburg.

We discussed our game plan in detail at this meeting. Everyone had to buy into it so that there could be no further confusion among management and the players. Although I could live with my two assistant coaches' different approaches to the game, I needed to find a balance between them in order for the players to understand what was required of them. If a coach has a strategy that a player thinks he cannot execute, there is no point in incorporating it into the game plan.

But the meeting went off well. Everyone had their say, and we all agreed that, as a team, the Boks were best at playing direct rugby. The way they liked to play was to take their time breaking down the defensive walls before playing running rugby, and a high premium was placed on territorial dominance. I had done profile tests on the players, so I no longer harboured any lingering fantasies about them being able to play the game differently. The meeting was also attended by players who had been drafted in as senior players, like Morné Steyn, for example. He had become a key factor in our game plan.

We studied Springbok history to establish how every successful Bok team had approached the game, starting with Philip Nel's legendary 1937 team, the only South African side to win a series on New Zealand soil. In that way, we established that all the great Springbok teams had played quite similarly. So, by the end of the meeting, we were all on the same page and started the Tri Nations as a unified force.

Perhaps the wisest thing I did in 2009 was to give the players maximum time off between the end of the Lions series and the start of the Tri Nations. Coaches often worry that there is a certain amount of work that they have to get through before a big game and forget that the players – certainly at Springbok level – don't play for just one team. So a player has to absorb a lot of the same technical instructions from various coaches.

With someone like Schalk Burger, you can change 40 line-out calls and he will have understood and absorbed all of it within two minutes. So if you have a 40-minute session planned, it means he is bored for 38 minutes of that time. And you just need to look at his face to confirm that he's lost interest.

We had three weeks for training as a squad before the Lions series. To my mind, that was time banked – we needn't cover the same ground again. The Lions series itself had been the actual foundation for the Tri Nations, as a game situation is the perfect match practice. In other words, there was no point in driving the guys too hard. And, also, the flight to New Zealand is very long, and the players travel there a couple of times a year, so they deserved additional time off. Thus, with four weeks left until the start of the Tri Nations, I sent them home. Let their families get on their nerves, I thought, so that they are happy to get back to the squad when the time comes.

I had to work hard at convincing my assistant coaches to accept my way of thinking. They both reckoned there was too much work left to do after the Lions tour for the players to have so much time off.

Remember, we had lost the last game in that series. I was also aware of the fact that some members of the SARU executive committee weren't happy with my decision. However, I cared only about what the players wanted. If more time off would help to motivate them for the task ahead, so much the better. And I think they appreciated the trust I placed in them.

So we travelled to Bloemfontein, the venue of the first Tri Nations test against the All Blacks, only a few days before the start of the preparation week. Everyone was now back from injury, so unfortunately there was no place for Adi Jacobs, one of my favourite players, in the starting team.

I always thought that Adi got a bit of a raw deal from the media, for which I partially blame Sharks coach John Plumtree. Because of Plumtree's attitude towards Adi, he was often written off. Plumtree didn't rate him, and it's a piece of information he shared with other players, who passed it on to Adi. And he didn't take it lightly. I am amazed at how long Adi's loyalty to the Sharks lasted, considering how badly they treated him.

Perhaps Dick Muir shares a bit of the blame for the fact that Adi came to be labelled as just a good bench player. It was while Dick was coaching the Sharks that Adi became a specialist impact sub. But I believed that Adi was good enough to start, which he proved on the several occasions he started for the Springboks. He was the sort of player who would always bail his team out of trouble.

I did consider moving Adi to inside centre for the 2009 Tri Nations, and I might even have gone ahead if he had been fit. But with Jean de Villiers and Jaque Fourie in the squad, we were well covered there. Funnily enough, I consider Jean a better outside than inside centre. I discussed this with him and suggested that I switch him. He was amenable to the idea, but on one condition: that he be allowed to continue wearing the No. 12 on his back. Because of his natural creative flair, I thought Adi was a better No. 12, but in the modern era, an inside centre is expected to be physical and crash the ball up, which was not his style. So I decided to stick with Jean.

I started the Tri Nations with Ruan Pienaar at flyhalf, but although he began the series with a strong all-round game, his inconsistent kicking forced my hand. Although I didn't exactly run out of patience with him, when the big games arrived, he just couldn't handle the pressure. So that was that. The question now was, do I play Ruan at No. 10 and get someone else to kick, or do I go with Morné Steyn, who had won so many games for the Bulls? Given our decision to play a more kicking-orientated game, it was obvious that Morné just had to play.

I sometimes think Ruan put far too much pressure on himself. He's the type of guy who, when it comes time to switch on, is on already. Morné can go and play golf and forget about rugby for a while. Ruan can never do that. So, given all these factors, after the first Tri Nations game, Ruan was never my first-choice flyhalf again.

We approached the Tri Nations very differently from the way we'd gone into the Lions series. No one mentioned the word 'winning' now, whereas against the Lions, winning was our only goal. Our emphasis had been only on the result. But for most of the four years of my tenure, we had the 2011 World Cup in mind – that was what we were preparing for. Our usual belief was that although you couldn't always exercise control over winning, you could control the way you prepared for a game. The Lions series was the one occasion on which everything depended on just winning those two games. What came afterwards did not matter.

So with the advent of the 2009 Tri Nations, we refocused on our long-term goal. Obviously winning was important, we knew that, but every result, like every performance, would be seen in the context of the build-up to 2011.

One of the factors in our favour was the confidence we had gained by beating the Lions. I think that privately everyone thought that if we could beat the British & Irish Lions, there was no reason we couldn't win the Tri Nations.

Also in our favour was the very good draw we had, as we were playing the All Blacks twice in South Africa. It is always difficult for the All Blacks or Wallabies to come to South Africa and win both their games. They tend to concentrate on winning one of the games, as they do in Super Rugby too. When they win that one, they gain the confidence to win another, and the game they target depends on where they are playing.

I didn't think they would target Bloemfontein, as the city is at altitude and they weren't very familiar with the place, as they never go there to prepare for Super Rugby. When overseas teams play against the Cheetahs, they tend to spend the preceding week at one of the cities at sea level – either Durban or Cape Town – and then fly to Bloemfontein either the night before the game or on match day. Again, the All Blacks spent the entire build-up to the match in Durban, which was quite ironic, as later in the competition the Kiwi media would give me loads of flak for not staying in Hamilton. Bloemfontein and Hamilton are similar in many ways.

We started well against the All Blacks, with Ruan Pienaar playing well at flyhalf, as I've mentioned. He missed several kicks, though, which made our task more difficult than it should have been, but then he scored an excellent try in the 26th minute that set us on our way. At 14-3 at half-time, we had built up a good buffer.

The All Blacks came back strongly in the third quarter, and it even looked like they might win at one stage, but we managed to stay ahead until, with eight minutes to go, Jaque Fourie was presented with an opportunity up the right touchline and he scored a spectacular try to seal a 28-19 win.

This victory was significant, as it allowed us to reclaim the number-one spot in the world rankings. I knew the All Blacks would now be under massive pressure for the Durban match. We reckoned that we could force them into making mistakes and playing the wrong game. And that was how it turned out. It wasn't easy, but we strangled them in the end. In fact, they were their own worst enemies. They tried to run from all over the place. It was suicide.

So, after two successive wins over New Zealand, we were suddenly in a very strong position on the log, with the game against Australia in Cape Town the last of the home leg. By this stage we were a settled team, and Morné Steyn was now assured that he was my number-one choice at flyhalf after his heroics against the All Blacks the week before, where he scored all the points in our 31-19 victory, which had been more convincing than the score line might suggest. After such a big win, we wanted to take the momentum into the Wallaby game. We knew that on the back of beating the All Blacks so comfortably, we would be up for the challenge. But as a coach, what do you say to the players at such a time? If you praise them too much and tell them they will win, you risk making them overconfident; and if you take a more cautionary tone, you might make them doubt themselves.

So I called in John Smit and Victor Matfield and told them that we must find a way of ensuring that we go into the game with a full tank of petrol and our tails up. There wasn't to be any negative talk. And again we won comfortably, with John Smit setting us on our way with a delightful little chip-kick that would have done justice to a flyhalf, and which resulted in a first-half try. It ensured that we were comfortably ahead throughout the game. Our 29-17 victory was a satisfactory way to end the home leg of our campaign, and we were able to head overseas with confidence

After three wins in a row, one might have thought I would be under less pressure, but that was not the case. Certain sections of the media now criticised me for the team's style of play, which they claimed was too conservative. Most of the criticism came from the Cape, where a few reporters seemed to think that all rugby consisted of was passing the ball to the wings.

But what matters to me is that I must like what I see when I look in the mirror; I must be confident that the decisions I make are for the good of the team and will improve their chances of doing well. And I wasn't going to be swayed by people who thought they could tell me how the team should play. I could make up my own mind about that, and the results were speaking for themselves. Some of my critics would probably have pointed out that we had only won our home games, but still, we had never before won quite so easily in the Tri Nations.

I'm a man who makes his own decisions, even though the selectors hated it and often argued with me. It was only when I doubted something that I sought advice. People simply didn't understand how I operated.

We had three games to play in the Antipodes, and I suspected that we might lose one of them – probably in Hamilton, in the last match against the All Blacks. I thought we had the ability to win both matches in Australia.

We surprised the Wallabies in our first tour game, played in Perth.

We had been playing conservative rugby up to that point, for which the Australian and Kiwi media had lambasted us. According to them, we were 'killing' rugby. So we wondered how our opponents would react if we suddenly did the unexpected and started running the ball …

Although we had planned to run the ball from the outset, to some extent the match in Perth also unfolded in a way that lent itself to that kind of game. We were still effective with our usual kicking game, too, and it played a massive part in our victory. The ball seemed to bounce just right for us, and Fourie du Preez's great decision-making was instrumental to our victory.

Jaque Fourie scored a brilliant try from a first-phase set move. It had been set up from one of the few scrums that we were given in the right area of the field that year. After we scored, the Aussies had to play catch-up, and that suited us just fine. By half-time we were out of sight and eventually won more comfortably than the 32-25 scoreline suggested. We already knew we had won the game when the Wallabies scored some late tries to salvage some pride.

But perhaps we'd won too comfortably, as we were overconfident the next week. We learnt a valuable lesson from that Brisbane defeat (6-21), where the Wallabies beat us at our own game and profited from a pinpoint kick-and-chase strategy.

Having lost that game, we had to win in Hamilton to clinch the Tri Nations trophy. Afterwards I reflected that, perhaps if we had won in Brisbane, we wouldn't have won on the other side of the Tasman Sea. I had some serious decisions to make before the final and deciding game of the Tri Nations: were we going to start preparing for the match from the Monday, or were we going to rely on the whole season's preparations to see us through, as we'd basically done against England the year before? Apart from five tough Tri Nations games, we had also played three tests against the British & Irish Lions, so I decided we'd go with the latter option.

I cancelled two practice sessions and instead we travelled to the Gold Coast for what turned out to be a mini holiday. We stayed in a very pleasant hotel with a very relaxed vibe about it, and the guys were able to completely escape from rugby for a few days. They surfed and swam and played touch rugby on the beach and had one hell of a time. In the end, we had only one training session in Brisbane before leaving for New Zealand.

My assistant coaches weren't happy with my decision, and I suppose you can't blame them. There we were, on our way to New Zealand, and we'd have only one practice session in Hamilton before playing the All Blacks in a must-win game. Although we could still win the Tri Nations if we lost by less than a certain margin, we wanted to do it the right way, by winning both the trophy *and* the match.

Fortunately, the break from rugby was of great benefit to us. When we arrived in New Zealand, their media tried to pile on the pressure. They knew we had a chance of beating them every time we played them, so the press tried to divide our unit. They attacked me mercilessly, alleging that the players and the assistant coaches were running the squad. But they couldn't split us, because I actually welcomed their attacks – they took the pressure off the players, who in turn rallied behind me, as they felt I was being treated unfairly. The guys often said that they didn't support me enough, but I told them that they could show their support by winning.

Apart from unsuccessfully trying to divide the team, the media also went bananas when I told them why I didn't want to base the team in Hamilton in the week preceding the test. As you all know by now, I am no diplomat – I just tell the truth when I'm asked a question. And there really isn't a lot to do in Hamilton. Ironically, as I've mentioned, those who were criticising me for finding Hamilton boring were the same people who hadn't wanted to spend time in Bloemfontein a few weeks earlier.

And it wasn't just the All Blacks and the local media we were up against in Hamilton … During the preparations for the game, Oregan Hoskins approached me and said that the IRB had informed him that they would not be able to vote for me as Coach of the Year, regardless of what happened in the last Tri Nations game. We had already won the series against the British & Irish Lions, so a Tri Nations win would have made us the top team in the world, but the IRB's decision didn't bother me. I don't coach for awards, I coach for the team.

Regan told me he hadn't wanted to tell me about the IRB's decision, but I said, 'So what? I don't coach for the IRB, I coach the Springboks!'

The reason why they didn't want me to be Coach of the Year was obvious – I was seen as an upstart. I had embarrassed the organisation with my comments about Schalk Burger in the eye-gouging controversy during the Lions series, and our little protest in the final test of that series against Bakkies's banning had probably been the last straw.

Later, after winning in Hamilton, we heard that an IRB official, who had attended the match in one of the hospitality suites, had said that it was a great pity we had won, as now they would have to make us Team of the Year. We were a bit hurt by that remark.

The Hamilton win will forever be remembered for the kicking exploits of Frans Steyn. Frans had played fullback for me in the first four Tri Nations games, but then, because he was heading overseas to play for Racing Métro 92, I decided to try Ruan Pienaar at fullback in the Brisbane match. I had called Frans in and told him I was leaving him out because I'd heard that he was going overseas and I wanted to find a way of fitting Ruan into the team. I thought maybe Ruan could handle the pressure better at fullback than he did at flyhalf.

Frans was open with me. He sat in my room and confirmed that he was going overseas. I told him I had no problem with that, even though I didn't want him to go. And Frans assured me that he was okay with being left out of the Brisbane match, but I knew he wasn't really.

When we arrived in Hamilton, and following the defeat in Brisbane, Ruan came to me and said that he thought I should play Frans, as it would be his final game. I told Ruan I had been considering recalling Frans anyway, but because of his generous gesture, I knew I was making the right decision. We played Frans, and he won us the match with his stupendous long-range penalties, which knocked the stuffing out of the All Blacks. That day, they learnt that they couldn't infringe even when 10 metres inside their *own* half.

After our 32-29 win, we celebrated much as we'd done earlier in the year, after winning the series against the British & Irish Lions. I stood apart from the players for a while, as I always did in moments when the team had triumphed, and then made my way into the changing room. We had won the Tri Nations and the series against the British & Irish Lions – surely no one could ask more from us?

Amid the celebrations, an incident occurred that I still find completely unacceptable: when Fourie du Preez wanted to have his photo taken with the Tri Nations trophy, some over-exuberant SARU officials spoilt the moment by snatching the trophy away from him so that they could have *their* picture taken with it. Funny how when you lose, no one wants to be part of the set-up or take responsibility, but when you win, somehow they make it their moment too ...

* * *

On a different note, by that stage the Eastern Cape team's bid to get into Super Rugby had become an issue again, and I knew that SARU's vice-president, Mark Alexander, was working closely with Cheeky Watson. I also suspected that Cheeky was continually working behind the scenes in an effort to oust me from my job, and I'd heard from Neels Liebel, our fitness advisor, who had good contacts, that they had set the end of the home leg of the Tri Nations as the deadline to dispose of me. They figured that the Boks would lose against the British & Irish Lions, and that subsequent home defeats in the Tri Nations would force SARU to fire me.

But we had won both series, so my enemies' plans had backfired badly. I imagined that they must have been seething. So I told Mark Alexander, 'You can phone your friend Cheeky now and ask him if he wants to take this trophy away from me too.'

After the second All Blacks home game, Neels said to me, 'Now you have really buggered up their plans.'

But I was still hearing how Cedric Frolick was telling people that he'd rather have a white coach who listened to him than a black coach who just did his own thing. Not that I cared too much about that – we had won the Tri Nations and reclaimed the number-one spot in the rugby world rankings.

18

A bump in the road

When I went into the changing room after the match, I was flushed with contentment for the players. They were so chuffed, and I was pleased for them that by winning the Tri Nations two years after winning the World Cup, they had finally ended the debate on whether they should be regarded as the finest rugby team on the planet. They had won everything that there was to win; there were no more barriers that needed breaking.

We had a heck of a party that night, and although we had to wake up at 5 a.m. the next morning to catch the plane to Auckland, the guys didn't hold back. People were running around cutting each other's clothes off. It was scary stuff, and I remember technical analyst Peter Maimane running for shelter with a terrified look on his face.

But nothing beat the feeling of pride when we landed at OR Tambo International Airport in Johannesburg. President Jacob Zuma had taken time off from his busy schedule to come and meet us. His appearance was the cherry on top and a moment we will savour for the rest of our lives.

But now the time had come for me to start planning for the World Cup, which was two years away. I had started to tick off items on my to-do list one by one as we had progressed over the past two years, but I still wasn't sure what the government expected of me. And arranging to meet with the Parliamentary Portfolio Committee on Sport and Recreation and the minister of sport was proving an impossible task. At the time, Makhankesi Stofile was still the minister, and the guys who had made up my reference or support group still had a big influence on the politics in South African sport, albeit behind the scenes.

I was keen to tell government about the plans I had for the Boks, as I thought the highest authority in the land should be informed of what I was doing. The newspapers were still criticising my transformation record, but it seemed to me that those who actually made the rules weren't keen to explain what they expected of me. It was as if they were giving me a blank cheque and then complaining when I spent the money.

Perhaps the problem was that no one had expected me to still be the coach, or perhaps the portfolio committee members were afraid that I was going to ask them for their support. But I would not have done so. Nevertheless, I found it odd that they couldn't find the time to speak to the Springbok coach. So I thought, 'To hell with you guys, then. I will just do what I feel is right.'

I also wanted to discuss my long-term future with SARU, as some of the players wanted to know whether I was staying on after the World Cup, but they weren't interested in discussing the matter at that stage. I had had a chat with Fourie du Preez about him taking over as captain of the Boks after the World Cup in order to facilitate the continuation of the team culture into the next era, but he was considering an offer from a club in Japan. Because my own future at SA Rugby was not assured, I had nothing to offer him as an incentive to stay.

But, most important of all, was setting up the structures for the World Cup. And that meant that the time had arrived to decide whether John Smit and Victor Matfield would be the team leaders for the next two years. I had promised John and Victor only two years in 2008, but I now knew that they both deserved to go to the World Cup. They were not only excellent players, but were also crucial to the team dynamic. The team revolved around those two, a factor that not many people outside of the inner circle comprehended. Half the players followed John, the other half Victor.

So if I played Bismarck du Plessis from the kick-off, I may have been starting with a superior hooker, but I would lack the leadership of the captain, who was an inspiration to his teammates on the field. When John wasn't on the pitch, guys like Schalk Burger missed both his presence and his leadership. Then, of course, there were the ambitions of the other players. When John and Victor were around, there disputing who the team leaders were. But when they weren't, of the senior players might have assumed that they could take ...... the role of team leader, making the leadership issue a lot more complicated.

Of course Bismarck du Plessis had every right to be pissed off at me for leaving him out of the starting line-up, but I simply couldn't afford to field him and, at the same time, have the other players misfire because John wasn't there to lead them. I wasn't prepared to take that risk, and in 2009 I was still reluctant to commit myself to a scenario that I might regret one day.

Had I known better at the time, I would have rested a lot of the senior campaigners for the end-of-year tour of Europe. But I made the wrong call. My judgement was impaired by the emphatic win we had scored against England at Twickenham 12 months earlier, which had been an important win for us in terms of how it contributed to our confidence and momentum going into 2009. But I didn't factor in the massive workload the players had had that year. Apart from the usual Super 14 tournament, the Tri Nations and also the last few Currie Cup matches, the Springbok players had been involved in an iconic series against the British & Irish Lions, which had exhausted them physically and, more importantly, emotionally. Their exhaustion was hardly surprising. Our season had started way back in January, and the players, particularly the Bulls guys who had won the Super 14 and the Currie Cup, had claimed every trophy that was up for grabs.

But there were also a few players who were approaching the 100-game mark – which was a bit of a problem. Although they were tired, they were eager to notch up the requisite test caps. And the public and rugby administrators also wanted to continue the momentum of the southern hemisphere season. Everyone knew Ireland would be targeting us in the big game of the tour, as they had a number of British & Irish Lions in their ranks who were smarting after losing the series. They had also enjoyed a successful season and were seen as our main competition for the IRB Team of the Year award.

So, given all these factors, I thought we should go out and win all the remaining games to cap off a resoundingly successful year.

Of course I knew almost from the outset that I was not doing the right thing. I should have taken Professor Noakes's advice to rest the top players, and I also might have temporarily lost sight of our long-term goal, which was to win the World Cup. If we had used that tour as an opportunity to blood a new team, we would have produced a much better Tri Nations performance in the World Cup year and would have been under less pressure in the build-up to the global tournament.

This is where South African rugby needs an expert advisor who runs a rugby department within SARU. I would have found it very useful to have had a person in that position who could have taken me aside and pointed out that, after such a brilliant year, the end-of-year results weren't so important. As we discovered the following year, you can take a relatively under-strength Springbok team on a northern hemisphere tour and still win major games.

The tour wasn't a complete disaster, though. In the midweek games, in which we fielded what was essentially a South Africa A-side, we could assess the players who potentially could start for the Boks. But, at the same time, I also realised the folly of giving cheap caps away.

We could argue forever about why the midweek losses came about, but the part that disturbed me was the lack of pride some players displayed in the Springbok jersey. And I was so shocked by the poor scrumming performance in the first game against the Leicester Tigers that I sent some of the front-row forwards home.

Jannie du Plessis, Chiliboy Ralepelle and Gurthrö Steenkamp were so passionless about their performances that I just got really fed up. Chiliboy was forced out of the tour with an injury sustained in the Leicester defeat, but I also sent Jannie and Gurthrö home, thinking that it might be the end of their international careers. The official explanation, which was reported in the press, was that they had injuries, but in reality I just couldn't tolerate how little pride they had in the Springbok jersey.

In my opinion, they had just given up in the game against the Tigers, and it made no sense to me how anyone could ever just give up when they are wearing the Springbok jersey. If I had ever been given a chance to wear it, I would have been prepared to die for the cause.

So when the medical team told me that these players had niggling injuries, I made up my mind to send them home. At the time, Jannie

sis seemed to think that he could be a Springbok just by going
the motions. Perhaps he didn't have enough competition at
prop. But some time afterwards, fortunately, he changed my
mind and became an anchorman among the forwards. In fact, he
would become my unsung hero in the 2010/11 team.

While I'd thought that was the end of the rugby road for those
guys, they both proved me wrong the next year. After the 2010 Super
14 tournament, they told me that being sent home had been a wake-
up call for them. Gurthrö worked so hard in the end that he won the
South Africa Player of the Year award in 2010. So if I treated them
harshly, at least it brought about a positive result.

Earl Rose was one of the players who did well in the midweek games,
and, in retrospect, I should have sent Ruan Pienaar home, as he did
not play at his best on that trip, and put Earl on the bench instead. But
it turned out to be Earl's last tour of my tenure. He seemed to fade away
quickly afterwards, which was tragic, as he had amazing talent. He was
a sad example of a black player who had been failed by the system. Part
of the problem is that few coaches understand the psychology of black
players.

I had a lot of time for Earl as a player. Along with Thabang Molefe,
he'd helped us win the IRB under-21 title in 2005. But he could be a
very emotional guy at times. At one under-21 tournament, Bismarck
du Plessis had to go home early after breaking an ankle, and Earl came
to my room in tears.

'You know what, coach? I realised today that every day is potentially
your last day, and every tour is potentially your last tour,' he said.

Critics often accused Earl of not caring enough about his rugby, and
that he was too happy-go-lucky in his approach. But I knew him to be
very passionate about and committed to the sport, and his emotional
reaction to Bismarck's misfortune during that under-21 tournament
was just one instance where he disproved the general perception.

On another occasion while I was coaching the under-21s, I gave
everyone in the squad a piece of paper on which they could write down
their problems as the first step in trying to overcome them. Earl was
the only player who actually signed the piece of paper, which was supposed to be anonymous. A lot of the other players had problems with

the captain as well as other issues, but Earl just wrote: 'I have no problems. Whatever the team decides, I'm in.'

As a player, Earl never let me down. At the end of my first year with the Springboks, I thought that he might be the transformational force our game needed. Not necessarily in the starting team, but certainly coming off the bench.

Over the years, the provincial unions have coached many black players with plenty of talent, but not always successfully, Mzwandile Stick, Adi Jacobs, Thabang Molefe, Thando Manana and the late Solly Tyibilika among them. But when I worked with those guys, I quickly realised what the real problem was. The system was the problem, not them. The white coaches who coached them at the unions didn't understand that they had creative minds and just saw things differently.

If you told Solly Tyibilika that you wanted him to set up a ball, he would want to know why. He would say, 'Agh no man, why must I do that when I can just go around the defender?' I had similar conversations with Earl Rose, but I soon figured out how to handle him. With Earl, you had to make him believe that he was the one making the decision. Let's say he is playing at fullback and running from the back more than you want him to – you sit him down and tell him how brilliant he is, but also ask why he ran the ball with so many defenders lined up in front of him. Chances are that he will then say that he shouldn't have done it. And he will make a note not to do it again.

Earl may be 10 years ahead of his time. He will run through you when he could have run around you, and while that may be criticised now, as it doesn't conform to the norm, perhaps in time it will be seen as a good thing. Schalk Burger is an example of a white player who is very creative. But if he wasn't white, selectors might have dismissed him as a stereotype and he may have found it more difficult to become a regular in the starting line-up. I am not denigrating Schalk or knocking his status as one of South Africa's truly great players – far from it. But Schalk likes to do his own thing on the field, and that has often been exactly what black players are criticised for. In our 2011 World Cup game against Samoa, we needed Schalk to drive us forward. Instead, he ended up being the guy who made the most passes. If someone like Solly Tyibilika had done something similar, he might have been

d because he wasn't following instructions. He would have been
red a problem player.

remains a factor in rugby, whether people want to believe it
or not. Often, too much notice is taken of a player's background and
origin, which can cloud your judgement. At the 2011 World Cup, we
turned a blind eye when John Smit and some of his fellow senior
players stole a signboard while on a road trip in New Zealand. The
incident made all the local newspapers, but we just laughed it off. After
all, the guys were just letting off steam. But what would the reaction
have been had Ricky Januarie stolen that sign? As Ricky was regarded
as a 'problem' player, the public might not have been as accepting.

I had plans in mind for Earl after the 2009 end-of-year tour, so I
wanted Dick Muir, who was coaching the Lions in the following year's
Super 14, to give him an extended run. Dick agreed with me about
Earl's potential, but then he left Earl out of the Lions team. I couldn't
understand why. That was one of the reasons I wasn't happy with Dick
coaching the Lions, despite the fact that I had initially supported the
idea. I'd thought that Dick was aware of how I wanted to operate; he
knew how frustrated I was that I had no support from the Super Rugby
coaches apart from Frans Ludeke at the Bulls. But Dick followed his
own head – so I guess I can't blame him, as I am much the same. It
irritated me that by not selecting Earl, as we had agreed, he sent out
the wrong message about the player.

But back to the end-of-year tour, where we lost both midweek
games (to Leicester Tigers (17-22) and Saracens (23-24)) *and* two of
the three tests. The game against France was a disaster right from the
start. The singer Ras Dumisani set the tone for the day when he made
a complete hash of our national anthem. I am still convinced it was a
ploy by the French, who can be quite crafty. Normally a touring team
is given the names of three performers from which it can choose the
singer, but we weren't given any choice before that match.

The singing of the anthem is extremely important to the Springboks,
as it is as inspiring to them as the haka is to the All Blacks. So when Ras
botched it up, it wasn't funny at all. I am not even slightly exaggerating
the importance of the anthem – if you talk to the Boks, they will vouch
for it.

The weather on tour was also particularly poor. It was bitterly cold and windy in Toulouse, and it was -2°C and foggy when we played Ireland in Dublin. For us South Africans, it just felt crazy to be playing in those conditions.

We had left our departure for France until the last minute, something we were criticised for, but that did not play a role in our defeat. Long-haul overnight flights to Europe are no problem, as jet lag isn't a factor. And leaving later allows for some extra training in the good weather back home.

In Toulouse, the French hit us incredibly hard – in fact, much harder than we were expecting. They came out with guns blazing in the knowledge that they were playing against the best team in the world. For us, it was just another game on the tour, and we slumped to a disappointing 13-20 defeat.

We had a tough time in the scrums, with the French camping on the offside line, which cut down our space. John Smit was still at tighthead then, but that experiment was about to be terminated. It would, in fact, stop the very next week, in the match against Italy in Udine.

After the disastrous opening midweek game, I'd sent Jannie du Plessis and Gurthrö Steenkamp home and had summoned BJ Botha from Ulster, with Adriaan Strauss replacing Chiliboy Ralepelle. Strauss was one of the unluckiest South African rugby players of my time. He was good enough to be in any other international side, but was kept out of the Bok side by players like John, Bismarck and Chiliboy. If a player is not good enough for international level, so be it, but in Adriaan's case, that was not true. He was just around at the wrong time.

The scrumming had been our Achilles heel on tour up till then, but fortunately it came right against Italy. The Italians had expected to dominate us in the scrums, as Martin Castrogiovanni, who had given us such a tough time in the Tigers game, was packing down at tighthead. But we handled him in the first 60 minutes, and then, when BJ Botha came on, he made a massive difference to our scrumming. John then moved to hooker, and we decided we'd stick with that front row for the following week's game.

So we beat Italy 32-10 before moving on to our final game of a momentous year with our confidence slightly boosted. Unfortunately, most of the players were by now running on empty. Normally the England game is seen as the big match of the end-of-year tour, but this time we weren't playing England – the match at Croke Park in Dublin was the one we were focused on. After all, the Irish were the reigning European champions.

We were aware of the fact that we weren't having the perfect build-up to the clash against Ireland, where we were expecting to play in front of 80 000 spectators. The weather was simply horrendous; it rained all the time we were there, and then, to make matters worse, Ireland came at us in much the same way France had. Gert Smal was Ireland's assistant coach, and although we had changed some of our strategies so that he would not be familiar with them, the former Springbok assistant coach must have done his homework on video, for he knew exactly where to stop us.

We might actually have won that game had Victor Matfield not got concussed. After that knock, he didn't know where he was. He couldn't even remember the line-out calls and got them wrong three times, including once right on Ireland's try line. I can't remember that ever happening at any other time with Victor. I suppose that pretty much summed up our tour – it was just a bridge too far at the end of a very long, eventful season.

I had sat John down before the game and told him that, as we were now okay at tighthead, I would like him to move back to hooker. I backed up my reasoning by pointing out that I had sent Jannie du Plessis home, which I would not have done if I didn't think we had adequate tighthead cover.

Just as I had asked John to put on weight for the switch to prop, I now asked him to lose weight, which he did. However, when John got back to the Sharks, he wasn't given much game time at hooker. I am not sure what happened there, but perhaps John should have decamped to the Lions, where he could have picked up the necessary experience in that position, thus avoiding the selection issue between him and Bismarck.

It should be noted that Bismarck and Jannie du Plessis come as a package, and I think some dealings conducted behind closed doors hurt John's standing at the Sharks. If the Sharks had been honest with

John and told him that he would now be a second-string player only, he could have moved to another franchise. Instead they appointed him captain so that he would feel there was good reason to stay in Durban. Had he moved to the Lions, we certainly would not have experienced the problems we did in the World Cup year, when he just never got enough playing opportunities.

On our overseas tour, we lost four of our five matches (including the two midweek games), yet it was not a massive setback in our World Cup preparations, as it was obvious that the players were exhausted. And we still won the IRB Team of the Year award, with Declan Kidney of Ireland deservedly being rewarded as Coach of the Year.

Although it was great to be named Team of the Year, we still arrived home feeling that we had let ourselves down on the tour.

19

A downward spiral

After a superb year in 2009, I was a little concerned that some members of my management team were getting ahead of themselves. The danger we faced after our previous successes was that we might think we had reached our goal and could now rest on our laurels. I had experienced this with previous winning teams, and evidence pointed towards it happening again at the end of 2009.

When a Springbok team loses, only the coach has to face the media, the public and the criticism. Whereas other management members are sheltered from the barbs of the critics and can get on with their lives, I have to prepare myself to address a press conference to explain what happened. Conversely, when the Springbok team wins, everyone wants to claim credit for it. After our successful year, everybody suddenly wanted to feature in the press. Management were falling all over one another to let everyone out there know how much they had contributed to our success. I suppose it was perfectly natural for them to want to take advantage of the situation and get some personal reward for the role they had played.

But their enthusiasm had to be curbed, or it would cause problems for the Springboks. And I said as much when I met with two Cape journalists, Ashfak Mohamed of the *Cape Times* and Stephen Nell of *Die Burger*, for a press briefing in Paarl in the early part of 2010. I wanted to convey to those concerned that although each and every member of management had a role to play, there was a structure that pointed to the tip, and the tip could only be strong if the base supported it.

In other words, I was saying that the players remained the most important factor in the Bok set-up, and that each member of the management team was there only because of them. I had told them exactly that at our first-ever meeting, in Somerset West, before our first training camp in 2008.

In the press briefing, I mentioned that a few harsh words might be exchanged within the management structure when we met up, but Ashfak ended up writing things I can only say were the product of his imagination. Stephen was there as well and yet his story differed completely from Ashfak's. While *Die Burger* printed what I had said, the *Cape Times* ran a front-page piece insinuating that I was not only having a go at the assistant coaches, but also wanted to get rid of one of them.

Gary Gold took exception to this and came out and saw me in Paarl. I told him the story was a fabrication and that I had no intention of sacking him. After all, as the person who had appointed him, it would be my judgement that would be called into question if he were now deemed not good enough. I assured him that all I had said was that we should all be humble after our success, and that my words had not been directed at him alone, or at Dick Muir, for that matter.

When we eventually got together, it wasn't even necessary for me to stress the point, as members of the management team raised the matter themselves by saying that the atmosphere in the group had changed. That gave me my platform. I said, 'No, the atmosphere hasn't changed. What has changed is that we have now tasted success, and success can lead people to think that they are now too important to perform the basic requirements that were part of their job from the start.'

That was really what all the fuss was about, but it started the year on a negative note for all of us, as the so-called rift in the management team the press were talking about had been cast into the public spotlight. Gary was also upset because I had praised the Stormers forwards coach Matthew Proudfoot in the *Cape Times* article, which no doubt made him feel a bit insecure.

But that hadn't been my intention either. I had said to the two journalists that I had started coaching the Boks with the intention of bringing in consultants whenever it was necessary for us to do so. I'd said that we must use the intellectual capital available to us in this country and, more as an example, I cited how well the Stormers forwards were doing. But I also praised the Stormers backs, so I don't know why that wasn't misconstrued too. Surely I was after the services of Allister Coetzee and Robbie Fleck too? But Ashfak didn't mention any other coach in his article – he just said that Proudfoot was being considered as an assistant coach.

Although Gary was upset with me for quite a while, I didn't take much notice of it. I knew what I had said and that I hadn't done any-thing wrong. Gary should have known by then how the media operated. I pointed out to him that Stephen Nell had also been at the interview and had written a completely different article to the one that had appeared in the *Cape Times*. As far as I was concerned, that was the end of it. If South African rugby needed Proudfoot, then I would have been duty bound to involve him, but only as a consultant, in the same way I'd utilised former French prop Pieter de Villiers the previous season. And when scrumming was a problem on the 2009 end-of-year tour, I'd brought Os du Randt in. I had actually called him in more for the psychological reinvigoration he could inspire in the forwards than anything else. As a two-times World Cup winner and a legendary Springbok, I thought he would lift the team's spirits. Scrumming is very technical, but a lot of it is also in the mind. If Os gives advice to a player, he thinks, 'I'd better pay attention … this guy has won two World Cups …'

Far from being dissatisfied with my assistant coaches, I was actually more than happy with them. I knew how hard both Gary and Dick worked behind the scenes and the value they brought to the team. I have mentioned the differences in their philosophies, but it wasn't a major issue. The essential difference between them was that Gary was the sort of guy who needed several paragraphs to say what was on his mind, while Dick needed a sentence. Dick lived his life spontaneously – he would go into town not knowing or caring how he was going to get back, whereas Gary wouldn't go anywhere without knowing that there was someone to pick him up to drive him home. Gary needed assurances. That was really all it came down to. The two of them actually got on tremendously well.

Time to relax – catching a Chelsea match at Stamford Bridge during the build-up to the Twickenham test in 2010

Annelee Murray

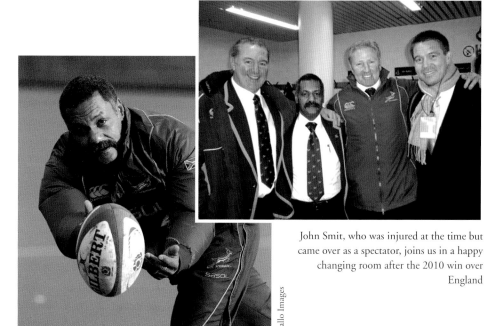

John Smit, who was injured at the time but came over as a spectator, joins us in a happy changing room after the 2010 win over England

Annelee Murray

Gallo Images

Showing the photographers that, even though it is some time since I last played, I can at least still pass the ball

Annelee Murray

Attending a post-match dinner with wife Theresa at Twickenham

Gallo Images

Handing out jerseys at the Nederburg Primary School in Paarl

Greeting Springbok fans from the Bok bus

Having a laugh with Pierre Spies on the practice field at
Ravensmead, Cape Town, 8 July 2011

Victor and John after beating
New Zealand in the 2011
Tri Nations – their last game
on home soil

Battle-scarred after beating Australia at Loftus in Victor's 100th
match: Jannie du Plessis, John Smit and Gürthro Steenkamp

AP Photo / SNPA, Ross Setford / Picturenet

Francois Hougaard scores against Wales, 11 September 2011

AP Photo / Themba Hadebe / Picturenet

Welsh coach Warren Gatland congratulates me after our nail-biting victory, 11 September 2011

Watching Wales play Ireland at the 2011 Rugby World Cup – with defence coach Jacques Nienaber and technical analyst Rassie Erasmus

We had a few trying moments along the way, but towards the end of my tenure as Bok coach, I had started getting on very well with Frans Steyn

Bryce Lawrence commiserates with Victor Matfield at the end of the quarter-final match against Australia, 9 October 2011

A portrait of me with team leaders Victor Matfield and John Smit that I keep in a proud place at my home in Paarl

The De Villiers family – me, daughters Odile and Claudia, and wife Theresa

Who knows what tomorrow will bring? With Bokkie at my home in Paarl

Later in the year I was to compromise my own principles when I agreed to look for alternative assistant coaches, but more on that later. At the time these stories appeared – during the 2010 Super 14 season – I had no intention of firing my assistants.

For the purposes of advancing Springbok rugby, the brilliant Super Rugby season both the Bulls and the Stormers experienced in 2010 was actually more of a hindrance than a help. Coupled with the fact that we were the Tri Nations champions and had won the series against the British & Irish Lions, two South African teams had advanced to the Super 14 final. It just added to the complacency that would trip us up at international level.

For some of the players, the definition of success was starting to become something other than the winning of rugby matches. It now revolved around the number of international caps a player could accumulate, or how many more sheep or cattle he could buy, or how much more money he could earn in order to pay for a lavish wedding.

This mindset had first emerged during the 2009 end-of-year tour, when some players were interested only in adding to their number of international caps instead of trying to win rugby matches. It was my mistake not to anticipate the consequences of the success we had enjoyed. Instead, I trusted the players to motivate themselves into a competitive frame of mind, which was a major reason why we would stumble in 2010.

The guys thought they just had to pitch up for a game and their opponents would roll over and die. They didn't understand that if you want to stay the best, you have to keep on improving.

In addition, I made some errors in my selections, which threw the team out of balance. We were without Heinrich Brüssow for the entire international season, and then Bakkies Botha was suspended. So we were essentially robbed of two fetchers, as I see Bakkies's role as a cleaner also as a fetching role. He hits the rucks so hard, opposition teams struggle to get the ball back quickly.

So once again, as in my first season as Bok coach, we had too many ball carriers and not enough cleaners and fetchers, with ball carriers now queuing up to carry the ball while no one was scavenging for it on the floor. It meant that we weren't able to react fast enough at the break-down, where New Zealand and Australia would now get the better of us.

Before kicking off the Tri Nations, we played Wales, France and Italy, and our results against Wales and France, in particular, just reinforced our perception that we were playing better than we actually were.

The Wales trip was detrimental for several reasons. I am not even sure why the tour was scheduled; the guys at SA Rugby blamed each other for adding it to our itinerary! There was no sense to such a trip, as it took place at the end of the week following the Super 14 final. Normally we would have used that time to regroup and assess injuries and start our planning for the season.

Nevertheless, I had an idea for the Wales game. In order to assess new and current talent, I wanted to take three Springboks from each of the major unions and combine them with a few younger players and a smattering of overseas-based players. However, injuries and other factors put paid to that idea. For instance, Andries Bekker was injured and I had to fly out Victor Matfield. And we fought for a whole week to get Butch James released by Bath. Joe van Niekerk also couldn't make the tour because of injury, and Frans Steyn arrived overweight and out of shape. After the Wales test, I realised that the pace of the game in the southern hemisphere had become too fast for northern-based players, and I still stick to that view.

We ended up fielding a team that was a mix between first-choice and second-choice players, which didn't do us any favours. When we won the game against Wales, there was the perception that we'd done so with a second-string team, which just further promoted the mindset within the team that they were just so damn good.

But at least some new talent was coming through. Gio Aplon and Juan de Jongh, two young Stormers players who had been outstanding in the Super 14, played for us in Cardiff, and they also played for us against France the following week in Cape Town.

We flew back to South Africa on the Sunday after the Wales test, which gave us only five days to assimilate those players who had not gone to Cardiff into our game plan. To make matters worse, when we tested all the players in the early part of the week, we found that they weren't fit enough for international rugby.

And yet we still smashed France by a huge margin. 'How good are we? We just need to pitch!' the players thought. 'One of our teams won the Super 14, we beat Wales with an under-strength team after a hugely disrupted week, and then we smashed France, who had beaten us the last time we played.'

All those things thrown together in the same pot was a recipe for disaster.

We went on to beat Italy in both our test matches, but we weren't particularly impressive in either of them. Playing Italy after seeing off Wales and France probably wasn't a good idea, as we knew we would beat them. So more grist to the mill ...

I had a lot of issues to consider, such as that John Smit and Victor Matfield were both approaching their 100th game during the Tri Nations. They needed to be managed in such a way that they would celebrate their milestone matches on different days, which was one of the factors that directed my decision to rest both players for one game each in the Italy series.

With an eye on the forthcoming World Cup, I also wanted to use the Tri Nations to experiment with new players and different combinations. But we never fired in the competition. In hindsight, I should really have used the Italian matches, when we could have worked on our combinations, to prepare for the Tri Nations. But at the time we weren't even prioritising the Tri Nations; we were looking further into the future.

I was meeting regularly with Professor Tim Noakes of the Sports Science Institute to discuss our approach to the World Cup, and he advised that we rest the top players as much as possible in 2010. But after talking to him I would meet with the players, who didn't want to buy into his advice. I was caught between the devil and the deep blue sea. Noakes recommended that each player play only a certain number of games in the Super Rugby tournament, but the players didn't believe he was right. Or they didn't *want* to believe he was right. A lot of them would realise later that he *had* been right – they had played too much. But by then it was too late.

None of the unions wanted to rest their players either. John Plumtree of the Sharks told me that although we could use the Tri Nations to prepare for the World Cup if we wanted to, his job was to get bums on seats for his union. They had a business to run. And he was right about that too. The only way this conundrum can be avoided in future is if South African rugby sets up a new structure in which Super Rugby and the Springboks can work together for the greater good of both parties. We have to find a middle ground that will benefit both the provinces and the national team. It's certainly not happening at the moment.

Looking back, I realise I had foreseen the problems that were to confront us in the Tri Nations. And, as always seemed the case, I had once again managed to say something that got me into hot water with the politicians.

The fallout was sparked by a comment I made before our departure for New Zealand. The FIFA World Cup was being played in South Africa at the time and, like the rest of the country, we got swept up in the excitement. We were in Cape Town on the opening weekend of the tournament for the game against France at Newlands, and the players and management all enjoyed the vibe.

I soon realised, however, that if we got too caught up in the emotion that was sweeping the country, it would not help our cause in the Antipodes. I pointed this out to the players, and then mentioned it to the media. I think I said that having a World Cup in South Africa was not going to win us the Tri Nations. The Springboks were also representing our country and our people expected us to win.

I'm still not sure why anyone took umbrage to what I said. After all, it was our job to focus on the task ahead. Perhaps it just got lost in translation. Butana Komphela went mad. He called Oregan Hoskins, who then called me to ask me how I could say something negative about the World Cup. I explained what I had said, but he didn't appear to listen. Every time Komphela spoke, Regan reacted.

I wondered why Komphela took this stance. Surely as the chairman of the Parliamentary Portfolio Committee on Sport and Recreation, he should have been pleased that the Springbok coach was so focused on winning …

And as if we didn't already have enough sideshows to distract us, shortly before we departed for New Zealand – in fact, at the airport while we were walking through the departure lounge – a meeting was held between SARU administrators and SARPA to decide who owned the commercial rights to the players.

The meeting worried me. 'What if it doesn't have the right outcome for the players?' I thought. 'How am I going to motivate them to face the All Blacks and Australia if they aren't happy?'

These thoughts crossed my mind as I waited in international departures for the players to arrive from the meeting. The Boeing 747 was warming its enormous engines in preparation for taxiing onto the runway when they eventually pitched up. And I'm not exaggerating – the rest of the squad was already waiting on the plane when the players concerned stepped on board.

It indicated to me that the administration, like the players themselves, now thought we were invincible and could do as we liked.

And we may well have been invincible had the team managed to play together in the tests leading up to the Tri Nations. We didn't make full use of a great opportunity to turn the team into a coherent unit, and we struggled as a consequence. Defence proved particularly problematic, due to the massive differences between the defensive structures of the Stormers, the Bulls and the Sharks. They had all concentrated on different aspects of defence, so we had some players who were used to the rush defence and others who were used to standing back. We lacked a unified approach, and it didn't help that the players had played a minimum of 13 Super Rugby games since we had last played together as a team.

Although we had been aware of the situation before the tour, we never had time to straighten it out in training and had to do most of the work on the blackboard. It was a real mission to get the players to drop the habits they'd picked up at their franchises. We needed much more time on the training field to impose our patterns, but that was impossible after the players had spent so much time playing Super Rugby.

So when New Zealand and Australia forced turnovers at the breakdown, players like John Smit and Pierre Spies suddenly looked like they were out of their depth. But the system was to blame.

Still, we went into the Auckland game in a positive mood and were confident of winning. After all, we had beaten the All Blacks three times the previous year.

But after we were defeated in that game, in which we were made to look decidedly second-rate by an All Black team that was fired up to avenge the previous year's losses and won 32-12, we found ourselves in a downward spiral from which we couldn't extricate ourselves. The Tri Nations is an unforgiving competition, particularly when on tour and having to play three games in a row. There was little time to correct the technical mistakes that had crept into our game.

Also, we didn't start the Tri Nations as a team, but as a group of individuals who had happened to be very good the previous season. The players struggled to play off one another and there was no cohesion. Before we knew it, we had been beaten by 20 points. It was a shock to all our systems. We had had the better of the Kiwis in the previous year's Tri Nations and in the 2009 and 2010 Super 14 seasons, and now this.

But the players believed they could turn it around. They didn't realise there was a bigger problem to solve, and we couldn't lay our fingers on what exactly it was that was going wrong in the actual games. It was only much later that we realised we were struggling because we didn't have a proper distinction between cleaners and fetchers. In training, the systems still worked like a bomb. However, in a match, we couldn't string more than three phases together, and the more we discussed the issue, the more convinced we became that we could improve our performances and come right in the next match. But it didn't work out that way. We followed the 20-point defeat in Auckland with a 14-point defeat in Wellington a week later, and by the time we got to Brisbane for the match against Australia, injuries were compounding the crisis.

As the tour progressed, the aspects of our game requiring work started to accumulate, and we soon got to a point where we couldn't cover every-thing in one session. But we continued to have meetings to discuss the issues and we continued to believe we would set things right.

To make matters worse, John Smit had been diagnosed with a neck injury, which would force him out of rugby for quite a while after the Tri Nations. However, we asked him to continue playing for the sake of the team. It didn't help his performance on the field, though, as he con-tinued to struggle until the last Tri Nations test, against the Wallabies in Bloemfontein, when he finally pulled his game together.

Had Francois Louw been in top form, we might not have missed Heinrich Brüssow, who was injured, quite so much. Louw had played well as a fetcher in the games against Wales, France and Italy, but when it came to the big tests against the All Blacks, he did not make an impression and was dropped after Wellington.

Once we got home, we had more time to prepare, and the upshot was that we were much improved when we played the All Blacks at the FNB Stadium – a huge game for us. John Smit was making his landmark 100th appearance in front of nearly 100 000 people. But a problem surfaced in that game that would also occur in some of the later games – we just couldn't finish off our scoring opportunities.

Despite leading for most of the time, the final move of the match cost us the game. The All Blacks had struggled initially, but gradually they managed to pick up some momentum and, when they drew level just before the final whistle, we thought they would settle for a draw. But they weren't finished, and when John Smit missed a crucial tackle, the All Blacks ran through to score the winning try in the last move of the match. The final score: 22-29. It was heartbreaking.

Fortunately we enjoyed a different scenario the next week at Loftus Versfeld, when Victor celebrated his 100th game and had a bit more luck than John. Although we fell well behind early on in the match, when we appeared to have massive defensive problems and conceded three early tries, we fought our way back to win, with Victor crowning his celebratory day with an influential performance in all aspects of the game. After what had gone before, it was with some relief that we celebrated our 44-31 win.

I had dispensed with Frans Steyn, who I thought was unfit, after the first game of the year, telling him to go and get his act together, and many critics slammed me for leaving him out. But I had planned to bring him back for the home leg of the Tri Nations, which I now did.

By the Loftus game, Frans was starting to become the consummate professional he was later to be. He would impress me a great deal at the 2011 World Cup. Unfortunately, earlier on, our relationship was embroiled in much controversy. Frans had shown how talented he was in my first year as Bok coach, but he had also been too individualistic on the field. As a result, he didn't make the cut with me in 2008. A player with such talent should add to the team, but Frans was playing just for himself.

At the time, I believed that Frans was being held back because he had achieved success at a young age without having had any proper life experience. I also believed that he was going to be one of the greatest Springboks ever, and, paradoxically, not only because of his prodigious talent, but because he had tasted success so young. I was hoping that he would go on to play 150 test matches for his country, so I didn't want him to leave South Africa, but his decision to move to France turned out to be the right one for him personally. His stay in Paris matured him. But as far as how many international caps he could achieve, it was the wrong decision.

In the first part of 2010, one could only get hold of Frans via his agent, Gerrie Swart, and I may be wrong, but Gerrie might not always have acted in his best interests. Because Springbok management had to make contact with Frans via Gerrie, it inevitably led to miscommunication. Whatever Gerrie relayed to Frans was either misconstrued or quoted incorrectly, and I also wasn't sure that everything Gerrie and I discussed in confidence stayed just between the two of us. Frans really believed in Gerrie, but in my opinion Gerrie didn't help Frans to get back to the Springboks.

Gerrie would come to an agreement with Andy Marinos, the SARU manager of national teams, but then something would happen that would throw a spanner in the works. So Frans stayed in France and we couldn't talk to him. If it weren't for that, he may have had 70 caps by now – it was what I wanted for him. But at first I had to be hard on the young man in order to be a good mentor to him in the long term.

But Frans didn't leave for France just because of me – other factors also influenced his decision. For example, the Sharks were using him in too many different positions. Before Frans made his decision to leave South Africa, he wanted to play inside centre. I was honest with him and told him that Jean de Villiers was my number-one inside centre, but as he was younger, stronger and faster than Jean and could also kick, he would probably replace Jean in time. But I told Frans that he needed to work hard in order for that to happen. I wasn't just going to select him on talent alone.

When I met with Frans when the team was together during the 2010 Tri Nations, and again when I went to meet with him and Gerrie in France before the World Cup the following year, I told him that I couldn't understand why all this nonsense was going on between us. I asked him why, if I could approach John Smit and Victor Matfield and get their support, I couldn't get his. Then he understood.

Frans often got very emotional during our conversations, but when I saw how much he had matured in 2011, I think I can say that I succeeded in what I'd set out to do. Our relationship improved to such an extent that by the time we reached New Zealand for the World Cup, he often sought out my company.

Frans's attitude might have changed during the home leg of the 2010 Tri Nations, but he still looked a bit rusty and couldn't help prevent the two losses we suffered in three home tests. The Wallabies even managed to break a long dry spell in South Africa by winning the final game with a late penalty from Kurtley Beale.

In the first half of that game, Australia scored at will; it was as if we weren't even on the field. At half-time, as I went down to the changing room with my assistant coaches to talk to the players, large sections of the Vodacom Park crowd yelled some really nasty abuse at me. Ag, they were very angry with me. But unlike two years earlier, when spectators had hurled abuse at me before my first test, there were no racial slurs on this occasion, so I could handle the comments. In fact, I understood the crowd's reaction completely. They are the people who indirectly pay our salaries and so have every right to be miffed when we're not producing the goods. In the second half, when we started fighting back, the crowd's attitude changed completely.

But a comeback can't last for 40 minutes, and once we'd caught up with Australia, who had led 31-6 just before half-time, chances were that we would not be able to sustain the momentum. As a rule of thumb, teams tend to ease back once they have drawn level after rallying from a deficit. The final score was 41-39 to the Wallabies, bringing to an end an unhappy Tri Nations campaign for us.

While we had a passage of play in the third quarter where we'd been unstoppable, much as Australia had been in the first half, we'd fallen behind early in a game far too often that season and it was clear that all was not well. We had a lot of work to do before we could even think about putting up a worthy challenge in the following year's World Cup.

A last place in the Tri Nations, with five defeats in six starts, was confirmation of how much we had slipped since the heady achievements of the year before.

20

Every man has his price

We were not only under pressure on the field during the 2010 Tri Nations – a lot happened off the pitch too. When we got back to South Africa, some major controversies were occurring that, had it not been for the performance clause I had had written into my contract, could have cost me my job.

But these events were foreshadowed by what happened in Australia in the build-up to the match in Brisbane.

I had been unhappy with the refereeing throughout the overseas leg of the competition, and had even exchanged words with some of the referees, which I will go into later. I had also ruffled a few feathers by saying publicly that we might have to cheat to be able to compete with New Zealand captain Richie McCaw at the breakdown. Everyone in rugby would have known what I meant by that – the openside flankers are always living on the boundary of the law. It's their job.

When Bakkies Botha was yellow-carded early in the opening game in Auckland, it was for a first offence in the red zone. It came soon after an incident that the referee hadn't picked up, when Bakkies had very stupidly headbutted All Black scrumhalf Jimmy Cowan. The Botha/Cowan incident was run over and over on the big screen at the stadium during a break in play. Referee Alan Lewis could not have missed it. Although Bakkies had been in the wrong, technically Lewis should not have sent Bakkies off for the minor red-zone offence, and to us it seemed as if he was reacting to what he had seen on the screen. As so frequently happened when we played in New Zealand and Australia, we seemed to be getting the short end of the stick in on-field refereeing decisions.

So it was an issue bubbling under the surface when I appeared on a rugby show on Australian television. I said the following in a video excerpt run on the *Rugby Club* television programme: 'I've got my own observations about the last two tests and I can't say it in public. But we do have a World Cup in New Zealand next year, and maybe it was the right thing for them to win the games so [that] they can attract more people to the games next year.'

Was I saying that there was a conspiracy and that the referees were cheating? I suppose you can interpret my words that way if you are shown only the part of the interview that was broadcast. But my words in their entirety were a different story. Of course, they were misinterpreted. I was accused of saying that the IRB was allowing cheating in order to fill seats at the 2011 World Cup. I acted quickly to refute this interpretation of what I'd said by issuing a statement.

It said: 'In no manner did I suggest that the All Blacks were being favoured – by match officials or anyone else – because their country was hosting the Rugby World Cup next year. I have stated many times during the past weeks that the All Blacks were better than us in their victories in Auckland and Wellington. Whilst I have also expressed unhappiness over some refereeing issues, this is a separate matter altogether and has no bearing on what I said.

'My comment during the *Rugby Club* interview was based on the general view that part of the success of any World Cup event rests on the fact that the host nation has a winning team. This view has been misinterpreted and I wish to make it clear that I had no other intention than to make that specific point. Nevertheless, I regret that this may have created the wrong impression and raised undue concern for South Africa, New Zealand and Australia Rugby (SANZAR) and the Rugby World Cup 2011 organisers.'

I thought that would be enough to put the matter to rest, but some of the media persisted in their view that I was claiming the existence of a conspiracy. On the basis of what I'd said in the television interview and in my statement, Simon Jelowitz of New Zealand, who worked as a citing commissioner out of Wellington, laid an official complaint against me with SANZAR.

But the communication experts at SARU and the acting CEO Andy

Marinos managed to obtain footage of the entire interview, and if you listened to all of what was said, it was clear that my words were being misinterpreted. SANZAR called a hearing, but by then we were back in South Africa and it had to take place by teleconference.

Jelowitz was part of the telecon, and my legal team asked him whether he had seen the interview in full. He said no, but that it hadn't been necessary, as he had seen what I had said on television and had read the newspapers. He was convinced that I was bringing rugby into disrepute. Of course that said it all for him. He was adamant that I was in the wrong.

And he remained adamant even when the judge, who was presiding over the hearing, explained to him that if he had read the entire transcript of the tape, he would have known that his case just wasn't going to stick. But even after hearing that, Jelowitz still wanted me to be fined and was very angry that I was going to be acquitted!

In the end, I didn't have to say anything in my defence. There were enough other people taking part in the teleconference who took Jelowitz on. And so the charge was dismissed. Andy Marinos was instrumental in getting me acquitted, as was my media manager at the time, Anthony MacKaiser. Apart from putting every effort into getting hold of the tape, they had also worked hard at obtaining other relevant documentation.

However, I again felt that SA Rugby was not making enough of my acquittal. Their attitude irked me, as it was obvious to me that although the New Zealanders and Australians couldn't stand each other, they would do everything within their power to work against South Africa when any kind of incident occurred. In contrast, we South Africans always seemed to be bowing and scraping to gain favour with them.

But on that occasion the media fuss around the incident worked to our advantage. Perhaps it favoured rugby too, for suddenly the spotlight fell on the referees and rugby refereeing became a talking point. The Australian Rugby Union coaching coordinator, David Nucifora, and Wallaby coach Robbie Deans even met with me in Bloemfontein during the home leg of our Tri Nations campaign to discuss the issue.

In fact, they told me that they felt the same way I did. Their suggestion was that the coaches should stand together against any indication that the international referees and the IRB were favouring New Zealand or, by the time all our teams arrived in New Zealand for the World Cup, the All Blacks might have an unfair advantage.

I told Robbie that I would throw my lot in with him, provided that we did indeed all band together and I would not be left as man alone again. Robbie then contacted some of the other international coaches, but as far as I can gather someone high up put an end to it. So nothing really changed.

On that same *Rugby Club* programme and pertaining to certain parts of the same pre-recorded interview, former Wallaby Brendan Cannon called me a clown, asking how the senior players in the Springbok team could 'listen to a clown like [Peter de Villiers]'.

The Springbok management thought this was quite rich coming from someone like Brendan, as he wasn't exactly a rocket scientist himself, but we called the television station, Fox, who were the rights-holders with SANZAR and, hence, effectively business partners with SA Rugby. When we threatened never to talk to them again, they quickly pulled Cannon into line and he had to make a public apology.

But that wasn't the end of the pressure I was under, nor was it the last time that year that I had to point people in the direction of the full transcript of a recording. It happened again when SARU's exco members wanted to dismiss me because of comments I'd allegedly made in support of Blue Bulls prop Bees Roux, who was arrested for murder and later convicted of manslaughter following an incident in Pretoria in which a Metro policeman was killed.

The story broke on the morning of our test against the Wallabies at Loftus. That morning, as I was heading to the gym in Pretoria, I saw the newspaper billboards and hoped that SARU would release a statement. In fact, I asked them to release one, but they refused because it 'wasn't their jurisdiction'. Bees Roux was a Bulls player, they said, and he was therefore the Bulls' responsibility.

I felt uncomfortable, because I knew the media guys would ask me about it at the first opportunity. Not being one to run away from any question with a 'no comment', you can understand my apprehension in this case. I can't, in fact, recall if I've ever used the words 'no comment'.

The tragic circumstances of the Bees Roux incident touched me deeply, and I talked about it in the team meeting on the morning of the test. The media were reporting that Bees had been violently drunk when the incident occurred, and I advised the players that if they wanted to drink, they should rather do so in their own bar at home, where they could drink as much as they liked without it affecting other people or placing them in harm's way. I told them about the dangers of drinking and the possibility that unscrupulous people could spike their drinks.

No one can condone the killing of another human being, and I for one am not callous enough to even suggest anyone should commit such an act. But I did say that circumstances beyond anyone's control sometimes warranted some sympathy for the perpetrator, as they could make a person act irrationally. I reminded the guys that they were always in the public eye and should thus make the right decisions in their lives. As long as they were representing their country, they couldn't expect to lead a normal life.

There was no mention of the Bees Roux incident at the post-match press conference after the Loftus test, but the subject was raised at the Monday press conference in Bloemfontein just as we started our build-up to the next game against the Wallabies. Fortunately the interview in which I had made the so-called offending comments had been conducted in Afrikaans.

After the game, which concluded our Tri Nations season, Oregan Hoskins asked to see me. Some of the other SARU board members were also present at the meeting in Johannesburg. And that's where I discovered that several administrators had been colluding behind my back.

Senior SARU office bearers Mark Alexander and James Stofberg, as well as chief executive Johan Prinsloo, were already there when I arrived. We waited for a while for Regan to turn up. During that time, Mark and the other guys were friendly and made a few jokes. I had no idea what was coming.

But when Regan walked in, you could see that he had hyped himself up for the meeting. He was very aggressive, which made it almost impossible to reason with him. He proceeded to scold me as if I were a schoolboy. In fact, he seemed to have completely pre-judged the matter at hand and acted as if I had no rights. I was told that he was fed up with how I embarrassed SA Rugby, and he took me on again for quoting the Bible. And several months after the actual event, he again brought up what I'd said during the FIFA World Cup.

The more he talked, the more negative I became. I didn't think that I owed Oregan anything – my duty was to the public of South Africa. It was clear that Oregan was playing to the crowd. 'To hell with you, man,' I thought.

'And this thing about Bees Roux ...' he continued. He was in my face. Hell, he was in my face. Up till that point, everyone from Butana Komphela, the sports minister, to the media and some members of the public had spoken a lot of shit about what I'd said about Bees Roux, but no one had actually called to ask me what I had *really* said, which was that although we supported Bees, we condemned the deed itself.

So I reminded Oregan that he was running one of the biggest sports organisations in the country. 'You have the wherewithal to get all the facts on this issue,' I said, 'but you haven't bothered to do that.'

I said that he was attacking me in order to fulfil an obligation to someone else, and he later confirmed this when he told me that Trevor Munday, a representative of the sponsors, had told him that the time had come to get rid of me. Fortunately, as I was leaving Paarl that morning, I had called Springbok media manager Anthony MacKaiser to ask him for the USB flash drive on which he had saved the recording of the Bees Roux interview.

I played the board members the recording, but Mark Alexander and Oregan said they couldn't understand what I'd said, as neither of them were proficient in Afrikaans. So I asked James Stofberg and Johan Prinsloo to explain to Mark and Oregan what I'd said – they were both Afrikaans.

'Please listen to it, James, and tell them exactly what I said that was wrong,' I asked.

So James started: 'What he said might have been interpreted ...'

'Hey,' I stopped him short, 'don't tell them what I *might* have said and how it *might* have been interpreted! Tell them *exactly* what I said.'

James concurred with me that what I had said in the interview did not correspond with what I was being accused of. Oregan was extremely upset. He knew he had been caught short and was severely embarrassed. It was like he was leaving with a black eye and, as he might have told everyone before the meeting that he was going to fire me, he probably felt he had lost face.

I was very thankful at the time that I had fought to include a performance clause in my contract in 2008. Because of the successes of the previous year, my win/loss ratio would not allow for me to be sacked. If they wanted to see the back of me, they would have to charge me for bringing the game into disrepute. But whenever someone tried to pin such an accusation on me, I managed to flat-bat it.

But Regan had to blame somebody, so he turned his attentions to Andy Colquhoun, the SARU director of strategic communications, instead. Andy had not come into the meeting but was sitting outside. He asked Andy why he hadn't listened to the interview, but of course Andy had been raised and educated in England and couldn't understand Afrikaans either.

SARU were looking for reasons to sack me, and they wanted to get rid of Gary Gold, Dick Muir and Neels Liebel too. The board members had identified replacements for each one of us.

After the Bees Roux showdown, there was a short break, which gave them time to regroup. Now getting rid of me was no longer the priority; I guess they realised I had the better of them on that one. They switched targets to Dick and Gary, as someone had to be the scapegoats for the Tri Nations failure.

Throughout my tenure, I reiterated time and again that I had brought those guys into the Bok set-up and my judgement would be called into question if I fired them. So I stood by them through thick and thin, even though the public and the press might have thought otherwise.

It was at that meeting that I realised I do, after all, have a price. I'd always insisted that I would stick by my principles, no matter what. But then SARU produced their trump card: if I wanted to save myself, I had to sacrifice either Dick or Gary, or both of them. I wasn't prepared for the ultimatum Oregan and Mark put before me.

It would be easy to say that I am only human and so justify the thoughts that went through my head – how much I was enjoying my job and that I did not want to give it up to save someone else. But I am not going to look for excuses or justify my actions. I let myself down. There is no other way to put it. As a proud, principled guy, I betrayed my principles when I was faced with the hardest choice. As a leader, I also let my followers down.

The main guys at SARU were telling me that they considered me to be the coach of the future. According to them, I could be the Springbok coach for many years to come *if* I was prepared to surround myself with the 'right people'. If I didn't, it would be my own fault if they had to let me go. Unfortunately, their strongest bargaining tool was the results from the season. They pointed out that the backline was not working, the scrum was bad ... They had all sorts of ammunition against the two assistant coaches – they even mentioned their drinking habits. It was as if they had been documenting Dick and Gary's every move.

Their new approach derailed me completely. They actually managed to make me forget that it was *me* they didn't want! The assistant coaches were just their second prize – they had to taste blood or they wouldn't be satisfied. With all the public pressure bearing down on them, the situation demanded it.

I was told to go and look for coaches who would be prepared to work with me. It was a very difficult situation, as I knew the right thing to do would be to call Gary and Dick and tell them what was going on. It was a catch-22 situation. And I didn't really want to start working with a new coaching team at this late stage.

But after that meeting, SARU kept asking me how I was progressing. They told me to go and see Allister Coetzee, the Stormers coach and former Springbok assistant coach. So I went to see him, and Coetzee was available. You can disregard what was written in the newspapers at the time – he was available. He did not say 'no' to me, as was reported. SARU told me Coetzee would be the next Bok coach, so I thought it would be good for him to be involved in the Bok set-up. And I told him as much.

I also went to see Frans Ludeke, whom I trusted, as he was the one Super Rugby coach who had always been helpful. But the administrators didn't want Frans. So those were the two people I saw: Allister Coetzee and Frans Ludeke.

I was also aware of the fact that Oregan had gone to Ireland to speak to Gert Smal, the other Springbok assistant coach from the

Jake White era. Oregan's trip was a renewed sign to me that they wanted to get rid of me too. They wanted all three of us out and not just my two assistants. I was rudely reminded that you couldn't trust anyone in SA Rugby.

Then the story got into the papers and exploded around Oregan. I was now caught in the middle – my two assistants no longer trusted me, and the administrators had bracketed me in with them and wanted me out too. Oregan lost it completely when Allister Coetzee confirmed to the newspapers that he had been approached.

'How can we trust this guy? He will never work in South African rugby as long as I am involved,' he vowed to me. I thought of those words later when Allister was overlooked when the new coach was appointed in 2012.

Although the media mentioned other names too, I only went to see Allister and Frans. I was also thinking about hiring John Mitchell, the former All Black coach who had taken charge at the Lions, as a consultant. I wanted him for the job that Rassie Erasmus ended up doing at the World Cup. But I had first approached Mitchell much earlier in the year, during the pre-season tournament involving the Stormers, Sharks and Western Force at Newlands. Mitchell was then still coaching the Western Force.

Mitchell was a New Zealander and thus had intimate knowledge of the country where we would be playing the World Cup. As New Zealand is not a great place in which to spend a full eight weeks, I was a bit concerned about the prospect, and I reckoned that having a Kiwi as part of the management team might somehow make it easier for us.

I am not big on employing foreigners as coaches, simply because I prefer to tap into our own talent pool for our top coaching positions. I believe South Africans have a passion for their country that no outsider can possibly have. Overseas coaches can just pack up and walk away when things go wrong.

So in this crisis period, with the exco guys breathing down my neck, constantly inquiring whether I was making any progress in selecting new assistant coaches, I decided to follow up the meeting I'd had with Mitchell in Cape Town and arranged to meet him in Johannesburg.

On the day I was due to see him, I phoned Kevin de Klerk, the Lions president, and told him I wanted to pop in to see him in his office. Kevin agreed to see me, so I made my way to Ellis Park. I told Kevin of my plans going forward, and that I was thinking of making Mitchell part of those plans. I asked him if he thought it was the right thing to do.

Kevin said no, it wasn't.

So I told De Klerk that if he didn't want me to meet with Mitchell, I wouldn't. But I asked him to please inform John of my decision. So instead of seeing Mitchell, I went off to my other meetings and never actually officially approached him for any position. But I lost some respect for John when, like Allister, he told the newspapers that I had approached him to be my assistant coach. I hadn't.

Frans Ludeke did the right thing and denied to the newspapers that I had approached him, even though I had. I had asked all the guys I approached not to say anything about it, as I told them we had to take other people's feelings into consideration, but Frans was the only one who kept his promise.

With all this going on, Oregan called a meeting in Durban in late September 2010. And hell, what a meeting that was – easily the worst one of my life! Oregan, Dick, Gary and I all attended. SARU bigwigs Mark Alexander and James Stofberg had been very outspoken about Gary and Dick at the Johannesburg meeting, where they had joined Regan in reading me the riot act. They had strong feelings, some of them quite valid, on the matter. But they weren't prepared to go to Durban to tell Gary and Dick to their faces what they thought, despite the fact that I asked them to attend. I said, 'Come on, guys, come [to Durban] and tell them how you feel.' They refused. I told Mark I was happy with my assistants, but perhaps he should tell them where he thought they were going wrong. But he wouldn't. So it was just the four of us, and the things that were said during those several heated hours did nothing to build trust among us.

Gary and Dick tore into me and I tore back into them; Regan tore into all of us, and we in turn tore into him. It definitely wasn't a good meeting for South African rugby, or for the Springboks. It felt as if the trust my assistant coaches and I had built up over a period of three years was being flushed down the toilet.

Dick really went for Oregan. This definitely wasn't the same Oregan I had seen in Johannesburg; it was now Dick who was the aggressor. Later in the year, when Oregan wanted to see us to chat about the referee issue (in other words, he was trying to help us), Dick still just wanted to grab him by the jugular. Whenever Dick came face to face with Oregan, it was like waving a red rag in front of a bull.

As a leader, I wanted my colleagues and players to trust me, but I felt as if I was no longer trustworthy, and I had caused the state of affairs myself. An untenable situation had developed because I had sold my soul to the proverbial devil.

I never did manage to get SARU the new assistant coaches they wanted. After that heated meeting in Durban, Oregan just said, 'Go on this tour and then we will talk further.' We were about to undertake a tour to the UK, where we were scheduled to play all four Home Unions.

It was unclear whether our jobs were on the line if we did badly on the tour; it was never said in so many words. But then I often learnt these things via the media. When rumours appear in the press and prove to be correct more often than not, you start to realise that the reporters are not just speculating – someone must be talking to them.

One major change was Jurie Roux's appointment as chief executive of SARU. He wanted to re-staff the review committee, as according to him the incumbents weren't sufficiently adept at the technical aspects of the game. The result was that we never had an official Tri Nations review that year, because we were bickering over who should be on the committee. Jurie kept on tossing out the names of guys who were keen on the Springbok coaching job. How fair would the review have been then? So up until this day, no review of the 2010 Tri Nations has been done.

* * *

With all this off-the-field nonsense going on, at least we had a decent amount of time to prepare for the end-of-year tour, unlike the little time we'd had before the Tri Nations. Although the Currie Cup final between the Sharks and Western Province was played just a week before our first match, against Ireland in Dublin (the match opened the new Aviva Stadium, effectively a refurbished Lansdowne Road), I managed to get those players who weren't in that game together for a camp. And because there had been a two-week break between the semi-finals and the final, we also managed to get the Sharks and Western Province players together for some planning sessions.

John Smit would not be touring, as he had undergone a neck operation, but we brought him in nevertheless to help with the strategising. So our preparations were all very positive and, even though several players were out injured, we left South Africa feeling confident.

We might have been under-strength due to the injuries, but everyone was on the same page and, anyway, there is only really one way you can play in the UK because of the prevailing conditions – you have to prioritise the basics, seek forward domination and have a good kicking strategy. Fortunately, our pack was brilliant on that tour. The Sharks front row continued the excellent work they had done in the Currie Cup, and Bakkies Botha's return meant we now had a cleaner. Despite the injuries we had in the backline, our strong tight five made all the difference in the northern hemisphere.

Juan Smith was also outstanding, and Willem Alberts, as a substitute, had a massive impact with his ability to shift the momentum of a game. When we were trailing against Wales, he helped us come from behind to win our second match of the tour. There were only four points in it at the end (29-25), but we had come back from a big deficit. We had started our tour with a good wet-weather win against Ireland (23-21).

Scotland, however, was a disaster. Of course the Springboks should never lose to Scotland, but you had to give them credit for the way they played on the day, as they scored a well-deserved 21-17 win. Two years earlier they had played magnificently against us at Murrayfield, and they did so again this time. But they were aided by the one thing all Springbok teams hate – icy-cold weather and pouring rain.

Our structures were better than they had been during our previous visit, so even though we were bitterly disappointed that we'd lost and criticism was raining down on us, we were still confident we could beat England. I knew the players didn't need any extra motivation to play them.

I heard through the grapevine that it was make or break for me with this match – if we lost, I was out. However, I wasn't informed of this officially and the squad didn't make a habit of reading the newspapers. We were just focused on England.

Although it was cold at Twickenham, it was not nearly as icy as it had been in Edinburgh, and a brilliant performance against our most hated enemy soon warmed us up. I knew England would be way too confident, as they had smashed Australia a fortnight previously and their press were treating them like world-champions-in-waiting. So we went onto the pitch and shut them down. We gave them no room to manoeuvre. As it was our last game together as a group in 2010, we wanted to go into the next season with confidence. We beat England 21-11, but it could have been a lot more, as our forwards were far more dominant than they had been in 2008, when we won 42-6. Nevertheless, it was the perfect conclusion to the year before the World Cup.

But on the plane heading back to South Africa on the Sunday after our final tour game against the Barbarians, I sat pondering one point of concern: Why were we still not converting our opportunities into points on the board?

21

Plotting, planning and politics

The period after the 2010 end-of-year tour was a time of much soul-searching and introspection; it was probably the toughest downtime in my four-year tenure. I was assailed by doubts and haunted by Oregan Hoskins's 2008 speech, which repeated itself over and over in my head.

It had been an incredibly tough year. Much had gone wrong. Now I had to ask myself some serious questions. At the top of the list was whether or not I should continue as the Springbok coach. Should I carry on fighting an uphill battle that might be costing Springbok rugby too much, or should I turn my back on the job and let someone else take the team to the World Cup?

The debacle with SARU over the assistant coaches and the sordid way it had been portrayed in the media had soured everything for me. Although we had enjoyed a relatively successful end-of-year tour, my relationship with my assistant coaches had been irrevocably damaged. I could hardly blame Gary Gold and Dick Muir if they didn't trust me any more; I knew how I would have felt if the roles had been reversed.

As always, I was conflicted between my own desires and the well-being of the group. If my intentions were only to try to prove a point, then it was better for me to step down as coach.

I had also received no reassurances from SARU. Reports had circulated that some of the SARU officials had asked the players what they thought of my coaching. And this after a tour that should have put an end to the theory that the senior players were running the show ...

After all, injuries had forced half the top players to stay at home, and yet we had won three of our four games!

When I got home in early December, I scoured the newspapers for an article that reported that I was at last enjoying SARU's full backing. But there was nothing.

I spoke to several people and got a lot of different opinions, but in the end I resolved that since I had started the job, it was my duty to finish it. While it was true that I had faced much criticism, I had at least also enjoyed some support.

Many people thought I had brought the race groups closer together in my attempts at making the Springboks the people's team. I felt like I was on my way to succeeding in my mission, so I felt obligated not to leave the job half finished. We had to keep the dreams of those South Africans who supported us alive.

At the same time, the set-up could not continue as it was. It had become clear that we needed an outside element to breathe new life into us after the difficult 2010 season.

In January 2011, I met with a lot of people in my quest to cover all bases for the challenging year that lay ahead. I saw sports psychologists and businesspeople such as Paarl businessman Jan Marais, and I spoke to Morné du Plessis and Professor Tim Noakes. I even had a meeting with Trevor Manuel, the former finance minister, who was then working in the office of the Presidency. I also met with some of the provincial presidents, and my good friend Francois Davids.

But although all those meetings were a huge help, something was still missing. It was that X-factor, that little bit extra …

One of my ideas had been to bring in Morné du Plessis as team manager for the World Cup. He had done the job in 1995, and that World Cup victory had become a golden moment in the history of our country. Morné possessed the statesmanlike qualities the team needed. He was also a consummate diplomat who could calm troubled waters in times of crises.

I envisaged a ceremonial role for Morné, but he would also motivate and inspire the players. Just the fact that he had been part of the 1995 victory was enough to get the players' attention and win their respect. He is a legendary figure in South African rugby.

Unfortunately, though, some of the other management members were against the idea, as most of our preparations had already been done and it would have been money wasted. That did not deter me, but then Morné contacted me and told me that, after a lot of consideration, he had decided not to take on the role. I respected his decision.

In the meantime, the Bok management got together in Paarl for planning sessions. I was determined that we would not leave anything to chance in our quest to create the best possible environment for the players at the World Cup.

I was also determined that, in a World Cup year, the players should prepare in a location that had a certain 'wow' factor. Although everything for the Bok management team revolved around the World Cup, it was different for the players. Yes, of course they were all focused on the World Cup, but at the same time that was just part of their workload – they first had to play Super Rugby and in the Tri Nations series too.

So, for their sake, I didn't want the pre–World Cup training camp to be mundane. It had to have something special about it. I travelled around the country and assessed various venues, but the Bafokeng Sports Campus near Rustenburg, where the England soccer team had stayed during the FIFA World Cup, was the obvious choice. Apart from the luxurious accommodation, they had a high-tech gym and an unbelievably well-staffed and well-equipped medical facility on the premises.

The initial plan was to stage the camp immediately after the Super 15, but then it quickly became apparent that the tournament would be too long and taxing for the players to assemble directly afterwards for a camp. It would have been counterproductive. I had met with the franchise coaches as part of my planning and had appealed to them to manage the players throughout the competition, but I did not get the response I wanted. John Plumtree of the Sharks said that I could use the Tri Nations as the build-up to the World Cup. I couldn't really blame the coaches – their jobs were on the line and winning was their bottom line.

The upshot was that when the medical assessments on the players were done at the end of the Super 15, we were shocked at the condition of so many of our key personnel. They had been played into the ground. This, though, offered us an opportunity – we could stage our training camp in Rustenburg during the away leg of the Tri Nations.

Obviously we would have to reduce any training component because of the poor condition of the players, but at least we could get the top players together under one roof and would be able to put our heads together and plan our strategies.

But there was a problem: if the camp was going to take place during the Tri Nations, the coaches would not be able to attend it, as we would be in Australia and New Zealand with the team. I had approached Rassie Erasmus, then the director of rugby at the Stormers, the previous year to ask him if he would be interested in taking up the position of technical advisor. I thought Rassie might bring me that elusive X-factor I was after, as he pays amazing attention to detail and has the ability to compartmentalise and then measure all the different aspects that comprise the overall performance of a rugby team. John Smit and Victor Matfield had told me that Rassie had made a strong contribution to the Springboks' 2007 success. Although he did not accompany the squad to France for the World Cup, he had done his bit with his technical innovations.

Rassie made his biggest contribution at a training camp in Cape Town at the start of the build-up to the 2007 World Cup, while the 'second-stringers' were overseas. I wanted him to do much the same in 2011. I respected Rassie's rugby brain and it would have been short-sighted of me to leave him on the sidelines when he'd said that he was available. Of course, we faced a battle with Western Province to release him, as we had when we'd tried to engage the services of Stormers defence coach Jacques Nienaber the year before.

I started negotiating with Rassie, and I approached Nienaber at the same time. He offers a great deal more than just his genius on defence. Indeed, I would say he is one of the sharpest rugby brains I have ever come across. He has an unbelievably good feel for the game. If SA Rugby does not contract him soon, some other country is sure to stumble upon his talents and steal him away from us.

Then there was Derik Coetzee. I was well aware of Derik's capabilities as a fitness trainer, as my national under-21 players had spoken of him often. Some might say he should have been part of the Bok set-up in the first place, but I had worked with Neels Liebel at age-group level and placed a high value on his holistic approach to player fitness. Neels is a biokineticist, but he could just as easily have been a physiotherapist. He has extensive knowledge of the body and human movement.

Neels is one of those guys who is constantly on the internet to research his field in order to keep ahead of the game. But he has a gentle side to him, which is sometimes too soft for some of the rugby stuff. In this World Cup year, I needed someone who would drive the players without taking any nonsense from them. I knew that a lot of the guys were very wary of Derik and considered him to be a real drill sergeant. He was exactly what we needed.

It proved to be a great decision, as Derik complemented Neels perfectly. While Derik took charge of on-field conditioning, pre-practice drills and warm-ups, Neels supervised the scientific aspects of getting the players into peak condition for the World Cup. It was almost immediately apparent that Derik's methods were giving the players renewed energy and interest in training.

These factors made a massive difference to the efficiency of our operation. With Rassie working on technical details and adding his excellent organisational touches to everything, I was freed to be more of a manager. For the first time I didn't feel like I was looking over my shoulder all the time – I could delegate with confidence. It even had an impact on how I dealt with the media. Whereas before I was often criticised for my 'tetchy' attitude to the press, this was no longer the case in the run-up to the World Cup.

We cut down on the time we spent in meetings, and the meetings themselves were handled a lot more efficiently. Dick Muir was in charge of attack, Gary Gold was put in charge of loose play, Jacques was responsible for defence and Rassie was responsible for bringing it all together. Then, of course, there were the senior players, who were also given responsibilities, with Victor joining Gary in taking charge of the line-outs, and John Smit and Gary looking after the scrums. Fourie du Preez oversaw our kicking game, and Schalk Burger and Jean de Villiers concentrated on defence.

It was not all plain sailing, though, as we soon encountered obstacles beyond our control. Our budget allowed for only so many assistants, so

I had to seriously consider who to take to the World Cup as part of my management team.

In 2010, I had brought Os du Randt in as a scrum consultant, as I wanted him, as a World Cup winner, to imbue the players with self-belief. But by the end of that year's final tour, the players' self-belief was in place and the scrum was working well. When SARU called me in for a progress meeting, they asked me what I had in mind for Os. I told them I would assess what I needed. Previously I had used former French prop Pieter de Villiers as my scrum consultant. Pieter had been excellent, but then our requirements changed when it became neces-sary to concentrate more on the mental than the technical side of the scrum. So Pieter departed, and by the end of 2010 Os had also done his job. I think he might have been a little frustrated about the amount of time he was given to work on the scrumming.

I also had to consider whether the time Gary Gold spent coaching on the pitch warranted retaining his services. There is, of course, only a limited amount of time available to coach each facet of play, and as far as consultants are concerned, timing is everything – in other words, you employ them only when they are most needed and can make the most difference.

And I had to motivate why I wanted Jacques Nienaber involved, as SARU official Mark Alexander asked me why I thought a defence coach was necessary. But by the time the international season arrived, every-thing had been sorted out, and I had my team in place.

Unfortunately our planning for the new season didn't take into account the number of injuries we'd have at the start of the international campaign. We knew the players would be exhausted, but the extended Super Rugby season was new territory for everyone. We didn't foresee the extent of the wear and tear on the players. And I think it was the same for all the SANZAR teams.

The injury problems forced us to rethink quite a few issues. The initial plan was to mix and match our selections for the World Cup so we could have young talent playing alongside enough old hands for there not to be too much disruption to the team. We had done the same when injuries forced us into a similar situation during the 2010 end-of-year tour.

But even before the end of the Super 15, I knew we were in trouble. Our tests had confirmed that Andries Bekker and Willem Alberts were nursing injuries. But the Super 15 tournament had by then reached a crucial stage and the franchise coaches needed all hands on deck. And then the Stormers' Duane Vermeulen, whom we wanted to select for the Tri Nations, got injured in their last league match in the competition.

But nothing had quite prepared us for the shock we got at the results of the medical assessments after the end of the Super 15. We seemed to be sitting on a potential time bomb, as just about everyone was carrying an injury. While some injuries were more serious than others, all of them could potentially rule the affected players out of the World Cup.

Apart from Andries and Willem, the injured list consisted of Victor Matfield, Jean de Villiers, Jannie du Plessis, Jaque Fourie, Wynand Olivier, Fourie du Preez, Heinrich Brüssow, Gurthrö Steenkamp, Bryan Habana and, of course Juan Smith, who had been injured early on in the Super 15. Guys like Francois Hougaard were also not 100 per cent. The list was endless.

Maybe some of the players could have played through their injuries, but that was too big a risk. If some of them were injured in the Tri Nations, we would have no chance of winning the World Cup. So we had to decide whether we wanted to go into the Tri Nations managing the players' injuries, or, with the World Cup in mind, we use the time to get the players properly rehabilitated. We chose the latter.

And it worked for us in one respect. Pat Lambie had not been in my initial plans, though I was planning to play him in the Tri Nations so that he could gain some experience for the future. In my opinion, he hadn't been settled in one position and was therefore difficult to assess. But by keeping a calm head while others around him were losing theirs during the disastrous away leg of the Tri Nations, Pat proved that I could rely on him if I needed him at the World Cup.

The many injuries forced us to take a brand new front row into the Tri Nations, including two new locks, and then the new guys also got injured! We had too many rookies in the squad and not enough cool heads on the field. Everyone was playing for themselves.

In a way, our poor Tri Nations performance underlined the concerns

I'd harboured at the start of the Super 15. I thought that the standard of play in the competition had dropped alarmingly. Aside from the Reds, who won the competition, the Australian franchises, with an additional team now in the mix, didn't seem to have any expectations and the New Zealand sides seemed weaker than before. Too many guys had left to play overseas, and even in a World Cup year it was glaringly apparent that there was a missing generation in our rugby, as a whole tier of experienced players who should have been playing a mentoring role to the youngsters had been lost to the northern hemisphere.

We wanted our backline to be better on attack, but this was impossible because of the inexperience up front. The fact that a young guy like Werner Kruger was suddenly considered the best prop in South Africa during Super Rugby summed it up. The so-called *hardebaarde* (wise old beards) weren't there to guide the youngsters and to facilitate the learning process by sorting them out on the field in provincial games.

With Rassie Erasmus now part of our management team, we were able to fully assess the players during the Super Rugby campaign and also in the Tri Nations. We could gauge where some players had improved, set goals for them and be clear on what was expected of them in training and in their game. Rassie's contribution was invaluable in this regard.

But while there was some measurable progress on several fronts during the Tri Nations, having to rehabilitate the injured robbed us of the players who would have intimidated the opposition. That all-important psychological edge was missing. So it was hardly a surprise to us that we did not do well in the overseas leg of the tournament. We were well beaten by both Australia (20-39) and New Zealand (7-40).

On our return, we were relieved to discover that all our top players were again available for selection, as after the disastrous results in the Antipodes, we were under tremendous pressure. At the same time, we knew we couldn't expect too much – the rehabilitated players hadn't played for several weeks, and there really is only one way to gain match fitness, and that is to play games. We suspected that we wouldn't have the legs to last the full 80 minutes in the match against Australia in Durban.

It nevertheless turned into one hell of a game. In the first half, our standard of play was encouraging. Unfortunately, though, 2011 would follow more or less the same pattern as 2010, when the bounce of the ball and the referees' 50/50 calls did not go our way. We needed to build up a points difference in the first half, and indeed we should have scored on several occasions in the first 40 minutes, but somehow we just couldn't get over the line. Without those points on the board and suspecting that we were going to run out of steam in the second half, we were pretty sure we weren't going to win the match by the time the half-time whistle blew. And so it proved, with Australia winning 14-9.

Our post-match assessments indicated that we had not achieved our objectives in four of the 12 areas (or systems) we had earmarked for measuring. We had a heck of a lot to improve on.

In direct contrast to the Durban match, everything went our way in Port Elizabeth against the All Blacks. Suddenly the bounce of the ball favoured us and our defence was top-notch, with the New Zealanders frequently being stopped when one more pass would have resulted in a try. Our 18-5 victory happened at just the right time, as we could now take some much-needed momentum into the World Cup. And there is nothing like a win over New Zealand to unite the South African public behind the Boks.

But then I was summoned to meet with the Parliamentary Portfolio Committee on Sport and Recreation, where I was asked why I did not play my best team in the Tri Nations. I explained that most of the senior players had been injured and in need of rehabilitation. I also stressed that we were working towards the World Cup.

But they didn't want to hear it. They called us a disgrace and said that our overseas defeats should not have been allowed to happen. Even Madiba was brought into the fray because we had lost the Mandela Challenge Cup to Australia. His name, I was told, had been denigrated. Of course Jake White had also played an under-strength team in the 2007 Tri Nations for the same reasons I did, but it seemed as if our politicians just couldn't see the bigger picture.

I explained that we hadn't set out to lose, and that most of the players we'd selected had plenty of potential and the experience would stand them in good stead for the future. But the most important point was that we were going to the World Cup with a mostly fit team. Although New Zealand would eventually narrowly win the World Cup, both the Kiwis and the Australians were plagued by injuries during the tournament.

While the committee was quick to criticise us for our approach to the World Cup, its members were unable to suggest how else we should have done it. How were we supposed to push the same players who had played in the Super 15 straight into the Tri Nations *and* still expect them to deliver at their peak in the World Cup? They couldn't say.

I felt very down in the dumps after that meeting. No one seemed to be 100 per cent behind us, and I also couldn't understand what the committee wanted from me. Of course we should go out and win every game we play, but surely everyone knows how unrealistic it is to expect that?

I was frustrated, as I thought I was doing what was best for SA rugby. I was also confused, as SARU and other South Africans seemed to have different priorities to those of the Bok management.

Earlier in the year I had a meeting with the SARU board, and Mark Alexander and Oregan Hoskins informed me then that they would not have a problem if I decided to select an all-white team for the World Cup. Needless to say, I was somewhat surprised at this. Oregan and Mark just wanted us to win the World Cup. They said government would not oppose my selections if we won the trophy.

I said that I knew very well what country I lived in, so I found what they said hard to believe. So they asked me who had told me that I *had* to choose a racially representative team.

I was disappointed with that question, as it was so ridiculous. I had spent four years working within certain transformation parameters only to be told by the national body that there had never been any!

But I strongly suspected that although they might be saying these things, they would never make such a statement in public. If I did choose an all-white team and it resulted in a political fallout, Mark and Oregan would run for cover. And anyway, in my mind, South Africans had come to accept the need for transformation. Had I now abandoned the parameters I had thought I was working within, it would have been a massive step backwards.

The politics that went on behind the scenes at SA Rugby was mind-boggling. During the local elections in 2011, the ANC candidate in Paarl went to see my father, who is a keen horticulturalist. One of the drains in his back garden had been overflowing for ages without the municipality doing anything about it. Every year he called the municipality up, and every year they failed to respond.

So my father, by now fed up, took on the ANC candidate and told him that the mayor and the rest of the municipality had never cared about him. They never bothered to pitch up at his flower shows, so why were they suddenly showing an interest in him now? He told the ANC candidate that he would vote for whomever he wanted.

On election day, my wife, our daughters and I drove to the different polling stations. We went to a number of places. At one location, one of my daughters saw a friend of hers sitting at a DA table and went to speak to her. I am not sure who my daughter voted for, nor do I want to know, as it is her business.

As a result of my daughter talking to her friend at the opposing party's table and my father's conversation with the ANC candidate, Butana Komphela called Oregan Hoskins to tell him to get rid of me before the World Cup. So Regan called me. I was stunned. What the hell did any of that have to do with rugby, or with the administrators? Regan told me he had heard my father had been rude, and that even my mother had been rude. He asked me for the facts, for goodness' sake!

I was now in the invidious position of having to go to my 80-year-old father and ask him if he had been rude. As stupid as I am, I did actually call him to gather the facts, and he had to explain to his son why he'd clashed with an ANC councillor. How ridiculous is that? This was four days after the results had been announced. The ANC didn't win in Paarl.

I couldn't believe how Komphela had behaved.

22

Blowing the whistle

There was another important matter I had to consider in the run-up to the Rugby World Cup – referees. Even way back in January, the issue of referees was constantly on my mind, as it was threatening to become one of the biggest obstacles in our quest to retain the Webb Ellis Cup. Of course, back in those summer months, in the heat of Paarl, I wasn't aware of just how accurate my concern would prove to be.

It's quite ridiculous how much time coaches spend assessing referees, but it's a reality of the modern game. As a coach, you have to be familiar with the style and quirks of all the international referees, or you risk neglecting a factor that could make the difference between winning and losing.

With the help of former referee Neville Heilbron, who attended most of the meetings I held with match officials, I conducted a thorough study of all the international referees. Then, when the referees for our World Cup games were announced, I also consulted with another former referee, Tappe Henning, who was involved with the IRB.

South African referees are the best in the world by some distance, but that doesn't help the Springboks, as the local referees don't officiate in our games. So we get all the 'less-talented' refs. And what makes matters worse, I am sorry to say, is that some of our own officials are far too keen to stay in favour with their overseas counterparts and the IRB. In my first days as Bok coach, André Watson was SARU's official in charge of referees, but rumour had it that he was angling for a job with the IRB. He seemed to be treading lightly around IRB referee chief Paddy O'Brien, but it didn't help much, as Lyndon Bray got the job in the end.

I remember talking to our local citing chief, Freek Burger, and saying that his Australian and New Zealand counterparts were always trying to find reasons why their players were *not* guilty of infringements rather than looking for reasons why they *were* guilty. Freek said my perception was correct, but then pointed out that the people he worked for (SANZAR and the IRB) lived in New Zealand. This summed up our problem – while South African referees may be the best (a point proven yet again when Craig Joubert officiated in the final of the 2011 World Cup), all the decision-making power is situated overseas.

I really do believe that the South African officials are too keen to please in order to stay in the good books of the 'right' people. Television match officials have even admitted that, when they have to make a 50/50 call, they rule against South Africa, as they want to officiate at the World Cup. In other words, some officials would let their country lose a match so that they can go to the World Cup. I just can't understand that kind of mindset – it makes no damn sense to me at all.

So I think refereeing standards have deteriorated over the past few years. Technology hasn't helped, either. When you consider the number of forward passes and other errors that have gone unnoticed by referees, all technology has done is to promote a laxness that didn't exist before. A few years back hardly anyone cared about who was officiating in a match, but with referees now seemingly more concerned about their own career prospects than their impartiality, it has become a massive issue.

Referee assessors have the same impact on rugby as the teaching inspectors I came across in my teaching career had on the teachers. In my view, the person who should be ascertaining whether the teacher is doing a good job is the school principal. The inspector should help and guide the teachers to improve their performances. But unfortunately in my day, the 'best' teaching inspectors were those who came up with the most negative reports, and referee assessors are much the same.

So, given the situation, we met with the referees and tried to find out how they refereed certain aspects of the game. I thought these were constructive meetings that would help them as much as they would help us, as we would understand and respect one another's viewpoint better.

Unfortunately, I soon found out that some of the referees were not always honest – as they would say one thing to us and something completely different to someone else. For instance, we had a meeting with Bryce Lawrence before the Lions series, which he described as the best meeting ever. But then Paddy O'Brien informed me later that Bryce had told him the exact opposite.

I am honest and like to speak my mind, and perhaps this came back to bite me with the referees. I hope this isn't true – should a person be penalised for being honest? Nevertheless, I had my moments with various referees down the years, and we often engaged in heated debate.

I had my first meeting with Paddy O'Brien in Johannesburg during my first year in charge, and my management team was also present. Paddy was a visitor to our country, yet when he walked into the room, his condescending attitude was immediately apparent.

'Peter, should I start this meeting?' he asked.

'No, Paddy, I will start it,' I said. 'You are in my country now.'

I then said something I don't think he was happy about.

'You know, Paddy, ever since [my schooldays] it has been a dream of mine to meet God. I now feel like that dream has [come true]. I feel God is finally in the same room as me.'

Phew, so that was the way the meeting started. Looking back, it probably wasn't the best approach. I informed Paddy that I would like to meet with the referees for a discussion. He snapped back that I would never meet the referees. So I ended the meeting there and then. I asked him who gave him the right to come to my country and dictate terms, and I said he should go and drink some beer with the other officials, as that seemed to be his main purpose for visiting South Africa. I added that he had become too self-important.

'We are nothing, you and I,' I said. 'The game has made us who we are.' I got ready to leave, but then O'Brien suddenly changed his attitude and said, 'No, no, come on, Peter, let's sit down and talk.' In the end I sat down and, with O'Brien now more amiable, I asked him why it had been necessary to arrive with such a haughty attitude. Why had he been so determined to show that he was in control? Fortunately, the meeting concluded on a more positive note.

But then we had the Bryce Lawrence meeting, and Bryce told Gary Gold that it had been constructive but then complained about it to Paddy. So I took Paddy on in a follow-up meeting.

'Paddy,' I said, 'this is exactly why I can't work with your referees – they are always too ready to bend the truth when it suits them.'

Of course he didn't like that, nor did he like it that I had had Neville Heilbron with me at the referees' meeting. But Neville had compiled all the data we required for the meeting, and I wanted him to present it to them first hand and to discuss the finer points. Perhaps the referees felt I was challenging their competency. I told Paddy that I thought the referees didn't want to take responsibility for their own decisions any more. Technology had made their jobs easier and, as a result, they were neglecting their fitness levels and were not as sharp on the field as they should be.

The deeper involvement of the touch judges, who have now become assistant referees, has not helped keep the referees on their toes either. Far from it. The referees have started to hide behind their assistants. Do shared responsibilities make the game better when referees aren't always man enough to take responsibility and pass the buck too easily?

Referees don't seem to understand the overriding principle of good refereeing: that the less they are noticed on the field, the better they are doing their job. And the game will be better off too. A lot of them may pay lip service to that principle, but too many of them are way too self-important. I said as much to Irish referee Alain Rolland, and we had a big fight about it. He said he didn't need rugby, that he had achieved a lot outside of the game. I disagreed, saying that he was recognised on the streets of Ireland only because of his involvement with rugby.

I didn't fight with referees because of the mistakes they made, but because they thought they were above the law. It's a weird situation when the presidents of countries can be criticised in the media but referees can't. If you do, you are blamed for bringing the game into disrepute. Yet it seems to me that they are the very people who are undermining the standing of the sport. Coaches and players can lose their jobs, but it appears as if referees are a protected species.

Also, I'm not always sure who benefits from some of the law changes. If you ask the players what they want, they will tell you that they want serious rucking; vigorous rucking has always been part of the game. I think it's the referees who can't handle it.

One of my biggest fights with a referee was with Alain Rolland during the 2010 Tri Nations series. As discussed in a previous chapter, Bakkies Botha had been sent off by Alan Lewis, Rolland's countryman, in the first test in Auckland. Although Bakkies had been guilty of an offence that he should deservedly have been sent off for, the referee hadn't spotted it. It was only during a break in play, when the incident was replayed on the big screen, that Lewis saw what had happened, and he then sent Bakkies off for an offence that didn't warrant a yellow card.

So I sat down with Rolland in the build-up to the next game in Wellington, which he was refereeing, and asked him: 'Are you really impartial, or are you influenced by the media? Do you think that if he hadn't seen the replay, Alan would still have sent Bakkies off?'

Rolland responded by saying that, yes, he would have sent him off. I didn't believe him, and I said so. We started a heated discussion. I heard stories afterwards that I had called a referee a racist in one of these meetings. Although I can't remember that, I suppose it's possible. I definitely told Rolland that he was 'stupid' for standing up for Lewis and that he was talking rubbish.

'Your reaction proves that I really can't trust you,' I said.

Perhaps I was wrong to remind him that he would be nothing without the game of rugby, but I wanted to make it clear that maybe we all think ourselves too important at times and forget how much we owe the sport, which we are blessed to be part of.

Rugby may once have cost me nearly everything in life, but I have come to realise that it's not the sport itself that cuts you down, but the people in the sport. Referees will make mistakes, but how can you expect a fair game when, for example, Bryce Lawrence is refereeing and the first thing he asks the TMO as he heads into the tunnel at half-time is what the penalty count is? And sure enough, there he is, immediately after half-time, trying to redress the balance by quickly awarding penalties to the other side for supposed infringements he never worried about in the first half. I raised this issue at a referee's meeting before the 2011 Rugby World Cup, and as a result an end was put to this trend.

I don't know how we are supposed to have any faith in the system when so many things are happening that are just patently wrong. As a coach your job is always on the line, but if after a game you know you have lost because of the mistakes of the referee, you have to pretend that it isn't an issue. The players and the coach can be criticised, but not the referee. Where is the justice in that?

Refereeing was a big issue at the World Cup, and not just for South Africa. I suppose it will continue to be for some time; I just hope the game can survive all the extra drama and controversy that is created by disputes over refereeing calls. Surely now that the game has become professional we have to be more vigilant in assessing the checks and balances?

The fanfare surrounding the Springbok squad as we departed Johannesburg for New Zealand in early September 2011 should have sent out an unambiguous message to the game's lawmakers about how important the sport has become to a great many people. That means the game needs to be properly governed and administered; it simply cannot afford to let refereeing play such a dominant role in determining results.

I have to admit that when I was first told about the send-off SARU was planning, I was uncomfortable with it. How can you be given a hero's farewell when you haven't achieved anything yet? It was not what I had wanted, but the SARU marketing people had organised the event, and by the time I was consulted the planning was too far advanced to change it.

I don't think any of us expected the enormity of the event. It blew my mind. There was intense television focus, and thousands had turned up at Mandela Square and along the route of our journey there to wish us well. For the first time in my life I was afraid to address a crowd. The occasion was just too big for me. I wasn't sure what to say.

I tried to wriggle out of speaking, but before I knew it, the microphone was in my hand. I just started talking as if I was at a political rally, and the positive reaction of the crowd put me at ease. It was then that it really hit home that I was not going to New Zealand just with the Bok team, but with the hopes and dreams of 50 million people. It made the pressure more real. We knew that if our departure evoked this kind of frenzy, we simply couldn't afford to fail our supporters.

This additional pressure was exactly why I had not wanted a farewell with too much fanfare, but in retrospect I don't think it was too much of a problem. The guys knew what the country expected of them and they were mostly experienced players who understood what the

World Cup meant to their people. After all, many of them had been on the open-top bus that had paraded the Webb Ellis Cup around the country four years previously.

The occasion did manage to erase any memory of the negative mood that had permeated the squad just a few weeks earlier, when the whole country thought we were facing a crisis in our rugby, and with the All Blacks awaiting us. Then the win over the Kiwis boosted our confidence, and the send-off lifted our spirits even further.

But we knew we faced an incredibly tough opening game against the rapidly improving Wales. We reckoned they would have fresher legs and be better prepared than us, as they had been away on a training camp and did not have a Tri Nations they'd had to contend with. The northern hemisphere teams also had the advantage of not having had an extra-long regional competition.

Welsh skipper Sam Warburton really surprised us in that game. He is a natural leader and put in a full 80 minutes of effort. It was clear that he had significantly changed the culture of the Welsh team. In most of the matches the Welsh played against us in the four years of my tenure, it had been a case of so near and yet so far for them. We had just managed to win some games, but they were now significantly better than before. And to return to the subject of referees, the Welsh can probably claim that they would have beaten us, had the penalty kick that they had been adjudged to have missed been awarded, as some of the television replays suggested should have been the case.

We had started well, and an impressive build-up and the early application of pressure saw Frans Steyn go over for a try. But after that, the Welsh fought like tigers. With Warburton giving us such a hard time on the floor, we couldn't get our hands on the ball. In the end, you could say that we were lucky to win.

But win we did, and after escaping with a victory when we had been outplayed in so many areas, we thought all the pieces of the puzzle were beginning to fall into place. We sensed that we would only get better from then on. Our planning was sound, and the foundation we'd laid was solid. We could now sit down and discuss some of the finer details with the players, for example where we thought they needed to improve.

Peter Maimane, our technical analyst, had the important task of setting up computer programs that enabled us to analyse and assess the statistics. We introduced a green vs. red report, whereby a player was given either the red or green light from the coaches and his fellow players after the game depending on whether he had succeeded or failed in attaining the ojectives that had been set for him. It was a fact-centred method in the sense that everything was measured statistically.

We hammered Fiji 49-3 in our second game, and such an emphatic victory over a team we had struggled against in the quarter-final in Marseille in 2007 boosted our confidence further. We were also sitting with a rather pleasant headache: the guys who had come on to replace the injured players had played really well. Bakkies Botha still had to come back from injury, but Danie Rossouw was in outstanding form, while Frans Steyn had revelled in wearing the No.12 jersey again, the same one he had worn at the previous World Cup when he'd replaced the injured Jean de Villiers.

Francois Hougaard had scored the winning try against Wales, and his brilliant form motivated the media to pressurise us into including him in the starting line-up ahead of Bryan Habana. There was also a lot of pressure on us to replace John Smit with Bismarck du Plessis.

I took a lot of flak for playing Smit ahead of Du Plessis, and I suppose the debate will continue after the way we exited the World Cup, but if I had to do it all over again, I think I would make the same decision.

Any coach would be pleased to have Bismarck in his side, as he is so physically aggressive. When he is allowed to dominate physically, his innate aggression simply destroys the opposition. But in the Super 15 I'd noticed that some teams were negating his impact by focusing on his flaws – and he has a few, mainly because he is just so big for his position.

Bismarck can be too upright when going into the rucks, and he sometimes carries the ball wrong because, with his physical strength, he feels he can hand off anyone. And on occasion he doesn't make the right decisions, off-loading at an inopportune time, or carrying too often and too far. No one will deny that Bismarck was a better rugby player than John Smit at the end of his Springbok career, but which one was the better player for the team?

John may have carried the ball three times less than Bismarck, but he got over the line more often. He also knew when to off-load and made better decisions. The bottom line was that the other players could play off John, whereas they didn't play off Bismarck as effortlessly.

So the matter wasn't as clear-cut as some people assumed. In South Africa, we often make the mistake of forgetting that individual brilliance isn't necessarily always what the team needs. In tests we conducted on the players, it emerged that in not having a personal agenda, John was quite unique. With him, everything revolved around the team. Bismarck differs from John in that respect. I think the competition with John over the years has hampered Bismarck's natural development. He's too determined to make a personal point.

I had to sit Bismarck down and tell him that the honeymoon was over for him: the other teams had figured him out. He would have to make adjustments if he wanted to retain his reputation as the best hooker in the world. And the challenge isn't over for Bismarck now that John is no longer playing. Chiliboy Ralepelle is also an excellent hooker who can make his mark at international level.

My advice to Bismarck would be to follow the example of All Black hooker Keven Mealamu and refine aspects of his game. When Mealamu first came onto the scene, he controlled the area around the rucks and mauls, but then opposition players worked him out. He made adjustments to his game that ensured his longevity in the All Black team and he arrived at the 2011 World Cup pretty close to the perfect player.

But as I said at the outset, Bismarck has immense potential, and it was great to have both him and John available to us. Everyone knows that the first 20 minutes are the toughest part of any game. If you start with a guy like John, he can weather the storm and then you can bring on Bismarck with all his attributes, knowing he is on for the rest of the match.

Having Bismarck, Willem Alberts and Francois Hougaard on the bench at the World Cup gave us the ability to change the momentum of a game just when such a change was needed, like in the second half against Wales. Of course there was an interesting dynamic in having the two Du Plessis brothers playing in the same team. Jannie and Bismarck come as a package, but I think Bismarck is the primary decision-maker in that relationship, meaning that Bismarck can handle whatever happens to Jannie, but not the other way around. When Jannie perceives his brother to be in trouble or thinks that he has been ill-treated, it impacts on Jannie's play. Jannie and Bismarck are both brilliant people, but they tend to make the same mistakes over and over and consider an apology sufficient compensation. I once told them that if you apologise for the same mistake too often, people will stop believing that you're really sorry.

Bismarck had every right to be upset about the situation at the World Cup. At times during the tournament he wore a long face, but I reiterated that we had discussed how we were going to play the two hookers at our first meeting in May. I had gone to see Bismarck in Durban and played open cards with him, as I did with John.

But our plans didn't work out perfectly, as we could not foresee all the injuries. For example, we hadn't planned on John being apart from the other players for so long when they were at the camp in Rustenburg. That caused a few problems during the home leg of the Tri Nations.

I made it clear that Bismarck would have to start a game before the World Cup, and I'd always intended it to be the test against the All Blacks in Port Elizabeth. Bismarck produced a brilliant performance, but the previous week in Durban was the first time he'd played at test level in several weeks. So I didn't think he would last the full 80 minutes in the PE game, and I called him off after an hour.

In the week leading up to the game, John hadn't been happy with me for leaving him out of the starting team. But I had to make decisions for the good of the team, and just as it was necessary to start with Bismarck, it was also necessary to bring John on when we had a good lead and needed to close the game down. That was not a situation that called for the X-factor; it called for John's experience. And this is exactly what happened in the PE test. None of the other coaches in the box agreed with me, but I was adamant that we needed John on the field. And his fresh legs indeed improved our scrumming, which meant that the All Blacks were on the back foot from first phase as they tried to chase the score.

But Bismarck disappointed me when he made it so obvious that he was unhappy to be taken off. I thought he'd behaved like a spoilt brat in that instance, and I called him in on the Sunday morning. He apologised immediately, as he always did in such circumstances, but I told him that by his actions he had conveyed to the country that he was not a team man. And we needed guys at the World Cup whose main interest was the team, not individual glory.

I told Bismarck that I would consider his behaviour a once-off, and that the next time he got so angry, he should rather hit me with a chair behind closed doors, as he was not setting a good example for the many youngsters watching the game.

The Sharks never did me any favours as far as Bismarck was concerned. By playing him ahead of John so often, they created expectations in his mind. I asked Sharks coach John Plumtree why he didn't give Bismarck and John the opportunity to play three games successively, but he told me that everyone had a different view and it was his job to do what was best for the Sharks.

When Bismarck apologised to me, he told me that he had played the PE game for his father, who was very ill at the time. This was something I did not know, but it wouldn't have changed my decision to take him off the field. The team always comes first. And at the World Cup, it was an important part of our strategy to have superior players on the bench who could lift the tempo later in the game. There is no rule book that says the best players have to start the match, and today's rugby games are contested by 22 players, not just 15.

Actually, I might have played Bismarck in the starting team more often during the pool phase of the World Cup had it not been for the way that the tournament progressed. In other words, had we not been under pressure right up to the last game of the pool phase with the possibility looming that we could have found ourselves on an early flight home if we lost to Samoa.

Although we won that game, the Samoan match was disastrous to our World Cup campaign, and I felt really aggrieved afterwards. I had never before experienced the same extent of off-the-ball thuggery that we had to put up with in that game, and it cost us the important figure of Frans Steyn. The IRB privately thanked us afterwards for not making a fuss about the many incidents of foul play. One of their staff passed the message on to me.

The IRB's silence on the matter concerned me deeply. Surely Samoa had brought the game into disrepute? Could there have been a clearer case? They had nothing to lose by going all-out with off-the-ball incidents in order to try to throw us off our game. It would have been an achievement for Samoa just to make the quarter-finals, beyond which they would not have been expected to advance, but we had a probable showdown against Australia looming, so could hardly afford to play Samoa at their own game and risk losing players to red cards or a citing.

I felt it was the IRB's duty to ensure that our rights were protected in that game, but Nigel Owens, the referee, just turned a blind eye. It wasn't a good advertisement for rugby, but somehow the man was rewarded by being appointed to referee a play-off!

It made no sense to me, and I found it hard to repel the suspicion that it was part of a strategy to throw our challenge off course. After the World Cup, even the highly respected sports scientist Tim Noakes questioned whether or not the quarter-final had been 'fixed'. Perhaps I'm naive to think it a possibility, but with all the money that's now involved in the game, maybe it's naive to think that it *can't* happen. People said the same about cricket just a few years ago ...

Bryce Lawrence was always a cocky referee – he was never shy to exchange heated words with me, for example – and yet in the quarter-final he was very subdued. He even spent half the match apologising to our players for missing some Australian infringements! So I disagree with Victor Matfield's view that he just 'froze'. Lawrence had way too much experience for that to have been the case.

That is not to say we did not also play a role in our downfall. We made some poor decisions, and I agree with those critics who said we should have won despite the referee. But in the silence that engulfed me in the weeks after the culmination of the World Cup, the refereeing question continued to haunt me.

And that I saw it coming long before the World Cup only made it harder.

23

A wonderful ride

It's the last day of January 2012 and thus the last day I will officially hold the position of Springbok coach. I always knew this moment would come and, as I have already said, I regarded myself only as a caretaker – the job was never mine to keep. You are appointed for four years and when that period comes to an end, you are no longer Springbok coach and someone else takes over. So while I know I will miss the Boks and the massive privilege of coaching my country, I am not leaving with any hard feelings or regrets. As I said at the beginning, it's been a wonderful ride.

Of course, once the emotions evoked after our return from New Zealand faded away and the silence returned, I had three months to sit and ponder how my dream had never really been fulfilled. It wasn't an easy time for me, as I have the frustration of knowing that we were peaking at the right time and, had we got through the Wellington match, we could well have won the World Cup.

The feeling that there was unfinished business to attend to motivated me to say publicly that I would be available to coach the Springboks again. Some people criticised me for that, but I certainly wasn't saying that I felt I had a *right* to carry on. I never had any expectations. I just felt I was a lot more mature and experienced than when I started the job and was willing to learn – and had learnt – from my mistakes. I just wanted people to know that I was willing to carry on serving my country if I was needed.

As a young child, I knew I couldn't be cross with my mother when I asked her for more bread and she said no. When you ask something of someone, there is always the possibility that they may say no. But then again, if you don't ask, you have *no* chance of getting what you want. I wanted SARU to know that I was available if they needed me, but if in their wisdom they didn't think I was the right man for the job, then it was their right to say no.

I actively worked on suppressing any anger once the World Cup storm had died down and I was back at home. There were several reasons why I never publicly criticised Bryce Lawrence after the quarter-final, and one of them was that I don't fight against things I can't change. What happened that day in Wellington was irreversible. But deep inside I wanted some clarity. How did it end where it did? Where did we go wrong?

So members of the management team studied some of Lawrence's games and discovered that while he makes an average of six mistakes a match, which is quite good, in Wellington he made 47. A match-changing error like the one made by Wayne Barnes, when he missed a forward pass when New Zealand lost to France in the 2007 quarter-final in Cardiff, is perhaps permissible once in a blue moon, but Bryce made six of those kinds of errors in his quarter-final. His 'mistakes' changed the game completely.

I think it's tragic when people allow negative incidents to change them as a person. I would be the loser if I allowed that quarter-final result to make me bitter. Fortunately, it hasn't done so.

Instead of my team playing in the World Cup final in Auckland, I ended up watching the game at home in Paarl, where I also watched the semi-finals. I observed the games analytically and unemotionally, as rugby coaches tend to do when their team is not involved. The important point, though, is that I didn't watch with any regret – it was almost as if I had never been part of the competition.

So what will tomorrow, the first day of my life after being the Springbok coach, bring? I'm not sure, for in the three months following the World Cup, I haven't done much rugby business or had much contact with SARU. In fact, if I do have a bit of bitterness in me, it is directed at SARU for not treating me like an adult and keeping me informed of their plans. I would have liked to have known where I stood in October, when we first arrived back from the World Cup.

Perhaps I could have started focusing on my future then instead of being kept in limbo for three months.

In November I was notified that my contract would be extended until 31 January. The rest of the management contracts expired at the end of December. Why this discrepancy, I have no idea. No one at SARU has explained it to me. So that's what I'm talking about – while I accepted that it was time to move on after the Wellington defeat, I kept getting mixed messages. And things that had been said to me during the last two years of my tenure also gave me some hope.

When SARU chief executive Jurie Roux announced that I was on the shortlist, I didn't really think that I stood a chance, but I did feel that after four years of service they could have paid me the respect of playing open cards with me. Instead there was little contact, except for when I was called into an interview with Jurie in mid-January, where I was asked a few questions. Nothing was really spelt out, though.

The confirmation that I would not be carrying on as coach arrived in the form of a letter from Oregan Hoskins, which was delivered to me by Dr Ismail Jakoet, a long-time employee at SARU. Regan thanked me for my 'four years of nation building', but said that the board had decided to take a new path.

If I have some advice for SARU going forward, a large part of it would revolve around the way they deal with the human factor in their business. The people who work for you are human beings and they deserve to be treated as such. Loyalty should be respected and rewarded, not trampled on.

I passed on some advice to Jurie and the organisation during my last year in charge, and I can only hope that they will act on it. However, at the time of writing it has become clear that they have not acted on the most important part of my advice, which was to arrange for a proper handover to the new coach and management.

My management team built a huge amount of intellectual capital over our four-year tenure, and the new management can only benefit from some of what we learnt. I'm not suggesting the entire management stay on to brief the new coach, but the head coach should be given the responsibility of ensuring that all the relevant information from the various departments is passed on to the new team.

Of course an official handover may cause a problem for the new coach, as taking advice from me could promote the perception that he is 'weak'. That's the problem, though – the current system is flawed in that too much is left open to interpretation. If it was standard practice to have a proper handover, then that problem wouldn't exist.

In South African rugby we don't make provision for the next generation – instead, we live only in the moment. For the good of our rugby, SARU must sit down and find a way to retain and store all the knowledge that's out there. Otherwise the four years, and the effort each coach puts in, just goes to waste. Even if the Bok coach doesn't want to draw on the experience and information accumulated by those who went before, there are other structures where this knowledge can be used.

Maybe I am being naive again, but surely the core business of a big corporation should be its primary focus? But over the years the headlines in newspapers have been dominated by peripheral stuff that has very little to do with the game itself.

When Andy Marinos was the acting CEO of SARU, I implored him to let my management team focus on our core business, which was the coaching and mental development of the players. I argued that if one got that right, then the financial and other aspects of the business would fall into place too. The next SuperSport television-rights deal is always finalised very quickly and seems to be given top priority, but when it comes to appointing a Springbok coach, the process drags on for so long that it negatively affects the preparations for the new season.

The top echelons of SARU need to intensify their focus on the game itself, starting with a dedicated rugby department that supports and advises the provincial unions and franchises so that they can grow and improve. There should be someone the Bulls can approach for advice when they have problems with their scrumming or the Cheetahs can go to for help with their kicking game.

Instead the unions are left to go it alone, and as a result they build up their own intellectual property and, because of it, in some cases become even stronger than SARU, who are sometimes regarded as a sixth franchise! The bottom line is that the provinces don't have as much respect for SARU as they should have, and that makes the job of the national coach so much harder.

In 2008, the 2007 World Cup–winning management team was decimated, and there were many times in those early days when I regretted it. The operation would have run so much smoother had there been a proper handover or if some of the guys who had been overseeing the efficient running of the Bok ship had stayed on.

Having said that, my own management team quickly picked up the pace and became super-efficient, and at the end of our tenure I thought there were many facets of our management that other professional sports in this country could benefit from.

Aside from the assistant coaches, about whom a lot has already been written, we managed to put together the best logistics, technical and medical teams. On the medical side, exhaustive studies were made on the medical history of the players. We went back as far as Craven Week to establish what injuries each player was likely to pick up. In the end, we were 80 per cent of the way towards knowing their anatomies inside out.

The logistics side of it became so efficient that the players were able to transition from the hotel to the airport and onto the plane without feeling like they were even travelling. A lot was done to make the players feel comfortable and good about themselves. While some would say they were spoilt, I think it was important for them to be free to concentrate on their primary business, which was playing at the top of their game.

I've said some negative stuff about SARU in this book, but I wouldn't say I had a terribly bad relationship with them. It was just the same as it had always been wherever I have worked, even in my previous life as a teacher – my colleagues and bosses struggle with my determination to be independent. I won't just kowtow to the whims of others before I have assessed whether it is the right thing to do.

I don't drink and I am not big on social commitments. I won't make small talk with the CEO or president of the union in the hope of getting some kind of favour. I just refuse to do it. Maybe I have overdone my quest to be independent, and as a result maybe I haven't allowed people to get to know or understand me better.

From my side, I felt I had an honest relationship with SARU, and I learnt that you can't blame rugby for the fact that there are many people in the game who allow circumstances rather than character to define them. Rugby will never belong to any one person, and those who think they can own the sport are making a very big mistake.

Rugby is a game to be respected and adored. It was because of rugby that I lost every material possession I had, but it is also why I am where I am today. Rugby does not define me, but we all need the sport more than it needs any individual. What I know for sure now is that although it is a privilege and often a joy to be the Springbok coach, it is one of the toughest jobs in the world. Heyneke Meyer is in for a very rough time, as the pressures and demands are huge, and they don't get any easier to deal with the longer you hold the job. Heyneke may have been successful with the Bulls and have a strong rugby pedigree, but the best bit of advice I can give him is that Heyneke Meyer needs to know who Heyneke Meyer is.

There are going to be many different stakeholders that are going to try to pressurise him or bend him to their will so that he will do what they want him to do. The only way to survive this is to know who you are and to observe the message behind that old Latin phrase *quisque sibi verus* – unto thine own self be true. Sometimes it's very hard to do this, and you may even hurt or anger a lot of people in the process, but in the end you do it so that you can survive.

Did I survive or, more importantly, did I win? Not winning the World Cup hurts. But winning the World Cup is not the only thing that can make a positive difference to your country. Hopefully I have inspired some people and brought hope to those who might not otherwise have had reason to feel hopeful. I spent a lot of time trying to get the little things right – making the Springboks more accessible to the people, for example – and hopefully in time SARU will find a way to promote the game to the broader population so that they, too, will come to understand and, eventually, love it.

Throughout my four years as coach, I sensed an undercurrent of support for the Springboks from all cultures and communities in our country, but a vast number of the population is supporting us without really understanding what the game is about. It would be wonderful if SARU could find a way of educating people about the game and so broaden its support base. As a matter of fact, I'd love to be involved in such a programme.

Right now I don't know what the future holds for me. But I do know that my future does not *have* to involve rugby, no matter how much I would like to continue with what I started. I am not the coach any more, but I don't think people will stop calling me coach. And I feel as if I have created a platform over the past four years from which I can make a positive contribution to our diverse but vibrant society.

When I was involved in rugby, I invariably got drawn into discussing rugby topics, but on many occasions, when I was in the company of sportspeople from other codes, I was asked for advice on other aspects of life. I therefore like to think that I am not just a one-dimensional personality – as I've said, there's more to life than just rugby.

Perhaps what I have said here may not be enough to convince you that I have answered the question on whether or not I see myself as having won anything, so I will conclude my story by returning to where I left off in the first chapter, with a description of the events around our exit from the World Cup.

* * *

As you can imagine, when we got back to the hotel on that Sunday evening in October 2011 after suffering the quarter-final defeat at the Wellington Regional Stadium, everyone was very emotional. And as a group, we went through one hell of a fraught night together, our last before we'd return to our country. The journey we had been on for four years had ended, and it had all happened so quickly. Even though we were to fly out of New Zealand before first light, we stayed up till late. We didn't have a conventional Contiki (the team 'court case' we hold after every game) that night.

Victor Matfield took charge of the proceedings, and he played his part brilliantly. After we'd thanked the liaison officers, everyone was given a chance to say something, and they all talked about matters dear to their hearts. I was very chuffed when the management team was thanked effusively time and again for running the show so efficiently throughout the four years. Of course it was also very nice to hear so many positive things being said about the role I had played. Derik Coetzee, who was new to the management team, having joined in 2011, was particularly direct: 'Coach Peter, I just want to tell you that there are lots of people talking nonsense out there [about you], but if anyone does it near me, I will stop it because I know you are a very intelligent guy. You know the structures, and these past three months that I have worked with you have been a real eye-opener on where rugby can be in this country.'

But I knew his was just one small voice, and that the next day, back home in South Africa, I was going to have to face the music. No matter what was being said at the Contiki, no matter how hard we were trying to console one another with kind words, we knew we had failed in our mission. As I said in the opening chapter, the press conference that awaited me at OR Tambo International Airport loomed as a particularly scary prospect.

And before that, there was the possibility that some rugby fans might turn up to meet us in the arrivals hall and give us a hard time. I had been booed at Kings Park in my first year as coach, something that I still remember as the nadir of my four years, and I was expecting it to happen again. As the Contiki drew to a close, Victor and John Smit had the last word, which was appropriate, as these were two giants of the game who were now bowing out.

Flying out from Wellington the next morning, I kept thinking about the massive send-off we'd received on our departure from South Africa. People had vested so much hope in us. It would be understandable if they were consumed with anger that we had failed them. I like challenges in life, but I felt a great deal of trepidation as we flew across the Tasman Sea to Sydney, and then, after a short changeover, onwards across the Indian Ocean to Johannesburg.

Sydney to Joburg, which encompasses nearly 15 hours of non-stop flying, is one of the longest flights there is. Most of the journey takes place in the daytime, but you have to try to find a way to sleep, which I managed to do on and off. But in between bouts of sleep, I kept on thinking, 'What the hell am I going to say to the media back home and to all those people who depended on us?'

I probably irritated assistant coaches Gary Gold and Dick Muir in the end, as I repeatedly asked them, 'Are we prepared to dance?'

They kept telling me that things would be fine and that I had nothing to worry about – everything would be okay, they said. But it was all right for them, as they weren't going to have to face the press alone and answer all the questions. They would not be in the line of fire. And someone had to take the rap.

It was hellishly difficult preparing for the presser, as I didn't want to be perceived as making excuses. But then, if they asked me why we had lost and I gave my reasons, wouldn't that come across as making excuses?

I wanted to bow out with my dignity intact. I felt I had done so at the post-match press conference the night before, but now I was about to face my own countrymen. What the hell do you say to them?

My sense of foreboding increased as we flew over the African coastline and then started our descent to OR Tambo. I had to keep telling myself to be strong, to be brave.

After we touched down, we were greeted by the police, who had come onto the aircraft. I thought that was odd and a little unnecessary. But then something happened that took me totally by surprise – they started asking for autographs. Some of them even wanted *my* autograph! One guy gave me a carving as a gift. What is this? I thought. This is not how you treat a pariah. It started to dawn on me that perhaps we did not have a repeat of Kings Park 2008 in store for us.

We were waved through passport control by very friendly home-affairs staff, who treated us like returning heroes. I thought I would now be taken straight into the press conference, so I was completely unprepared for what happened next. As we walked into the arrivals hall, we were suddenly surrounded by people – and there were more packed onto all three of the landings above us. There wasn't room for a mouse.

Boy, it's hard to explain how I felt, and I am sure the rest of the guys were just as emotional. I had to bite down hard to contain the feelings coursing through me, or I would have had tears in my eyes. Someone threw something at me, which I caught. It was a flower. Hah, now I was really at a loss for words. Our send-off seven weeks earlier had been massive and perhaps there had been more people in attendance there, but this was more humbling. Did these people not know that we were home early because we had lost the World Cup and that the tournament would be continuing in New Zealand for the next two weeks without us?

Those who have listened to me speak at public events over the years probably know I have a small speech impediment. The less excited I am, the more voice I seem to have. But when I am excited, my voice starts squeaking and eventually disappears altogether. So when I was asked to say something, I doubted my ability to do so. It was like the day of our departure in Mandela Square all over again. I wanted to just slink away and not say anything, but all these people had honoured us by turning up to greet us, and I had to say *something*.

'I know we let you down,' I began, 'and we should have done you more justice than we did, but we tried our best. I am just sorry that on the day our best wasn't good enough.'

I went on to honour our two 'statesmen', John and Victor, and ended up speaking for about two or three minutes – it felt more like 10 hours, though, as I was finding it hard not to choke up. The fact that there was none of the anticipated booing and jeering just made me even more emotional. Instead of a hubbub of noise, the entire building just seemed to be engulfed in a deathly quiet as people listened to what I was saying.

After I'd finished, some children came up to me and women gave me flowers – people from all backgrounds and cultures stepped forward and embraced me and the players and commiserated with us on our loss. For the first time in the four years I had been the Springbok coach, I felt really valued as a human being in my own country. It seemed that not even the disappointing defeat we had suffered in Wellington could detract from people's humanity. It made me feel even guiltier for not having taken the team further.

I knew the prevailing mood of those present was not necessarily going to last or carry over to the population at large, so just as I tried not to take my critics personally, I tried not take the events of that day at OR Tambo personally either. And the press conference still loomed large – there were questions to be answered.

Much to my surprise, apart from being aggressively questioned on my supposed resignation at the press conference in Wellington a day earlier, even the media seemed to have caught the positive vibes. A most unusual spirit of togetherness appeared to be sweeping the nation!

It was an experience I felt very fortunate to be a part of, and I made the most of the moment. It was such a far cry from the negativity that had surrounded me and forced me, even at an early stage, to reconsider my future as Springbok coach (I am referring to after our defeat against New Zealand in Wellington in 2008). And it was light years away from being booed by the Durban crowd later that same season, an incident that coincidentally also followed a loss to Australia. We may not have won the World Cup, but the two vastly different reactions three years apart to defeats by the same nation suggested that my four years had not been completely wasted. Perhaps my mission to make the Springboks the people's team had been successful.

The passing of time will determine how history will judge the team and me as a Springbok coach, but on the day we got back from the World Cup, which signified the actual end of my tenure, I knew that even the really bad days can be very, very good indeed.

And knowing that made me feel like a winner.

Index

Do you have any comments, suggestions or
feedback about this book or any other Zebra Press titles?
Contact us at talkback@zebrapress.co.za

*

Visit www.randomstruik.co.za and subscribe
to our newsletter for monthly updates and news